Learning to Salsa

Learning to Salsa

*New Steps in
U.S.-Cuba Relations*

Vicki Huddleston
Carlos Pascual

BROOKINGS INSTITUTION PRESS
Washington, D.C.

Library of Congress Cataloging-in-Publication data
Huddleston, Vicki.
    Learning to salsa : new steps in U.S.-Cuba relations / Vicki Huddleston, Carlos Pascual.
    p.   cm.
  Summary: "Drawing on simulation exercises involving role playing and extensive
debates, explores how major developments within or outside Cuba might open
opportunities for the U.S. to reengage with the island nation and support Cuban actors
in initiating change from within, and reveals specific challenges to crafting a new U.S.
approach"—Provided by publisher.
    Includes bibliographical references and index.
    ISBN 978-0-8157-0389-1 (pbk. : alk. paper)
    1. United States—Foreign relations—Cuba.   2. Cuba—Foreign relations—United
States.   3. United States—Relations—Cuba.   4. Cuba—Relations—United States.
5. Engagement (Philosophy)—Political aspects.   6. Political games.   7. Role
playing—Political aspects. 8. Cuba—Politics and government—1990–   9. Cuba—
Social conditions—1959–   10. Social change—Cuba.   I. Pascual, Carlos.   II. Title.
    E183.8.C9H83 2010
    327.730729109'0511—dc22   2009052539

2 4 6 8 9 7 5 3 1

Printed on acid-free paper

Typeset in Sabon and Strayhorn

Composition by R. Lynn Rivenbark
Macon, Georgia

Printed by R. R. Donnelley
Harrisonburg, Virginia

Contents

Foreword

Two thousand nine is the fiftieth anniversary of the Cuban Revolution that brought Fidel Castro to power. On New Year's Day 2009, his brother and successor, Raúl Castro, vowed that the socialist slogan "*Socialismo o muerte*," "Socialism or death," would guide Cuba for another half century.

Yet change was in the air even as he spoke, for Raúl had announced a series of reforms since assuming the presidency in February 2008. Cuban citizens could enter tourist facilities where most of them had previously been barred; they could purchase cell phones, computers, and other electronic equipment that gave them more contact with the outside world; modest improvements in salaries and the leasing of idle state-owned agricultural land to independent farmers created the possibility of new opportunities for grassroots economic activity.

By the summer of 2009, however, it was clear that these measures would not by themselves set Cuba on a path toward sustainable economic growth. While loosening control in some aspects of national life, the government was tightening the screws in other areas. Indeed, downgrading the socialist slogan to "*Ahorro o muerte*," "Savings or death," the government reduced already meager food rations and cut back a range of social programs, decreed that air conditioning was to be turned off in the workplace, and closed nonessential factories. Emerging frustration with these cutbacks, together with heightened expectations for change, rising inequality and social stratification, and a decline in state capacity to provide education, health, and housing, is increasing tensions in Cuba. The question is whether this combination of tensions and expectations will create pressure for deeper change.

The possibility of genuine change in Cuba is resonating with changing attitudes in the Miami area, home to 800,000 Cuban Americans and the capital of the Cuban American community. The rise of a new generation of leaders within the community brought with it an ideological shift. Frustrated with the U.S. embargo on Cuba, in place for almost five decades, prominent Cuban Americans are looking for an alternative approach that would focus less on isolating the Cuban government and more on supporting the well-being and political rights of the Cuban people.

Washington, too, is more open to rethinking policy—not least because January 2009 brought a new American president who, in his inaugural address, challenged dictatorships with a promise to "extend a hand if you are willing to unclench your fist." He recognized, as did many Americans, that the freeze in U.S.-Cuba relations had for too long disproportionately dominated American diplomacy toward the hemisphere.

Taken together, these trends constituted the most significant opportunity for a reassessment of U.S.-Cuba relations since 1959—this book could not be more timely. In the best tradition of Brookings research and prescription, it provides policymakers with fact-based analysis and pragmatic recommendations, and it helps informed citizens better understand the realities, opportunities, and risks that their government is dealing with.

The book grew out of an eighteen-month Brookings project, U.S. Policy toward a Cuba in Transition, directed by Carlos Pascual, vice president and director of Foreign Policy at Brookings, and Vicki Huddleston, a visiting fellow at the Institution. They set out to identify ways to break the stalemate in U.S.-Cuba relations and inject new ideas into the debate on how to best support a strategy for change driven from within by the Cuban people.

The Brookings project brought together a fully independent advisory group of nineteen distinguished academics, opinion leaders, and diplomats from diverse backgrounds and political orientations to seek ways to advance a new U.S. policy toward Cuba that would better serve the interests of the United States, the Cuban people, and the broader hemisphere. All members served in a personal capacity only and none represented any organization or government.

Having sat in on some of the deliberations of the group, I can testify that *Learning to Salsa: New Steps in U.S.-Cuba Relations* captures the spirit in which the nineteen advisers came together to develop a roadmap of policy recommendations. Over a period of eighteen months, they held six simulation exercises and discussions in which they modeled and analyzed the decisionmaking processes of various strategic actors and stakeholders in a future transition in Cuba. In a unique, forward-looking approach, the simulations applied the advisers' expertise across a range of subjects to a series of hypothetical future scenarios, allowing them to create dynamic recommendations for policy. The chapters of this book reproduce the deliberations and findings of each simulation: how different U.S. policy responses would affect a Cuban transition, and how the Cuban hierarchy, independent civil society, and the international and Cuban American communities might act and react to internal and external events that would logically be expected to occur in the near future.

Over the course of its work, the group united behind an overarching conclusion: the United States should adopt a policy of critical and constructive engagement toward Cuba. In April 2009, the project launched *Cuba: A New Policy of Critical and Constructive Engagement*, a pathbreaking report providing a comprehensive roadmap of executive actions that would allow the president to align U.S. policy with that of the rest of the hemisphere and restore normal bilateral relations over time.

The deliberations from this project had an impact even as the work proceeded. A Brookings Commission on Latin America, co-chaired by the former president of Mexico, Ernesto Zedillo, and the legendary American diplomat Thomas Pickering, adopted key findings of the Cuba project. Senator Richard Lugar, the ranking Republican on the Senate Foreign Relations Committee, embraced the proposed focus on critical and constructive engagement in a congressional report issued in February 2009.

A number of people outside the group of advisers who were soon to join the Obama administration were engaged throughout the project. Indeed, one of the simulation exercises conducted under the auspices of the project, in October 2008, turned out to be good preparation for issues that arose in June 2009 in the context of the Obama administration's dealings with the Organization of American States and Cuba. Some ideas generated by the project found their way into the perspectives of other nations' policies through the interaction of foreign participants with their governments. Thus, the book not only suggests new steps in U.S.-Cuba relations but has already had significant impact—a key goal of everything we do at Brookings.

Carlos and Vicki brought their own significant experience and expertise to the endeavor, and they also guided the advisory group toward achieving consensus on a set of recommendations on a subject that elicits powerful political passions. Carlos is now ambassador to Mexico, and Vicki is the deputy assistant secretary for Africa at the Department of Defense. So it is especially important to stress that their work here reflects their personal views and the research they conducted during their time at Brookings, and was completed before they took up their current posts. The views contained herein do not represent those of the U.S. government.

On behalf of Brookings, I wish to thank the members of the core group of advisers (listed at the end of this foreword) for contributing their time, depth of expertise, and rich experiences to this project. The group's policy recommendations would not have been possible without the assistance of Robert Muse and Richard Popkin, who helped the advisers navigate the maze of relevant embargo laws and regulations. We are also indebted to Hugh Gladwin, Katrin Hansing, and Guillermo Grenier for their research and polling work on Cuban American opinion in Florida. Within Brookings, Dóra Beszterczey was instrumental in writing and editing this book, drafting individual chapters with scholarly insight and analysis, and guiding the manuscript through to publication. Other assistance throughout the course of the project was provided by Amélie Rapp, Michael Bustamante, Dan Sullivan, Jason Trentacoste, Danielle Barav, Tiziana Dominguez, and Jessica Despres. The authors are also indebted to Mauricio Cárdenas, Carol Graham, Ted Piccone, and Diana Negroponte, who were a constant source of ideas throughout the project, as well as the support of Brookings's Foreign Policy staff, particularly Charlotte Baldwin, Peggy Knudson, Gail Chalef, Ian Livingston, Maggie Humenay, and Shawn Dhar. They also extend their appreciation to Bob Faherty, Mary Kwak, Janet Walker, and other colleagues at the Brookings Institution Press for their excellent work in bringing the manuscript to publication.

The project benefited from the information and opinions generously shared by a wide range of individuals during the simulation exercises and other project-related events, including Frank Almaguer, Fulton Armstrong, Anders Aslund, Paul Cejas, Alex Correa, Margaret Crahan, Isabel Estrada-Portales, John Ferch, Alan Flanigan, Joe Garcia, Colonel Sam Gardiner, Robert Gelbard, Tom Gjelten, Guillermo Grenier, Orlando Gutierrez Boronat, Peter Hakim, Alcibíades Hidalgo, Caryn Hollis, José Miguel Insulza, Kirby Jones, Brian Latell, Bruce Levy, Abe Lowenthal,

John McAuliff, Carmelo Mesa-Lago, Captain Michael Mohn, Carlos Alberto Montaner, Frank Mora, David Mutchler, Despina Manos, José Pascual Marco Martinez, Carlos Ricardo Martins Ceglia, Eusebio Mujal-León, Angelos Pangratis, Michael E. Parmly, Phil Peters, Albert Ramdin, Dan Restrepo, Riordan Roett, Arturo Sarukhán Casamitjana, Jack Sheehan, Wayne Smith, Jaime Suchlicki, Julia E. Sweig, Jay Taylor, Octavio Tripp, and Michael Wilson.

Finally, this project would not have been possible without generous support from the Liberty Mutual Group; the Cleveland Foundation; the Cuba Study Group; Chuck Robinson, a Brookings trustee; and other donors. Chuck and another trustee, Tom Ramey, were especially engaged in encouraging the innovative course of analysis from the very conception of the project.

STROBE TALBOTT
President
The Brookings Institution

Washington, D.C.
December 2009

Members of the Core Group of Advisers

Codirectors

Carlos Pascual
*Vice President and Director of Foreign
    Policy*
Brookings Institution

Vicki Huddleston
Visiting Fellow
Brookings Institution

Project Advisers

Gustavo Arnavat[1]
Attorney at Law

Ann Louise Bardach
Author and Journalist
*University of California–
    Santa Barbara*

Ramon Colás
Codirector
*Center for the Understanding of
    Cubans of African Descent*

Jorge I. Domínguez
*Antonio Madero Professor of
    Mexican and Latin American
    Politics and Economics*
*Vice Provost for International
    Affairs*
Harvard University

Daniel Erikson
*Senior Associate for U.S. Policy
    and Director of
    Caribbean Programs*
Inter-American Dialogue

Mark Falcoff
Resident Scholar Emeritus
American Enterprise Institute

Damián J. Fernández
*Provost and Executive
    Vice President*
Purchase College

1. Gustavo Arnavat completed his role as adviser to this project prior to being nominated by President Obama to serve as the United States executive director to the Inter-American Development Bank.

Andy S. Gomez
Nonresident Senior Fellow
Brookings Institution
Assistant Provost
University of Miami
Senior Fellow
Institute for Cuban and
    Cuban American Studies

Jesús Gracia
Former Spanish Ambassador to Cuba

Paul Hare
Former British Ambassador to Cuba

Francisco J. (Pepe) Hernández
President
Cuban American National
    Foundation

William LeoGrande
Dean
School of Public Affairs,
    American University

Marifeli Pérez-Stable
Vice President for Democratic
    Governance
Inter-American Dialogue

Jorge R. Piñón
Energy Fellow
Center for Hemispheric Policy,
    University of Miami

Archibald Ritter
Distinguished Research Professor
    Emeritus
Department of Economics and
    Norman Paterson School of
    International Affairs
Carleton University

Andrés Rozental
Former Deputy Foreign Minister of
    Mexico
Nonresident Senior Fellow
Brookings Institution

Carlos Saladrigas
Cochairman
Cuba Study Group

Learning to Salsa

CHAPTER ONE

Introduction

If one compares outcomes to stated objectives, U.S. policy toward Cuba may be the most significant failure in the history of American foreign policy. An almost five-decade embargo and numerous attempts to isolate and undermine the Castro government have not produced democratic change. In February 2008, Fidel Castro successfully orchestrated a succession, handing power to his younger brother, Raúl. Today the United States has little leverage to promote change in Cuba. Indeed, Cuba enjoys normal relations with virtually every country in the world, and American attempts to isolate the Cuban government have served only to elevate its symbolic predicament as an underdog in the international arena. A new policy of engagement toward Cuba is long overdue.

Launched in September 2007, the Brookings project U.S. Policy toward a Cuba in Transition developed a strategic step-by-step program to break this stalemate of failure. This book was completed under the auspices of that project and reflects more than eighteen months of research, analysis, and debate conducted with a group of nineteen leading experts who formed the project's core advisory group. For the first time, opinion leaders in the Cuban American community joined with leading academics and international diplomats from diverse backgrounds and political orientations to seek common ground on the divisive and emotional issue of U.S. policy toward Cuba.

In the spirit of developing policy ideas that would support the emergence of a peaceful, prosperous, and democratic Cuba in which the Cuban people shape their political and economic future, the project featured a series of simulation exercises to identify critical components, both internal and external, that should be considered in the formulation of future U.S. policies toward Cuba. While the primary objective of the simulations was to facilitate a process of dynamic learning, the process also led the group to reach consensus on its recommendations for U.S. policy.

The fundamental premise of the project was that sustainable democratic change must come from within Cuba and that the American people and their government can serve as a catalyst to foster an environment in which the Cuban people will be able to determine how they wish to be governed. Encouraging broader and deeper knowledge through friendships and family ties will better prepare Cubans to participate in a transition away from the Castro era. In the three decades since 1980, an internal impetus for political change has dominated most power transitions in a number of countries; witness the collapse of the Soviet Union, the emergence of the Orange Revolution in Ukraine, and the consolidation of successful democracies in Central Europe. In China and Vietnam, change from within—though certainly not constituting "political change"—was what drove China's and Vietnam's willingness to engage globally, even as other domestic political actors sought to insulate both countries from global uncertainties. The pathways of political change may resemble wandering roots. But only such internal roots can eventually spread, grow, and nurture democratic change.

The timing of the project was based on the conviction that an unprecedented opportunity was presenting itself. The combination of change within Cuba and within the Cuban American community creates the most significant opening for a reassessment of U.S. policy toward Cuba since 1959. Demographic and ideological shifts inside Miami's Cuban American community underscore frustration with the embargo and a growing sense that a more effective alternative must be sought, one that shifts the focus of policy away from isolating Cuba to supporting the well-being and political rights of the Cuban people. Many in the Cuban American business community, too, seeing international actors who have already positioned themselves to take advantage of market openings, fear that they may be shut out from playing a role in a future Cuba. Polling within the community reflects that, across the political spectrum, Cuban American opinion is now converging in favor of increased engagement with the island at all levels, creating a growing political space to challenge traditional orthodoxy on U.S. policy toward Cuba. A Florida International University poll conducted in November 2008 in the aftermath of the American presidential elections found that, by substantial margins, a majority of Cuban American voters favor ending restrictions on their travel and remittances to Cuba and support a bilateral dialogue and normal diplomatic relations with the Cuban government (see appendix B).

Across the Straits of Florida, Raúl Castro remains committed to the continuation of the Revolution and the preservation of power. Yet Raúl also sees that he cannot succeed by means merely of charisma—he cannot exhort the Cuban people to continue to make sacrifices in the name of the Revolution unless he has an external enemy. Thus, Raúl initiated a process of incremental reforms in order to relieve pressure for political change. The more the United States is committed to engaging Cuba, the less Raúl Castro can use a presumed U.S. threat to justify his authoritarian rule. President Barack Obama is extraordinarily popular among Cubans. His changing tone in U.S. policy shifts the responsibility for how well or badly Cuba is governed from the United States and its policies to Cuba's leaders themselves. If Raúl is to consolidate his rule, he will need a stronger and wider base to govern from, and will need to mobilize the Communist Party and the Revolutionary Armed Forces to disseminate, explain, and enforce the decisions of the Cuban hierarchy. This imperative will be all the more important in an environment where reforms that permit greater economic openness may create new, unpredictable challenges to the status quo.

The international community should not delude itself. Raúl's preference is to be a Cuban Deng Xiao Ping, not Mikhail Gorbachev. His desire is to extend the life of Cuba's authoritarian government, not to preside over the crumbling of one of the world's remaining authoritarian regimes. The central question is whether the Cuban government will be able to control a modest opening of Cuban society, or whether incremental reforms will gather the momentum to unleash a process of irreversible change. The focus of U.S. policy and of international initiatives should be on this new internal dynamic in Cuba. How can U.S. policy be framed so as to give sustenance to actors within Cuba who have the potential to use these small openings to widen the prospects for change? How should the United States engage the international community to challenge Cuba to allow true democratic participation?

Thus, the objective of U.S. policy and broader international engagement with Cuba is not to flirt with Cuban authoritarianism but to challenge it. If the United States and the West hold up their values to be compared to

Cuba's, which values will prevail? Freedom, openness, and the chance to pursue one's aspirations, or state control over political and economic life? These dual tracks of engagement and moral challenge have a solid grounding in history and policy. Ronald Reagan challenged Mikhail Gorbachev to "tear down this Wall," while simultaneously using his direct contacts with the Soviet premier and working with other conservatives like Margaret Thatcher to build pressure to do so.

Through the lessons learned in the project simulations, Brookings advisers came to the unanimous conclusion that the United States should adopt a proactive policy of critical and constructive engagement toward Cuba. Its focus should be on facilitating change from within Cuba. Specific measures, the group concluded, should be phased in unilaterally by the U.S. president on the basis of U.S. judgments, in order to delink U.S. interests from attempts by Cuba to thwart or block U.S. objectives. The more the United States specifies expectations of reciprocal Cuban policy actions, the less the chance that Cuba will take those steps. Instead, the group created a consensus road map of executive actions comprising short-, medium-, and long-term initiatives that would allow the United States to align its policy with that of the rest of the hemisphere and restore normal bilateral relations with Cuba over time. The road map should serve as a clear statement of U.S. intentions to Cuba and the international community. The president of the United States, the group agreed, should decide how and when to move forward along this road map.

Methodology

Over a period of eighteen months, project advisers carried out a series of six simulation exercises and discussions to enhance their understanding of the complex political realities in Cuba and the United States. Each exercise is described in a chapter of this book. Taking a forward-looking approach, the exercises sought to apply the advisers' expertise across a range of subjects to a series of hypothetical scenarios in which participants tested how different U.S. policy responses would affect a Cuban transition, and how the Cuban political hierarchy, independent civil society, and international and Cuban American communities might react to internal and external events that could logically be expected to occur in the near future.

By modeling and generating analyses of various strategic actors' and stakeholders' decisionmaking processes, the simulations identified factors that might influence the success or failure of specific policy options. Those lessons, explained at the end of chapters 3 to 8 in this book, provide policymakers with perhaps the most extensive and systematic set of policy exercises, deliberations, and resultant recommendations for Cuba policy that has ever been created. Whether or not policymakers agree with the specific recommendations, these scenarios reveal not only opportunities that can lead to more effective outcomes but also possible constraints and potential mistakes to be avoided.

The first exercise, in chapter 3 ("U.S. Policy: Constraints of a Historical Legacy"), tested the limits of a policy based on isolating Cuba to respond to major external developments that could open an opportunity for change inside the island. The past fifty years are a strong indicator that a continuation of an isolationist policy will not produce change in Cuba. If, however, change were to arise exogenously, would "isolationist orthodoxy" provide a useful means to help usher in a process of democratic self-determination in Cuba? To assess the possibilities and limitations inherent to this strategy, we simulated how the U.S. government might respond to an exogenous shock, Fidel Castro's death, if it had to stay strictly within the confines of policies prevailing during the George W. Bush administration. Assuming the role of cabinet secretaries at a meeting of the National Security Council, simulation participants aimed to formulate a diplomatic response and shape a public message while taking precautionary measures to avoid mass migration to the United States. Would instability within Cuba support or hurt the cause of democratic transition? How could the United States bolster the work of civil society leaders seeking political change on the ground? To what extent could the United States mobilize the international community to coordinate pressure to advance political reforms? One of the biggest lessons learned in the exercise was that the historical policy of isolation—characterized by little engagement with Cuba, little policy space to expand such engagement, and little international credibility to influence others—left the United States few levers to act effectively to promote change, even when opportunities arose.

The second exercise, in chapter 4 ("U.S. Policy: A New Strategy toward Cuba"), reviewed options for policy under a new U.S. administration. A replay of the National Security Council meeting explored policy options without setting predefined constraints; instead, advisers could propose policy options and evaluate their viability on their individual merit. Participants debated whether formulating a long-range strategic policy of engagement would be politically viable without positive Cuban responses. How might the United States formulate a unilateral strategy that balances support for economic liberalization with a commitment to keeping political reform and human rights on the table? Participants considered a new and important strategic reality: Cuba's potential to develop its oil reserves and sugarcane ethanol industry within the next three to five years. With energy revenues, Cuba's vulnerability to outside pressure, from either the United States or Venezuela, will diminish, and state power will be reinforced, bolstering the Cuban government's credibility to maintain political control. This reality suggests that the time for bold U.S. action may be now, before U.S. influence diminishes further.

The third exercise, in chapter 5 ("Understanding the Cuban Leadership"), called on participants to put themselves in the shoes of an inner circle of advisers to Raúl Castro as they meet to discuss how to consolidate their leadership and continue the next phase of the Revolution. Focusing on the internal dynamics, motivations, and decisionmaking processes of the new Castro government, the exercise assessed the possible political and economic strategies Cuba might adopt in the immediate future. Participants probed how the Raúl Castro government might secure its legitimacy and address citizens' rising expectations for improved livelihoods and economic opportunities without undermining the authority of the state. Will the government seek to broaden voices within the Communist Party and rule from a wider institutional base? How far could the government go to address grievances without inviting strong economic dislocations or eroding the social achievements of the Revolution and the socialist nature of Cuban society? How might Cuba reduce its single-source oil dependence on Venezuela, and what might be the costs of closer relations with the United States?

The fourth exercise, in chapter 6 ("Transforming Disparate Voices into a Dynamic Civil Society Coalition"), simulated a meeting of diverse representatives of Cuban civil society convened to analyze the potential of civic movements to advance change in Cuba. By evaluating the interests, strengths, and weaknesses of key sectors of civil society and testing potential motivations and points of division as they endeavor to unite in pursuit of a common agenda, U.S. policymakers will be better placed to craft more effective strategies to support a peaceful transition with Cubans defining the island's future. Advisers assessed ways that groups might infuse legitimacy and mass appeal into a broad-based movement, the pros and cons of accepting foreign support, and possibilities for constructively engaging disaffected segments of the population while preserving the interests of those most vulnerable to dislocations.

The fifth exercise, in chapter 7 ("Coordinating U.S. Policy with the International Community"), tested whether a group of key U.S. allies represented by foreign ministers convened by the U.S. secretary of state could come together to forge a coordinated approach toward Cuba. The aim was to assess potential spoilers and constraints to forging new directions, including ways to avoid a high-profile change in policy being perceived as rewarding the Cuban government. Participants debated whether the United States would be more effective in promoting democracy in Cuba if it were willing to work with the international community to place democracy and human rights in a wider context of shared interests that include trade, migration, security, the environment, and civil society. They assessed whether allowing Cuba to participate in international and regional organizations would provide incentives that would change Cuba's behavior by linking it more closely with international standards on democracy, transparency, and human rights. Finally, they examined American potential to forge a multilateral framework to manage an unanticipated breakdown of internal order in Cuba.

In the final exercise, in chapter 8 ("Creating Consensus in the Cuban American Community"), a broad base of leaders from Miami's Cuban American community assessed whether the new dynamics within the community—ideological and demographic shifts demonstrating increased support for engagement with Cuba—would translate to a consensus agenda that would allow the community to play a critical role in shaping a new U.S. policy. Would emerging Cuban American leaders accept possibly being bypassed as Cuba policy is returned to the prerogative of the administration as foreign—not domestic—policy? Could they prioritize recommendations for the administration and come to a consensus on their expectations of Cuban responses on human rights and democracy, and the new administration's resolution of the issues of Guantánamo Bay and expropriated property? Advisers were able to flesh out a broad unilateral and multilateral agenda for engagement rooted firmly within the framework of the views of the Cuban American community. The recommendations that emerged from this simulation paved the way for the completion of their policy report issued in April 2009.

Crosscutting Challenges

Three crosscutting challenges to crafting a new U.S. policy emerged from the simulations and form the backbone to this book.

The first arises out of the recognition that change in Cuba will have to come from Cuban actors. This fact mandates framing a new objective for U.S. policy, and also raises the question of what policy initiatives might increase the capacity of those working for change within Cuba. How can the United States—lacking insights about grassroots political dynamics and the interests and organizational capacities of civil society actors— structure policy to reach out to actors in civil society so that they have the will and confidence to carry out effective strategies that lead to a more representative government? How might civil society organizations in the United States help build their capacity and get the most appropriate resources into their hands? Facing such constraints, U.S. efforts to assist Cuban civil society should avoid micromanagement by the U.S. govern- ment and encourage direct contact and communications between U.S. and Cuban entities to foster relations with a diverse cross section of Cuban society. U.S. policy, therefore, should be based on a three-pronged approach: first, it should aim to foster contacts between the citizens of both countries through travel and the engagement of a broad cross- section of Cuban civil society entities by their U.S. counterparts; second, it should enhance the economic well-being and livelihood of the Cuban people through support for grassroots economic activity and unlimited material assistance; and third, it should increase the access of the Cuban people to the free flow of ideas, information, and communication.

The second challenge stems from the fact that the Cuban state can reduce at will the civic and political space critical for the development of pro-democracy movements struggling to grow within Cuba. What type of a strategy can the United States implement to counter the Cuban leader- ship's inclination to ensure its own survival by squeezing out dissenting voices? U.S. policy to "isolate Cuba" has cut off the Cuban people's ac- cess to resources and information, yet the Cuban state still has access to these very same information channels. Part of the intent of engaging Cuba is to level the playing field on the side of civil society. Nevertheless, U.S. policymakers must acknowledge that engagement does not guarantee success. Exogenous factors will play a part in whether and how Cuba evolves to democracy. The Cuban government has no desire to open up its political system in ways that will lead to its demise. And the rewards of its present marriage of convenience with Venezuela may soon give way to a bigger bounty: if Cuba's projected energy reserves are proven and its oil and ethanol industries become operational in three to five years, external influence—whether from the United States or Venezuela—over a newly economically viable government will diminish further.

Thus, a policy of engagement may not bring immediate results; success will require a confluence of three factors that over time will drive openings for change in Cuba: the growth of civil society; a change in leaders' attitudes; and changes in the relationship between Cuba and the international community. If Cuban civil society is to gain capacity and form broad-based movements for change, the Cuban government must allow more internal space for this. For this to occur, Cuba's leaders will have to find, or be given, reasons to view improved relations with the Cuban people and the international community as being in their own interest. These factors—the growth of civil society and the Cuban hierarchy's acquiescence to its expansion—will have to converge with a third: the reshaping of international perspectives about Cuba such that it is seen not as an underdog but as a holdout against change. This final critical factor must help compel the Cuban leadership to enact change in order to sustain its positive relations in the international arena.

The test for U.S. policy will be to facilitate the emergence of these three factors concurrently. The United States will need to engage a broad cross-section of Cuban civil society actors and help reduce the dependence of the Cuban people on the state through increased economic opportunity and improved material well-being. Second, it should engage the Cuban leadership on a wide bilateral agenda based on mutual respect to foster contacts at all levels of the government and reduce the Cuban government's resistance to change. And, third, U.S. policy should be shaped within a multilateral framework combining international pressure for the opening of civic spaces and respect for human, civil, and political rights and provide incentives to the Cuban government to enact change.

The third challenge arises out of the widely held view that an engagement policy without preconditions rewards the Cuban government.

More precisely, if the United States changes its approach to encourage greater contact and communication with the Cuban government, how should U.S. policy deal with the perception that in reducing or removing sanctions that contribute to Cuba's isolation the new strategy is "making concessions"?

This book's recommendation of a proactive, unilateral policy is predicated on an assessment that it is in the interest of the United States to seek ways to set both countries on a path that leads them out of the stalemate in bilateral relations. While the United States ultimately hopes to see consistent and irreversible political and economic openings on the island, to prescribe these objectives as preconditions for engagement is folly as it boils down to a reactive stance in which Cuban inaction determines U.S. action—or inaction. Indeed, inaction is in the short-term interest of a Cuban government focused on preserving power. And since the Cuban government will not pursue any reciprocal conditions established on paper, the United States should make clear the direction of policy it wishes to take, and decide when it wishes to take those steps. The United States would assess and judge Cuban actions that are fundamental to the conduct of foreign policy. On the basis of these unilateral judgments, the United States should decide on measures that will advance U.S. policy without making itself hostage to Cuban resistance to U.S. benchmarks.

It is therefore up to the United States to open a new chapter in bilateral relations. The new goal of supporting the emergence of a Cuban state in which the Cuban people determine the political and economic future of their country through democratic means would serve as the key criterion in assessing U.S. measures. In this context, changes in policy that engage Cuba are not "concessions" but strategic tools to advance policy objectives. A strategy that simultaneously engages the Cuban leadership and the Cuban people and strengthens civil society on the island is integral to this approach.

The U.S. president's leadership will be essential to forge a long-range strategy of engagement that may require quiet negotiations with the Cuban government. Contrary to the popular myth that Congress must legislate to change U.S. policy toward Cuba, the president has ample authority to loosen the embargo and put in place a policy of engagement, including the necessary carrot of increased commercial activities. Working closely with Robert Muse and Richard Popkin, two attorneys who specialize in embargo-related law, the project advisers formulated a road map that relied almost exclusively on unilateral executive actions. This approach is grounded in the understanding that the Helms-Burton Act of 1996 (the Cuban Liberty and Democratic Solidarity Act), which codified the embargo, also preserved and codified the authority of the secretary of the treasury to license all prohibited activities. Therefore, the president can order his secretary to modify, rescind, and change embargo regulations, including permitting broad categories of travel to Cuba and two-way trade in a wide variety of goods and services. (See appendix A for a review of the legal basis for executive action.) Executive action can accomplish a significant amount before the president has to go to Congress for legislation to remove the embargo and lift all restrictions on travel.

The Task of This Book

The second chapter of this book presents the consensus policy recommendations that emerged from the project; it is the only part of this book where the project sought to obtain consensus.

The process whereby all nineteen advisers came together to endorse a set of recommendations broadly acceptable to domestic constituencies in the United States and to the international community represents a strategy that may be replicated. The setting for debate and engagement provided by the simulation exercises led advisers to a common perspective, and the evolving convergence in their views in a sense reflects the deliberations within the Obama administration and in the wider U.S. political environment. A combination of frustration, experience, and new opportunity is leading to incremental change in U.S. policy. The first steps taken by the Obama administration in 2009 were to lift all restrictions on travel and remittances by Cuban Americans to Cuba, and to negotiate a change in OAS policy to rescind Cuba's exclusion and put the onus on the Cuban government to reactivate its membership. Equally significant is that the administration has not engaged in hostile and ultimately counterproductive rhetoric with Cuba. Still, these important measures will not achieve the new policy objective laid out earlier if they are not combined with a longer-term strategy of strategic engagement that further reduces barriers to a normal bilateral relationship.

As noted, chapters 3 to 8 review the main lessons learned from each simulation exercise. Appended to each chapter are documents that help capture the context and dynamics of each simulation: the scenario used for each simulation, the instructions and setting given for each exercise, and an abridged set of minutes that tracks the development of the discussion. The simulation summaries are analyses that reflect the views of the project team at Brookings and not necessarily the views of the full advisory group, though the chapters themselves were reviewed by the group. The cumulative insights reflected within these chapters were critical to the process of formulating the consensus recommendations presented in chapter 2.

The book includes two important appendixes that influenced the advisers' views on the potential for making constructive changes in U.S. policy toward Cuba. Appendix A, "Understanding the Legal Parameters of the U.S. Embargo on Cuba," presents information on the scope for changing policy toward Cuba within the limits of existing laws. An op-ed piece published by project directors in the *Miami Herald* on February 24, 2009, and a summary of embargo regulations present an underappreciated perspective: current law allows the president of the United States extensive leeway in changing policy toward Cuba without legally dismantling the embargo or seeking legislative action. Such flexibility is a crucial tool in constructing a policy that is nimble and dynamic. Appendix B, "2008 Florida International University Poll of Cuban American Opinion" describes the results of the 2008 Florida International University (FIU) poll of Cuban American opinion on U.S. policy toward Cuba and the U.S. elections. Conducted in the aftermath of the U.S. presidential elections by the Institute for Public Opinion Research of FIU and funded by the Brookings Institution and the Cuba Study Group, the poll shows that for the first time since FIU began polling Cuban American residents in 1991, a substantial majority of Cuban American registered voters favor ending current restrictions on travel and remittances to Cuba and support a bilateral dialogue and normal diplomatic relations with the Cuban government.

We offer this book to a broad range of readers—U.S., Cuban, and international policymakers as well as Cuban American and other general readers—in the belief that the lessons learned over the course of the project can be used as a tool set for future work on Cuba. We believe that our deliberations will be useful for U.S. policymakers as they seek to devise an effective policy toward Cuba. The simulations present plausible outcomes based on various policy approaches and provide insights into the strengths, weaknesses, and interests of a set of key strategic actors in and outside Cuba, thereby providing useful approximations of how policy-makers can expect the Cuban government and the international community to respond to different policies. We also hope our analyses will be of interest to Cuban policymakers themselves as they confront the realities of historic change and new dynamics within Cuban society. In addition, we believe this book will be useful to international policymakers who, attuned to the difficult task facing the United States as it reorients its policy toward Cuba, are called on to play a key role to defuse direct tensions between our two countries and advance the aspirations of the Cuban people on a coordinated front. Finally, we offer this book to the Cuban American community. The community has the potential to play an active role to shape U.S. policy toward Cuba. Cuban Americans can be the best ambassadors for reconciliation on both sides of the Florida Straits. But will the proliferation of voices and interests within the Cuban American community allow it to reach the consensus necessary to help lend coherence to U.S. policy?

Political opportunity is never a guarantee for political action or policy coherence, but for the first time in decades there is a convergence in political self-interests in Cuba and the United States that could break a legacy of stalemate. *Learning to Salsa: New Steps in U.S.-Cuba Relations* is written in that spirit, but it is also rooted in realism. The simulations captured in this book highlight not only positive potential but also resistance to political change. Cuban leaders will not want to relinquish power. Within the United States, adherents to isolating Cuba do so out of conviction, trapped by entrenched views. Still, the potential for building coalitions among younger Cuban Americans, business interests, and centrist Republicans and Democrats creates a new political dynamic. *Learning to Salsa* injects into the policy debates on Cuba perspectives that can take advantage of these political openings to increase the odds that the phrase "Cuba in transition" is grounded in reality.

CHAPTER TWO

Cuba: A New Policy of Critical and Constructive Engagement

U.S. policy toward Cuba should advance the democratic aspirations of the Cuban people and strengthen U.S. credibility throughout the hemisphere. Our nearly 50-year-old policy toward Cuba has failed on both counts: it has resulted in a downward spiral of U.S. influence on the island and has left the United States isolated in the hemisphere and beyond. Our Cuba policy has become a bellwether, indicating the extent to which the United States will act in partnership with the region or unilaterally—and ineffectually. Inevitably, strategic contact and dialogue with the Cuban government will be necessary if the United States seeks to engage the Cuban people.

This book proposes a new goal for U.S. policy toward Cuba: to support the emergence of a Cuban state where the Cuban people determine the political and economic future of their country through democratic means. A great lesson of democracy is that it cannot be imposed; it must come from within. The type of government at the helm of the island's future will depend on Cubans. Our policy should therefore encompass the political, economic, and diplomatic tools to enable the Cuban people to engage in and direct the politics of their country. This policy will

This chapter reproduces the Brookings report released in April 2009, "Cuba: A New Policy of Critical and Constructive Engagement," which presents the core group of advisers' consensus recommendations for U.S. policy toward Cuba. It is the only aspect of this book on which project directors sought the consensus of advisers. The original report has been slightly updated to reflect developments between April and August 2009.

advance the interests of the United States in seeking stable relationships based on common hemispheric values that promote the well-being of each individual and the growth of civil society. To engage the Cuban government and Cuban people effectively, the United States will need to engage with other governments, the private sector, and nongovernmental organizations (NGOs). In so doing, U.S. policy toward Cuba would reflect the hemisphere's and our own desire to encourage the Cuban government to adopt international standards of democracy, human rights, and transparency.

Engagement does not mean approval of the Cuban government's policies, nor should it indicate a wish to control internal developments in Cuba; legitimate changes in Cuba will only come from the actions of Cubans. If the United States is to play a positive role in Cuba's future, it must not indulge in hostile rhetoric nor obstruct a dialogue on issues that would advance democracy, justice, and human rights as well as our broader national interests. Perversely, the policy of seeking to isolate Cuba, rather than achieving its objective, has contributed to undermining the well-being of the Cuban people and to eroding U.S. influence in Cuba and Latin America. It has reinforced the Cuban government's power over its citizens by increasing their dependence on it for every aspect of their livelihood. By slowing the flow of ideas and information, we have unwittingly helped Cuban state security delay Cuba's political and economic evolution toward a more open and representative government. And by too tightly embracing Cuba's brave dissidents, we have provided the Cuban authorities with an excuse to denounce their legitimate efforts to build a more open society.

The Cuban Revolution of 1959 is a fact of history that cannot be removed or unlived, but over time, Cuba will change. As the Cuban people become inexorably linked to the region and the world, they will themselves come to play a larger role in the way they are governed. Mortality and time, not U.S. sanctions, have already begun the process of change. A new generation of Cuban leaders will replace the Castro brothers and those who fought in the Sierra Maestra. Although Cuba is already undergoing a process of change, the Bush administration's decision to cling to outmoded tactics of harsh rhetoric and confrontation alienated leaders across the region.

Cuba policy should be a pressing issue for the Obama administration because it offers a unique opportunity for the president to transform our relations with the hemisphere. Even a slight shift away from hostility to engagement will permit the United States to work more closely with the region to effectively advance a common agenda toward Cuba. In the run-up to the April 17, 2009, Summit of the Americas in Trinidad and Tobago, President Obama announced that he "seeks a new beginning with Cuba"; at the meeting itself he announced a lifting of all restrictions on family travel and remittances to Cuba, authorized increased telecommunications links with the island, and revised regulations on gift parcels. In so doing, the president proved that he had been listening to the region, a commitment he can underline further by engaging in dialogue with the Cuban government, as promised during his campaign. By reciprocally improving our diplomatic relations with Cuba, we will enhance our understanding of the island, its people, and its leaders. However, while these measures will promote understanding, improve the lives of people on the island, and build support for a new relationship between our countries, they are insufficient to ensure the changes needed to result in normal diplomatic relations over time.

If the president is to advance U.S. interests and principles, he will need a new policy and a long-term strategic vision for U.S. relations with Cuba. If he is prepared to discard the failed policy of regime change and adopt one of critical and constructive engagement, he and his administration will lay the foundations for a new approach toward Cuba and the rest of Latin America. Like his predecessors, President Obama has the authority to substantially modify embargo regulations in order to advance a policy of engagement that would broaden and deepen contacts with the Cuban people and their government. He has the popular support, domestic and international, to engage Cuba, and, by so doing, to staunch our diminishing influence on the island and recapture the high road in our relations with the hemisphere.

Although it will take Cuban cooperation to achieve a real improvement in relations, we should avoid the mistake of predicating our initiatives on the actions of the Cuban government. The United States must evaluate and act in its own interests. We must not tie our every action to those of the Cuban government, because doing so would allow Cuban officials to set U.S. policy, preventing the United States from serving its own interests.

The majority of Cuban Americans now agree with the American public that our half-century-old policy toward Cuba has failed. For the first time since Florida International University (FIU) began polling Cuban American residents in 1991, a December 2008 poll found that a majority of Cuban American voters favor ending current restrictions on travel and remittances to Cuba and support a bilateral dialogue and normal diplomatic relations with the Cuban government by substantial margins.

The United States is isolated in its approach to Cuba. In the 2008 United Nations General Assembly, 185 countries voted against the U.S. embargo and only two, Israel and Palau, supported the U.S. position. Although the international community is opposed to the embargo, it remains concerned about Cuba's poor human rights record. At the February 2009 Geneva Human Rights Council, Brazil, Chile, and Mexico asked Cuba to respect the rights of political opponents and give an "effective guarantee" of freedom of expression and the right to travel. The European Union has long maintained a policy of critical and constructive engagement in its Common Position yet continues to engage the Cuban government in an effort to obtain the release of political prisoners and ensure greater freedoms for civil society, including access to the Internet. If the United States were to align its policies with these governments—with the addition of Canada—it would enhance our united ability to forcefully make shared concerns known to the Cuban government.

The prospect of significant revenues from oil, natural gas, and sugarcane ethanol in the next five years could further integrate Cuba into global and regional markets. While in the short term Cuba will continue to be heavily dependent on Venezuela for subsidized fuel, in five years, offshore oil reserves, developed with Brazil, Spain, Norway, and Malaysia, combined with the potential for ethanol production with Brazil, may increase net annual financial flows to Cuba by $3.8 billion (at $50 per barrel of oil and $2 per gallon of ethanol). If democratic countries increase their economic stakes in Cuba, they will simultaneously enhance their political influence with its current and future leaders. To be relevant to Cuba, the Obama administration will need to shape its policies now.

The April 2009 Summit of the Americas provided President Obama with an opportunity to enhance U.S. credibility and leadership in the region by signaling a new direction in U.S.-Cuba policy. Rather than continuing to demand preconditions for engaging the Cuban government in the multilateral arena, the president should encourage the Organization of American States and international financial institutions to support Cuba's integration into their organizations as long as it meets their membership

BOX 2-1. Summary of Results of Survey of Cuban American Opinion on Future Relations between the United States and Cuba

A survey of 800 randomly selected Cuban American respondents was conducted in December 2008 in Miami-Dade County, Florida, by the Institute for Public Opinion Research of Florida International University. It was funded by the Brookings Institution and the Cuba Study Group, a nonprofit, nonpartisan organization.

Ending the U.S. Embargo against Cuba

44 percent of registered voters and 53 percent of those not registered to vote oppose continuing the embargo.

72 percent of registered voters and 78 percent of those not registered to vote think the embargo has worked not very well or not at all.

Restrictions on Travel and Remittances

54 percent of registered voters and 69 percent of those not registered to vote favor eliminating current restrictions on Cuban Americans sending remittances to Cuba.

56 percent of registered voters and 63 percent of those not registered to vote favor ending current restrictions on travel to Cuba by Cuban Americans.

58 percent of registered voters and 63 percent of those not registered to vote support open travel to Cuba for all Americans.

Engagement with Cuba

56 percent of registered voters and 65 percent of those not registered to vote support reestablishing diplomatic relations with Cuba.

72 percent of registered voters and 85 percent of those not registered to vote would like to see direct talks between the U.S. and Cuban governments on issues of bilateral concern.

Election Results

38 percent of Cuban Americans voted for Barack Obama.

51 percent under forty-five years of age voted for Barack Obama.

See appendix B for a more detailed account of the survey's findings.

criteria of human rights, democracy, and financial transparency. If Cuba's leaders know that Cuba can become a full member upon meeting standard requirements, they would have an incentive to carry out difficult reforms that ultimately benefit the Cuban people.

The United States successfully engaged the Soviet Union and China from 1973 onward. With those governments the policy objective was to further U.S. interests by reducing bilateral tension, expanding areas of cooperation, fostering cultural contacts, and enmeshing the Soviet and Chinese economies in international linkages that created incentives for improved relations with the West. We continued to voice our commitment to democracy and human rights, and enhanced that argument by pressing the Soviet Union to live up to international obligations. By working with the region and the international community, we can do much the same in Cuba. But as the cases of the Soviet Union and China demonstrated, this approach can only be effective if we are prepared to engage bilaterally and multilaterally.

A New U.S. Policy of Critical and Constructive Engagement

The advisory group of the Brookings Institution project U.S. Policy toward a Cuba in Transition came to the unanimous conclusion that President Barack Obama should commit to a long-term process of critical and constructive engagement at all levels, including with the Cuban government. We believe that only through engagement can the president put into place a strategic vision that would permit the United States to protect its interests and advance the desire we share with the hemisphere to help the Cuban people become agents for peaceful change from within the island. A decision by the president to engage the Cuban government would not reflect acceptance of its human rights abuses or approval of its conduct. Instead, it would prove a realistic evaluation and recognition of the extent to which the Cuban government controls Cuba—essential to the implementation of a new policy that would permit us to work with the region, enhance our influence with the Cuban government, and seek to help Cuba's citizens expand the political space they need to influence their future.

Engagement should serve to enhance personal contacts between Cuban and U.S. citizens and permanent residents, diminish Cuba's attraction as a rallying point for anti-American sentiment, and burnish our standing in the region and the wider international community. If we engage, the Cuban government will no longer be able to use the U.S. threat as a credible excuse for human rights abuses and restrictions on free speech, assembly, travel, and economic opportunity. This in turn would encourage the international community to hold the Cuban government to the same standards of democracy, rights, and freedoms that it expects from other governments around the world.

The Cuban hierarchy will not undertake openings or respond to pressure from the international community or the United States if it considers that doing so would jeopardize its continued existence. The key to a new dynamic in our relationship is to embark on a course of a series of strategic actions that aims to establish a bilateral relationship and put the United States on the playing field—to counter our hitherto self-imposed role of critical observer. Our priority should be to serve U.S. interests and values in the confidence that if we do so wisely and effectively, Cubans in the long run will gain as well.

The Way Forward

It should be understood that engagement, while having as a goal evolution to a peaceful and democratic Cuba, does not promise an overnight metamorphosis. Rather, it is a process, a pathway with various detours and obstacles that over time arrives at its destination.

The road map for critical and constructive engagement is a long-term strategic vision made up of baskets of short-, medium-, and long-term initiatives; all are within the authority of the executive branch to enact. Each of the initiatives we suggest would advance one or more of the following objectives:

—Facilitate contact and the flow of information between the American and Cuban governments to enhance the U.S. response to internal developments that directly impact the well-being of the Cuban people and the interests of the United States.

—Promote a constructive working relationship with the Cuban government to build confidence and trust in order to resolve disputes, with the longer-term objective of fostering a better relationship that serves United States interests and values.

—Support the well-being of the Cuban people and civil society by pro-moting enhanced people-to-people contact and grassroots economic activity.

—Support human rights activists, independent journalists, and the development of Cuban civil society and grassroots democracy.

—Engage Cuba through multilateral initiatives in a process that will lead to its reinstatement in multilateral and regional organizations if it meets the criteria for reinstatement and/or membership.

The conduct and timing of foreign policy remains the prerogative of the president. In order to create a new dynamic in our bilateral relation-ship, we prefer that all the initiatives in the short-term basket be carried out in President Obama's first eighteen months in office. We acknowledge that it is likely that the president and his advisers will assess the impact of the new policy on the United States, Cuba, and the international com-munity prior to moving on to the medium- and long-term baskets. On the basis of their assessment, they will determine how quickly to proceed with the medium- and long-term baskets of initiatives. If the Cuban re-sponse is not encouraging, they might carry out only a few of the sug-gested initiatives or lengthen the time frame. However, it is important that they continue to move toward a full normalization of relations, because doing so would most effectively create conditions for a demo-cratic evolution in Cuba. Equally important to the process is garnering the support of Cuban Americans and congressional leaders.

Given the strong sentiments and expectations that Cuba engenders, it would be preferable for the executive branch to proceed discreetly. The president might first announce the principles he hopes to achieve in Cuba through a policy of engagement that promotes human rights, the well-being of the Cuban people, and the growth of civil society. To carry out the president's vision, the secretary of the treasury will then have the responsibility to write and publish the changes to the Cuban Assets Con-trol Regulations by licensing activities designed to achieve these ends. The secretary of state can quietly accomplish many diplomatic initiatives on a reciprocal basis without any need to publicize them. This quiet diplomacy might be complemented by a refusal to engage in what some refer to as "megaphone diplomacy," in which our governments trade insults across the Straits of Florida, and which only contributes to making the United States appear to be a bully.

The president's leadership in carrying out a new Cuba policy is essential because by law and practice it is his responsibility to determine the overall conduct of U.S. foreign policy. In the case of Cuba, he has ample executive authority to put in place a policy of engagement. If he wishes, he can expand bilateral diplomatic relations, remove Cuba from the list of terrorist countries, and rescind the current policy that grants immediate legal residency to Cubans who enter the United States without visas. Should bilateral relations improve, he could choose to negotiate the unresolved expropriated property claims of U.S. citizens and review the status of Guantánamo Bay Naval Base.

Despite the myth that Congress must legislate to change U.S. policy toward Cuba, history has shown that presidents routinely take actions to strengthen or loosen the embargo as they see fit. Thus, like his predecessors, President Obama can change regulations in order to modify the Cuban embargo without the need for an act of Congress. He would, however, ultimately need to require Congress to legislate in order to remove the embargo and lift all restrictions on travel.

The Helms-Burton Act (H-B) of 1996 defines conditions Cuba must meet for the United States to end the embargo. The act codified embargo regulations, including the provision that states that all transactions are prohibited except as specifically authorized by the secretary of the treasury. Accordingly, the secretary of the treasury may use his licensing authorities to extend, revise, or modify the same regulations. President Clinton did so by instructing the Treasury to issue licenses for various categories of travel, regulations that were subsequently codified by the Trade Sanctions Reform and Export Enhancement Act (TSRA) of 2000. In view of the fact that, unlike Helms-Burton, the TSRA did not provide the secretary of the treasury with the authority to modify its content, legislation is required to remove or expand travel beyond the provisions of the TSRA. Nevertheless, the president can significantly expand travel to Cuba by reinstating provisions authorized by law but rescinded under the Bush administration and interpreting more broadly all categories of travel codified in the TSRA. The Cuban Democracy Act (CDA) of 1992 also legislated certain prohibitions, most notably on U.S. foreign subsidiary trade with Cuba, which, too, can only be revoked by an act of Congress.

In sum, the president does not have the authority to end the embargo or lift the travel ban, but he can effectively dismantle the current commercial embargo by using his licensing authority to permit U.S. exports of certain goods and services, encourage two-way trade in a wide variety of goods and services, and allow broad categories of travel to Cuba.

The Engagement Road Map

The road map to engagement with Cuba comprises short-, medium-, and long-term measures.

Short-Term Initiatives

During his campaign President Barack Obama made clear that the Cuban government must release all political prisoners if the United States is to move toward normalized relations. The initiatives in this first basket would permit greater interaction between the two governments and their citizens, thereby setting the stage for improved understanding and bilateral relations and the potential for enhanced U.S. influence on the island.

The more open travel and remittance measures put in place by the Clinton administration in 1998 and continued by the Bush administration until 2003 contributed to creating the conditions that brought about a more open political atmosphere. During the period now known as the "Cuban Spring," Oswaldo Payá, leader of the Varela Project, worked with Cuba's human rights activists to collect 11,000 signatures on a petition that requested a referendum on the Cuban constitution. Former president Jimmy Carter gave a speech at the University of Havana in Spanish in which he asked Fidel Castro, who was sitting in the front row, to permit the vote; the speech was broadcast live throughout the island. Martha Beatriz Roque, an important dissident leader, held a national assembly to advocate reforms to the Cuban government. Religious groups, with help from their American counterparts, provided equipment, food, and medicines to sister organizations that bolstered outreach to their communities. Students from colleges throughout the United States studying in Cuba were engaged in a lively discussion with students, academics, and people across the island.

The presence of licensed American and Cuban American visitors provided moral support, advice, and assistance to diverse civil society institutions, allowing them to expand and more effectively assist their membership. And interventions by U.S. government and private sector personalities with high-level Cuban officials resulted in reducing repression against dissidents, human rights activists, independent journalists, and librarians. This more fluid and open atmosphere was essential to the growth of civil society and to the freedoms and creation of spaces in which human rights activists and dissidents could operate.

President Obama should replicate these conditions through unilateral and unconditional actions that promote enhanced human contact by generously licensing all categories of travel permitted in the TSRA. He should, first, follow his campaign promise to grant Cuban Americans unrestricted rights to family travel and to send remittances to the island, since Cuban American connections to family are our best tool for helping to foster the beginnings of grassroots democracy on the island. Further, the president should expand travel for all American citizens and permanent residents by instructing the Office of Foreign Assets Control (OFAC) to license people-to-people travel for educational, cultural, and humanitarian purposes.

Cuban citizens should also be permitted to travel to the United States for a variety of purposes—including family, academic, and cultural visits—in order to enhance their understanding of our open and democratic society. The secretary of state should instruct the Department of State and the United States Interests Section (USINT) in Havana to use standard criteria applied around the world for awarding non-immigrant visas to Cubans. This more tolerant approach would strengthen the bonds of family and culture while helping the Cuban people improve their lives and grow the social organizations necessary for a democratic civil society.

Diplomatic travel and interaction must be reciprocally expanded so that our diplomats in Havana have the knowledge, access, and expertise needed to predict, evaluate, and deal with any eventuality in Cuba. This requires permitting comparable opportunities to Cuban diplomats posted in Washington. There is little the United States has to fear by allowing Cuban diplomats to see for themselves the realities of American life. To reduce illegal migration, enhance our security, and conserve our fisheries, the State Department should resume migration talks at the deputy assistant secretary level and begin a dialogue between the respective heads of the interests sections on other issues of mutual concern, including the environment, health, and counternarcotics measures.

The devastation caused by hurricanes that struck Cuba in 2008 generated considerable concern among Cubans in the United States and among the broader American public. Unfortunately, disagreements and distrust between our governments prevented the United States from assisting with relief efforts. In order to avoid a recurrence of this impasse, the Department of State should seek an understanding or agreement with the Cuban government that would permit U.S. assistance to Cuba for natural disasters.

Measures are now in place to ensure that public resources that provide support to the Cuban people are well used by USAID grantees. However, large contracts concluded in the final months of the Bush administration with nonprofit organizations and private companies that are said to promote or manage a transition in Cuba may not reflect the current administration's objectives. A review should be conducted to determine whether these contracts should be continued, modified, or canceled.

Additionally, although OFAC has always had the authority to license the importation of lifesaving medicines developed in Cuba for testing by the Food and Drug Administration (FDA), it has made the process cumbersome and lengthy. The sad conclusion is that OFAC has been more concerned with the financial benefits that might accrue to Cuba than with the potential of these medicines to treat children with brain tumors and adults with lung cancer or meningitis. To reduce bureaucratic hurdles and permit the speedy entry of lifesaving medications into the United States, OFAC regulations should be modified or reinterpreted so that the only barrier to the entry of Cuban manufactured medicines is that they meet FDA standards—the same criteria that apply to all medical imports.

The president should also seek to promote the free flow of ideas and information, including the creation of music, films, and other works of art as embodied in Representative Howard Berman's 1988 Free Trade in Ideas Act. Despite the prohibition against the U.S. government restricting the importation of all informational materials, successive administrations have narrowly interpreted the Berman Act in order to prohibit Americans from creating music, films, and other artistic works with Cubans. These prohibitions were not intended by the statutes and should be removed.

The aforementioned initiatives are noncontroversial and widely supported by the American public. More controversial—although still enjoying widespread public support—would be licensing the sale and donation of all communications equipment, including radios, televisions, and computers. The CDA recognized the importance of expanding access to ideas, knowledge, and information by authorizing the licensing of telecommunications goods and services. U.S. government financing of books and radios that are distributed to Cubans throughout the island demonstrates

---

BOX 2-2. Short-Term Initiatives

Remove all restrictions on family and humanitarian travel to Cuba.

Permit and expand specific licenses for people-to-people travel for educational, cultural, and humanitarian purposes.

Reinstate remittances to individuals and independent civil society organizations in Cuba.

Allow all Cubans who meet the requirements of U.S. immigration law to travel to the United States.

Promote normal diplomatic activities on a reciprocal basis, including in-country travel, official meetings, exchange of attachés, and sponsorship of cultural and educational exchanges.

Open a dialogue between the United States and Cuba, particularly on issues of mutual concern, including migration, counternarcotics enforcement, the environment, health, and security.

Develop agreements with the Cuban government for disaster relief and for environmental stewardship.

Conduct a review of the purpose, content, and implementation capacity of the new contracts awarded to private companies and nongovernmental organizations during the last months of the Bush administration.

Modify current licensing regulations so that tradable medicines developed in Cuba are subject to standard FDA approval and no longer require separate Office of Foreign Assets Control (OFAC) authorization.

---

a belief that breaking down the barriers to the flow of information is critical to promoting change in Cuba. The president should therefore instruct the Department of Commerce and OFAC to internally change their respective licensing policies with regard to Cuba from a "presumption of denial" to a "presumption of approval" with respect to items deemed to be in the U.S. national interest for Cuba to receive, including laptops, cell phones and other telecommunications equipment, computer peripherals, Internet connection equipment, as well as access to satellite and broadband communications networks.

The following initiatives that would provide assistance for civil society and for activities that help the Cuban people become agents for change would require in some cases a formal understanding with the Cuban government and in others at least a willingness to permit the activity. We believe that if these activities were permitted by the United States and the

Encourage the free exchange of ideas, including the creation of art, cinema, and music, by amending OFAC regulations to allow the "Free Trade in Ideas Act" ("the Berman Act") to reflect its original intention, which was to forbid any U.S. law from restricting the creation and free flow of informational materials and ideas.

Modify internal Department of Commerce and OFAC licensing policies and regulations as necessary to permit the donation and sale of communications equipment to Cuba and Cubans under a general license, and license the provision of telecommunications services as provided for in the Cuban Democracy Act.

License Cuban state and nonstate entities to access satellite and broadband communications networks.

Establish an assistance program for civil society entities and license the transfer of funds for activities that support human rights, the rule of law, micro-enterprise, and professional training.

License providers of U.S. government and private assistance to advance the goals of U.S. policy identified in this chapter.

Do not object to an OAS dialogue with Cuba on the status of its membership. Permit Cuba to participate in specialized and technical OAS agencies and in knowledge-building seminars at multilateral institutions.

Review the evidence to determine whether Cuba should continue to be listed as a state sponsor of terrorism.

Cuban governments, they would help to prepare the Cuban people for assuming a greater role in their governance.

The U.S. government should act to enhance the flow of resources to the Cuban people. It should license U.S. nongovernmental organizations and private individuals to transfer funds to individuals and civil society organizations in Cuba that work to foster a more open society. The United States should also encourage the creation of multilateral funds that promote the same objective. Such assistance should not be subject to an ideological test but rather be available to Cuban civic entities in the form of micro-credit for small businesses and for salaries of persons engaged by civil society to provide community services, among others.

Although the U.S. government currently manages an assistance program for Cuba, it is limited by sanctions regulations and is narrowly focused. Much of the assistance, amounting principally to in-kind goods, is difficult to deliver due to the opposition of the Cuban government either to the type of assistance or to the groups or individuals receiving it. In order to better serve the needs of civil society in Cuba, the U.S. government should seek to obtain the approval of the Cuban government for an assistance program that would provide financial and in-kind assistance for activities that advance human rights and the rule of law, encourage micro-enterprise, and promote educational and professional exchanges.

The issue of whether Cuba should be classified by the U.S. government as a terrorist state has many supporters and detractors. However, the reasons listed for Cuba's inclusion on the list appear to be insufficient, thus leading to charges that the list is a political tool for appeasing domestic constituencies. In order to ensure that this important vehicle in U.S. policy is used appropriately, a review of the evidence should be conducted. If Cuba is legitimately found to be a terrorist state based on the evidence over the last five years, it should remain on the list; if not, it should be removed.

Finally, it is in our interest to see Cuba reintegrated into the Organization of American States (OAS) if it meets membership standards of democracy, human rights, and transparency. To this end, and in order to provide incentives for reform, the United Sates should not object to the OAS secretary general's discussing with Cuba the requirements for reinstatement as a full member. In addition, the United States should not object to Cuba's participation in OAS specialized and technical agencies.

Medium-Term Initiatives

The second basket of initiatives is distinct from the first because it moves beyond enhancing the ability of Cubans to take a more proactive and informed part in their society and government. The initiatives in the second basket seek to build a foundation for reconciliation by beginning a process of resolving long-standing differences. A number of these initiatives could serve as incentives or rewards for improved human rights, the release of political prisoners, and greater freedom of assembly, speech, and rights for opposition groups and labor unions. Initiatives that fall within this category include allowing Cuba access to normal commercial instruments for the purchase of goods from the United States.

None of the initiatives, however, should be publicly or privately tied to specific Cuban actions. As the Cuban government is on record as rejecting any type of carrot-and-stick tactic, it would be counterproductive to do so. Rather, the United States should decide on the actions that it wishes to take and when to carry them out. Doing so will give the president maximum flexibility in determining how and when to engage.

The first two initiatives simply encourage a broadening of U.S. government public and private participation in activities that assist the growth of Cuban civil society and should be carried out regardless of Cuba's conduct. The U.S. government should expand the assistance envisioned in the first basket by encouraging other governments, multilateral institutions, organizations, and individuals to support educational exchanges as well as the improvement of human rights and the growth of civil society. In addition, in order to enhance access to knowledge, the U.S. government should allow private individuals, groups, and the Cuban government access to normal commercial credit for the sale of communications equipment and connections to satellite and broadband networks.

Licensing U.S. companies to provide services for the development of Cuban offshore oil and gas would provide benefits to the United States and Cuba. (At this point it should be noted that the secretary of the treasury has always had and continues to have the authority, as embodied in OFAC regulations, to license any transaction found to be in the U.S. national interest. This power has been used over the past fifteen years by various Republican and Democratic administrations to license a variety of commercial transactions between the United States and Cuba). The following are some of the reasons we might wish to become engaged in developing Cuba's offshore oil and gas: First, if U.S. and other reputable companies are involved in Cuba's offshore oil development it would reduce Cuba's dependence on Venezuela for two thirds of its oil imports. Second, it is preferable that U.S. oil companies with high standards of transparency develop these resources rather than, for example, Russia's notoriously corrupt oligarchy. Third, U.S. influence in Cuba is likely to increase if U.S. companies have an economic relationship on the ground. Fourth, our companies have the technology and expertise to develop Cuba's offshore oil and gas.

As we have pointed out, our actions should not be constrained by linking them to specific Cuban responses. Nevertheless, the following initiatives will depend on a significant change in bilateral and multilateral relations. Membership in regional and multilateral organizations ultimately depends on Cuba's meeting membership criteria and gaining approval. Therefore, if Cuba meets the membership criteria of the OAS, it should be

---

BOX 2-3. **Medium-Term Initiatives**

Encourage and fund a wide variety of educational exchanges and scholarships that
   promote understanding and provide training in diverse fields such as the arts, economics, and journalism.
Permit commercial credit terms without government guarantees for the sale of communications equipment.
Allow licenses for U.S. companies to participate in the development of Cuban off-
   shore oil, gas, and renewable-energy resources.
Encourage and participate in multilateral organizations that further human rights and
   the growth of civil society in Cuba.
Do not object to the lifting of Cuba's suspension by the Organization of American
   States if the OAS General Assembly consents.
Seek to recover executive authority to permit Cuba's participation in international
   financial institutions.
Work with Congress to restore executive branch authority over travel to Cuba.
Upgrade the United States' diplomatic relations with Cuba.
Open bilateral discussions on the resolution of claims relating to expropriated
   property.
Open bilateral discussions to reach an agreement that satisfies mutual concerns
   regarding Guantánamo Bay Naval Base.

---

reinstated. The same should be the case if Cuba meets the standards of international financial institutions. However, Helm-Burton instructs the U.S.
government to oppose Cuba's membership, even if it has complied with
institutional standards, if it has not met specific criteria relating to our
bilateral relationship. We believe that the authority for the U.S. government to determine how it will vote in international institutions should be
returned to the executive branch of government. The Helms-Burton language on OAS reinstatement is slightly more permissive than that regarding the international financial institutions—"The President *should* instruct
the United States Permanent Representative to the Organization of American States to oppose and vote against any termination of the suspension
of the Cuban Government from participation in the Organization until the
President determines . . . that a democratically elected government in Cuba
is in power"—in contrast to "The Secretary of the Treasury *shall* instruct
the United States executive director of each international financial institu-

tion to use the voice and vote of the United States to oppose the admission of Cuba." In both cases it would be preferable if Congress would return these prerogatives to the president.

Since this book deals solely with initiatives within the realm of executive authority, lifting the travel ban was beyond its scope. Nevertheless, the majority of the advisers felt that the ban had been counter-productive and should be lifted. In an effort to reach consensus and also maintain our initiatives within the realm of executive authority, we have recommended that the president seek to regain the authority to determine what, if any, travel restrictions should apply to U.S. citizens and permanent residents who wish to visit Cuba. In doing so, the executive branch would decide the timing and degree to which to expand licensing for additional categories of travel or to lift the travel ban altogether.

As for bilateral relations, if the conditions are right, we would prefer the exchange of ambassadors and the establishment of embassies. A stronger presence in Cuba would strengthen our capacity to assess political and power relationships, make local contacts, advocate directly with the Cuban government over issues that are in our interest, understand opportunities for Cuban entrepreneurship, and explore areas where the international community can engage to promote reform. However, since we have limited the recommendations to actions that the executive branch can take unilaterally, we have not suggested the exchange of ambassadors because confirmation is required from the Senate. It is our hope that, at the appropriate time, the president and the Senate would agree to move forward in this area. However, should this not be the case or should the president desire a different approach, he can on his own initiative improve and upgrade our relations by sending a more senior envoy to lead the United States Interests Section or by naming a special envoy for Cuban relations.

Finally, the United States cannot ignore indefinitely the issues that have bedeviled the U.S.-Cuba relationship for decades: property claims and sovereignty over Guantánamo Bay. The United States should open discussions on the claims of United States citizens for expropriated property. Equally difficult but just as compelling will be to initiate dialogue on the issue of sovereignty and use of the territory currently occupied by the U.S. Guantánamo Bay Naval Base. The administration should begin discussions to provide a broad framework for resolution of these issues.

BOX 2-4. Long-Term Initiatives

Open Cuban and American consular offices in major cities in the United States and
  Cuba, respectively.
Provide disaster relief, rehabilitation, and health assistance to the Cuban government.
Provide general licenses for the export to Cuba of additional categories of American
  goods and services such as products that enhance the environment, conserve
  energy, and provide improved quality of life.
Permit the import of additional categories of Cuban goods.
Support Cuban and Cuban American efforts to promote the reconciliation of the
  Cuban nation.
Reach a mutually acceptable settlement on claims for expropriated property.
Reach a mutually acceptable solution for restoring Cuban sovereignty over the terri-
  tory of Guantánamo Bay.
Achieve full diplomatic relations between the United States and Cuba.

Long-Term Initiatives

This last basket of initiatives may be taken by the president, but it would
be preferable if our bilateral relationship were such that Congress had
already taken steps to remove the final barriers to a normal diplomatic
relationship. This would include removing Cuba from the Trading with
the Enemy Act (TWEA) and rescinding or modifying Helms-Burton, the
TSRA, and the CDA. If Congress were receptive to a review of the aforementioned laws but not yet prepared to move forward, the president
should continue to deepen our engagement by expanding our diplomatic
presence and by permitting the reciprocal opening of consular offices in
major cities. Foreign assistance to the Cuban government is restricted by
the Foreign Assistance Act of 1961, with the exception of the provision of
assistance to any government for internal disaster relief, rehabilitation,
and health. The president could also license further categories of goods
and services for export, and the importation of certain Cuban goods in
addition to medicines approved by the FDA.

President Obama has stated that full normalization of relations will
depend on improved human rights and progress toward democracy in
Cuba. A truly successful and mutually beneficial relationship between our
countries will also be determined by the degree of reconciliation between

Cubans in exile and Cubans on the island. Concerns about illegal acts and human rights abuses on both sides must be reviewed and solutions must be found. This is also true in the case of expropriated property, made more complex by Cuban claims of damages for injuries allegedly caused by the embargo. Leaving these issues unresolved would not only stunt trade and investment, it would deprive the Cuban people of fully utilizing their talents and improving their lives. Resolution of claims for expropriated property, as well as the restoration of Cuban sovereignty over the territory of Guantánamo Bay, is essential to a prosperous and democratic Cuba and to the achievement of a healthy and normal relationship between our two countries.

CHAPTER THREE

U.S. Policy:
Constraints of a Historical Legacy

On February 7, 2008, the project hosted the first of six simulation exercises to assess the scope, limitations, and potential of the United States to promote an enabling environment for peaceful democratic transition in Cuba. The focus of the simulation was the question, Can U.S. policy, bound as it is by historical constraints—the embargo and restrictions on travel, remittances, and limited diplomatic engagement—promote political change in Cuba? Since U.S. policy has been relatively constant since 1961, there is little reason to expect that continuing it would produce different results from those we see today. Instead, the interesting question is to assess whether a policy rooted in isolating Cuba would advance or hinder U.S. interests in the event of an exogenous shock, such as Fidel's death.

The following key questions emerged from the first simulation:

—Do U.S. attempts to isolate Cuba create policy leverage for the United States or do they reduce U.S. capacity to influence events and policies in Cuba?

—Can the United States eliminate the tension between its short- and long-term policy objectives: migration deterrence and prevention (a short-term objective) versus the promotion of democracy and a coherent set of policies to advance freedom in Cuba (a long-term objective)?

—In the event of instability on the island, how can the United States effectively discourage a mass migration without seeming to legitimize the Cuban government's control over its citizens or altering its own migration policies (the wet foot, dry foot policy, which followed the 1995 revision of the Cuban Adjustment Act, whereby a Cuban detained on the waters between the two nations, that is, with "wet feet," would summarily be sent home or to a third country, whereas one who makes it to shore with "dry feet" got a chance to remain in the United States, and later would qualify for expedited "legal permanent resident" status and U.S. citizenship)?

—Given key allies' opposition to components of current U.S. policy toward Cuba, is there space for multilateral cooperation?

—What measures should the U.S. government take to obtain the information it needs to make informed policy decisions?

The Exercise

July 28, 2008. Fidel Castro is dead. President George W. Bush has asked his National Security Adviser to convene a meeting of the principal officers of all U.S. government agencies dealing with foreign affairs. Their task is to determine how to respond to Fidel's death and assess how the United States can seize the opportunity to advance U.S. policy goals then in place with respect to Cuba: promoting freedom on the island while isolating the regime. This scenario was designed to assess the strengths and weaknesses of policy options within the constraints of the Bush administration's Cuba policy. (For all simulations [chapters 3–8], see the "Simulation Documents" at the end of the chapter for a detailed description of the scenario; the instructions given to participants for the exercise; and the "minutes" of the exercise.)

President Bush's speech of October 24, 2007, was used as the baseline for the administration's policies. With this speech the president aimed to reorient a policy that had fallen behind the times, having been caught off-guard by the succession from Fidel to Raúl Castro. The expectation that a violent uprising by dissidents and a huge exodus of Cuban refugees would be set off when Fidel Castro died or left power has failed to materialize. The administration—assuming that Fidel was terminally ill and would die quickly—has remained silent while Raúl consolidated his control over Cuban institutions, established his own relationships with world leaders, and opened unprecedented dialogue with the Cuban people about their visions for a future Cuba.

The president's speech underlined two central tenets of his strategy toward Cuba. First, he emphasized that the U.S. embargo and travel restrictions would remain in place until Cuba undertakes significant political reforms, so as not to reward the Cuban government or reinforce its capabilities. Second, he pronounced that the operative word in policy would be "freedom," not "stability." In declaring that the United States is on the side of freedom and democracy, not stability, he intimated that the United States would side with (and possibly foment) instability in Cuba. He underscored this notion with a direct appeal to the Cuban people to continue to resist the regime, and with a statement to the Cuban government, armed forces, and police that if they positioned themselves on the right side of change, they could play a role in a future Cuba.

In that speech, President Bush offered three initiatives for fomenting internal change but gave few details as to how they might be made operational, since each requires the approval or reciprocity of the Cuban government. The United States will

1. License nongovernmental organizations and faith-based groups to provide computers and Internet access to the Cuban people contingent on Cuba's lifting restrictions on Internet access.

2. Issue an invitation to Cuban youths whose families suffer oppression to join a Latin American scholarship program, if the Cuban government allows their participation.

3. Create a multilateral fund to finance Cuban reconstruction and entrepreneurial activities, contingent on Cuba's adoption of fundamental freedoms and free and fair multi-party elections.

Simulation Exercise No. 1:
A Meeting of the National Security Council, July 28, 2008

The simulation sought to test the effectiveness of U.S. policy responses to Fidel's death and the extent to which they could advance the Bush administration's policy goals. Will the president's rhetoric—holding out political change as a precondition for engagement and creating incentives that were potentially out of line with the interests of the Cuban government—be effective? Would the administration's proposals strike a chord inside Cuba and with the international community?

Participants were not allowed to offer policy options that contradict core precepts of the Bush administration's views, an approach that helped focus attention on the limits of U.S. policy. Although the group found that it could work within the current policy framework to avoid further deterioration of U.S. relations with Cuba, it could not further the goal of advancing the role of the Cuban people in defining the political and economic direction of the island.

Managing Migration Risks

Participants agreed that a mass migration of Cubans to the United States was unlikely to materialize in the event of Fidel's death. Nonetheless, if a mass migration were to occur, all expressed confidence that the administration had an effective operational plan in place to handle the most probable migration levels.[1] Staging of Coast Guard ships and strong public statements that migrants would be stopped and returned were considered critical measures to head off a mass migration. Participants found that the possibility of U.S.-based militants seeking to enter Cuba posed a greater risk than incoming migrants from Cuba, though the likelihood of this has radically decreased since the 1990s.

Public diplomacy after Fidel's death will affect migration incentives, and the administration would hope to avert a large inflow of migrants into the United States. Participants recommended that the United States deliver a public message to underscore its commitment to a free Cuba shaped by the Cuban people, implying that Cubans should stay on the island. Some worried, however, that Washington could not credibly make this assertion while continuing the seemingly open invitation to migration it offers under the wet foot, dry foot policy. Even though Congress is unlikely to repeal the Cuban Adjustment Act, the administration could modify the wet foot, dry foot policy to discourage migration, since this aspect of the legislation is controlled by the executive branch.[2]

---

1. The scale of a future migration is difficult to predict with any certainty and is affected by many variables. The Coast Guard may have modeled scenarios of future migrations, but if so, the figures remain classified, as far as we know. The last exodus, in 1994, involved approximately 37,000 Cubans. A future migration could exceed this level. In fact, according to the Institute for Cuban and Cuban-American Studies, between October 2005 and September 2007, 77,000 Cubans reached American soil, more than twice the number of the 1994 exodus. Today, Homeland Security Task Force Southeast stands poised to deploy Operation Vigilant Sentry in the event of a sudden mass migration.

2. The Cuban Adjustment Act, first passed in 1966, permits all Cuban nationals who have been in the United States for over a year to adjust their status and become permanent U.S. residents. The law can only be modified or repealed by Congress. The wet foot, dry foot policy, on the other hand, remains under the authority of the executive branch.

Instituted by the Clinton administration, the wet foot, dry foot policy stipulates that all Cuban nationals who make it to U.S. territory are free to remain in the United States and eventually to adjust their status under a revision in 1995 to the Cuban Adjustment Act of 1996. Under the revision, those who are picked up at sea are to be interviewed by immigration authorities and then returned to Cuba. If the administration decided to modify the policy, it could announce that Cubans who arrive on dry land would be interviewed by immigration authorities under the same procedures as those picked up at sea, before admission to the country and without the possibility of applying to change their status. Most would not qualify for refugee status and would be returned to Cuba. This action would decrease the more visible migrants, the *balseros*, those who navigated the Florida Straits on balsawood rafts, but it would not change the situation of those entering the United States through third countries, particularly Mexico and Spain, who would still be allowed to apply for a legal change of status under the Cuban Adjustment Act.

The next question would be how to return migrants to Cuba. Participants debated how the administration might engage the Cuban government on this issue, in light of its accusations that the United States has repeatedly violated its commitment under the bilateral migration accords to return those arriving by irregular means. Participants urged the administration to proceed cautiously, recommending, first, that it not publicly demand that the Cuban government act to prevent a mass migration, lest it appear to legitimize the Cuban government's control over its citizens, and, second, that it deal with migration discreetly. Absent signs of an exodus that would require forthright action, they agreed that the administration should not make migration policy the first U.S. response to an event of this magnitude in Cuba—Fidel's death; such a response would create a poor first impression to a region watching closely. The first U.S. statement should be about the political environment.

Tension in Policy Objectives:
Migration Deterrence versus Promotion of Democracy

The discussion highlighted the conflict between short- and long-term U.S. interests: migration deterrence and prevention on the one hand (a short-term goal), and the promotion of democracy on the other (a long-term goal). If the United States demonstrates that its principal concern is migration prevention, it reinforces the value of an authoritarian government in Cuba that has the will and capacity to keep its population within its boundaries. If the president's objective is to focus on bringing democracy to Cuba, the administration should not indicate that it values the capacity of the Cuban government to prevent migration so as not to undercut the president's longer-term objective of democratization.

Within this context, participants debated the trade-off between freedom and stability. A commitment to stability on the island, though potentially out of line with administration policy, would be important to discouraging migration and to bringing the Cuban American leadership in line with Washington policy and to neutralizing elements in the United States that may be looking for an opportunity to destabilize the island to bring about regime change. A quiet attempt to reinforce stability through the offer of emergency humanitarian aid, a gesture of goodwill from the American people to the Cuban people, would be an appropriate first response, but the Cuban government would likely see it as a Trojan horse; a multilateral package may be more effective.

Attempting to work without the Cuban government would be problematic: not only does the United States lack information about the capacity and dynamics of broad-based civil society actors who would carry the momentum for change from within, but engaging dissidents to advance U.S. policy goals also jeopardizes the legitimacy of such actors in Cuba. Given these tensions between freedom and stability, how could the administration make the core precept of freedom—democracy promoted by Cuban actors—operational?

Managing Public Diplomacy

Given the narrow parameters of an isolationist policy, the best advice participants could provide was for the administration to reaffirm its commitment to freedom and democracy in Cuba. A public statement from the administration might read as follows: "The Cuban people deserve to be free. This is an opportunity for the people and institutions of Cuba to move toward fully engaging their country in the international community. The United States government reaffirms its current policy and is ready to work with other members of the OAS to develop relations with Cuba based on the principles of mutual respect, national self-determination, institutional democracy, and the rule of law."

The First Diplomatic Response

Sending a high-level delegation to Fidel Castro's funeral, while unlikely to bridge all policy differences, might provide U.S. policymakers with a chance to open spaces for renewed discussions with allies in Latin America and the European Union about building a more unified approach to Cuba. Participants rejected a number of proposed delegations (one suggestion was Jimmy Carter and George H. W. Bush or Colin Powell) because they seemed to legitimize the Cuban government and thus were inconsistent with current policy. Most opted for the safer approach of sending lower-level representation from the administration with members of Congress who have traveled to Cuba on previous occasions.

Limits to Regional Cooperation

Forging collaboration within current policy parameters will be difficult, even if regional partners in principle agree on a common goal of freedom and democracy for Cuba. Yet working with the region in pursuit of U.S. policy objectives is an important goal. Continuation of the U.S. trade embargo as well as the prolonged symbolic resonance of the Cuban saga within Latin American domestic politics will compel many regional partners to distance themselves from the United States on this issue. Perceptions of failed American attempts at democracy promotion elsewhere in the world further complicate the matter.

It is important to bear in mind that many Latin American countries—Brazil and Mexico in particular—have demonstrated a keen desire to forge new ties with Cuba under the leadership of Raúl Castro. To the extent that these ties help decrease the influence of Venezuelan president Hugo Chávez, they could be considered to advance U.S. interests and may offer a way for Washington to gain important interlocutors. Unfortunately, participants found that even modest options to encourage intermediary interlocutors contravened the stated goal of isolating the Cuban government and could not be pursued.

Impact on Political Prisoners

Participants agreed that the United States cannot suspend its scrutiny of human rights, and the administration would continue to demand the release of political prisoners. Unfortunately, participants found that they possessed few tools to back up the rhetoric. Direct support to dissidents is difficult to achieve. Providing material support to human rights and civil society activists is blocked by both the Cuban government and the current embargo. Furthermore, there is always the danger that assistance to dissidents will compromise the perception of their independence. Rhetorical demands have even less impact, given the negative image of U.S. internment facilities at Guantánamo Bay. In addition, other regional players may be less likely to ally themselves with the United States position on human rights because of disagreement on other issues.

Which Cubans Will Carry the Democratic Torch?

Participants agreed that a democratic movement must come from within the island's population and be led by the Cuban people, but there are innumerable obstacles to making such policy operational. Policymakers lack information about the political dynamics and organizing capacities of possible opposition voices in Cuban society, and existing dissident factions are often weak and divided. Moreover, because of the U.S.-imposed isolation, U.S. policymakers lack not only contacts but also the ability to identify channels to provide support to moderates in government, including members of the military who may be sympathetic to the prospect of a more open political system. The capacity may exist to provide limited support to some dissidents, but this assistance at most helps them organize for the future; it does not achieve real change in the short run, and these groups also take long-term risks by receiving external assistance. Participants reached the conclusion that current policy objectives will need to be recalibrated to take stock of these severe limitations.

Considerations for U.S. Policy

Although Fidel's death had long been anticipated as a moment that would present Cuba and the region with historic and strategic opportunities, project advisers found that, in the event, a U.S. policy rooted in isolating Cuba would allow for remarkably few options for decisive action. Unable to directly engage Cuba, the United States risked growing more isolated internationally, at a point when other nations were seeking to advance regional and commercial interests. Significantly, as other nations took proactive steps to influence developments in Cuba, any sizable change in U.S. policy remained contingent on actions by the Cuban government. Such a framework ultimately gave Havana, not Washington, the upper hand.

Across the board, in every single policy area, participants found their ability to make sound policy judgments hamstrung by a lack of detailed information about key Cuban institutions and individuals. Limited direct insights about the relationships among key individuals and among the Communist Party (PCC), the Revolutionary Armed Forces (FAR), the intelligence services, and other elites constrained the capacity of participants to judge the strength and longevity of the regime after Fidel. Particularly limiting was the lack of information about the military, since it must maintain security and it may make or break the ability of a new government to survive.

Participants considered several options to create clearer information flows, including: relaxing current travel restrictions on U.S. and Cuban diplomats; facilitating greater official contact between diplomats and their governments, especially on matters of mutual concern such as migration, organized crime and counternarcotics, and the environment; promoting more contact with Cuban civil society (and not simply the dissident community) by U.S. Interests Section diplomats as well as by Cuban Americans; and allowing free travel by Cuban Americans to Cuba. Although many participants believed that such measures would help make the Cuban people "champions of democracy," ultimately the measures were rejected as inconsistent with isolationist policy approaches. On the economics side, the United States has few levers in Cuba, because assistance packages are contingent on political reforms that the government is unlikely to make, and options to increase trade were outside the Bush administration's solution set.

In sum, participants felt that the best they could do under the restrictions of current Bush administration policies was to tread water. The more a new Cuban leadership takes a moderate stance on reforms—providing grounds for other countries to deepen their engagement—the greater the risk of U.S. isolation.

SIMULATION SCENARIO NO. 1
CONTEXTUAL BACKGROUND OF EXERCISE

The following scenario was given to participants:

July 28, 2008. On the morning of July 26, 2008—the fifty-fifth anniversary of Fidel Castro's failed attack on the Moncada Barracks in Santiago de Cuba on July 26, 1953—Raúl Castro announces Fidel's death. He says the Cuban government and people will observe a month of mourning and invites world leaders to join him at the state funeral, to be held in Havana the following week. He calls on the Cuban people to mourn Fidel by remaining calm and continuing to work for the Revolution. Raúl concludes his remarks by stating that he will continue as interim president of the Council of State until the National Assembly can meet to formally decide Fidel's successor in February. There is no doubt that the National Assembly will name Raúl president of Cuba; he is the head of the Communist Party, minister of defense, and acting president since July 2006.

Despite media reports and telephone calls from families in Cuba describing some street celebrations, the overall mood is somber as Cubans mourn and the country prepares for a major funeral that will be attended by many world leaders. The event is expected to be far larger than the Pope's visit in 1998. The United States Interests Section (USINT) reports an unusually heavy police and security presence, particularly along major roads, perhaps to ensure that there will be no large-scale movement of people, either into the cities or toward the coast.

In the run-up to Fidel's death, rumors have circulated that his health was failing, but the international media have been unable to provide confirmation. The Bush administration has been gaming scenarios on Fidel's death for years, yet has never been able to decide on a strategic response beyond preparations to close Florida ports to prevent or discourage a mass migration into the United States.

In reaction to the news of Fidel's death, President George W. Bush briefly remarks that the United States government remains committed to a true democratic transition in Cuba and will not change current policy, which supports freedom on the island. When asked about the possibility of a mass migration, he replies, "The best way to prevent mass migration and internal violence is for Cuba to have free and fair elections."

As anticipated, some members of the south Florida delegation as well as public officials in Florida publicly gloat over Fidel's death. A gathering of remembrance and celebration is planned for the Orange Bowl on July 29, sponsored by the Miami municipal government and the Cuban American community. Florida's three Cuban American congressional representatives—Senators Martinez and Menendez and Secretary of Commerce Gutierrez—plan to speak at the event, and Cuban American leaders from across the political spectrum are to attend. Florida police are expecting another mass rally like those that took place during the Elián González crisis.

Florida Republicans are concerned about eroding popular support for sustaining a hard line on contacts, trade, and travel with Cuba, especially given the interest of Cuban Americans in visiting and helping their families on the island. Some conservatives would like to increase the pressure for regime change—in effect, to help spark an internal revolution that produces radical internal change, as occurred in the Soviet Union in 1991—in order to wipe the slate clean and allow the emergence of a new government.

The majority of Cuban Americans are more moderate. Although they lament the fact that Raúl Castro will continue the Revolution's authoritarian tradition, they believe that the United States should engage the Cuban government and people.

As interim president Raúl does not enjoy significant popular support because the reforms he announced, while welcome, did not improve the well-being or opportunities of the vast majority of urban Cubans. Farm output and income did increase in moderate terms as thousands of individuals leased land for agricultural use.

Raúl's inability to improve economic conditions stems from divisions between "economic reformers" and "hard-line Revolutionaries" allied with Fidel, most notably Ramiro Valdéz Menendez and Foreign Minister Felipe Pérez Roque, who believe that structural reforms would jeopardize the Revolution by leading to demands for political space and greater contact with the outside world. In the same vein, Bush administration critics blame U.S.-Cuba policy for strengthening the Cuban hard-liners and reducing the influence of reformers by keeping tensions high and reducing the space for reform. The dissident movement led by Oswaldo Payá has successfully completed a drive for 20,000 signatures on a petition that presents a request for reforms.

Spain and Mexico have recently expanded ties with Cuba. Spain's conversations on human rights have contributed to the release of political prisoners; approximately one hundred remain incarcerated. Venezuela continues to provide subsidized oil with a value of several billion dollars annually. There is considerable sympathy for Raúl Castro's new government among delegates to the United Nations and the Organization of American States.

But Cuba remains wary of the United States and, as the chief of the Cuban Interests Section in Washington reiterated in the previous month, is not interested in improving relations with the United States until President Bush leaves office. And the U.S. administration remains concerned about the high level of illegal migration from Cuba, principally through Mexico. The U.S. Coast Guard has fewer assets in the seas around the Yucatán, and the Mexican mafias control the overland transport of migrants.

Role-Play No. 1: "A Meeting of Principals at the National Security Council"

Characters in the Role-Play–

National Security Adviser (Chair)
Secretary of State
Secretary of Defense
Secretary of Treasury
Secretary of Commerce
Secretary of Homeland
	Security
Director of National
	Intelligence
White House Chief of Staff
Chairman of the Joint
	Chiefs of Staff

USAID Administrator
Deputy Secretary of State
Deputy Secretary of Defense
Deputy Secretary of Commerce
Assistant Secretary for Western
	Hemisphere Affairs
Coordinator, Office of Cuban Affairs
National Intelligence Officer for
	Latin America
Commandant, U.S. Coast Guard
Combatant Commander, U.S.
	Southern Command

Instructions: Background and Meeting Agenda

Participants received instructions in the form of a description of the background and the meeting agenda. Knowing these instructions increases understanding and helps readers interpret the course of the dialogue.

The president sees the current situation as an opportunity to take full advantage of a weakened Raúl Castro in order to seek the collapse of the Cuban Revolution. He remains committed to the policy he outlined in October 2007, underlining that freedom will not be sacrificed for stability. U.S. government policy will thus remain closely aligned with the provisions of the Cuban Liberty and Democratic Solidarity Act (Helms-Burton Act), which makes the normalization of relations contingent upon Castro not holding power and the existence of a democratic transition well under way in Cuba.

The president continues to maintain that the U.S. government will respond to tangible reforms in Cuba, but until the release of political prisoners and progress toward democratic elections, U.S. policy will continue to be to deny resources and U.S. government support, to pressure Cuba's leaders to abdicate or reform. In the longer term the president envisions a stable and prosperous Cuba governed by an elite friendly to the United States. To date, the Cuban government has not requested assistance from the United States government.

The president is concerned that Fidel's death will erode the European Union's desire to continue to place sanctions on Cuba. He notes that Venezuela (and President Hugo Chávez as the ideological heir of Castro's Communist Revolution) provides critical financial support that ensures the survival of Raúl Castro's government. The president is also concerned with Cuba's friendship with China, Russia, and Iran.

I. Achieving the President's Objectives

The president has asked the principals attending the NSC meeting to provide specific recommendations on the following topics:

IMMEDIATE ACTIONS

At least initially, Cuba and the United States share the objective of avoiding a mass migration. Although there are no indications that a mass migration is imminent, the president has ordered the deployment of the Coast Guard and supporting assets to ensure a rapid response to any signals that a mass migration could be about to occur, such as vessels headed to Cuba or Cubans seeking refuge in embassies.

POSSIBLE STRATEGIES

In July 2006, Secretary of State Rice submitted the report of the Commission for Assistance to a Free Cuba to the president. The report endorsed the statement that the ultimate guarantor of stability in Cuba would be the rapid restoration of sovereignty to the Cuban people through free and fair elections. It stated: "The notion that the consolidation of continued dictatorship under Raúl Castro or other undemocratic successors will lead to stability is an illusion."

—What actions can the U.S. government take in the near term to restore sovereignty to the Cuban people?

—How can the United States bolster the influence of those on the island seeking a real transition to democracy to Cuba? What actions can lead to the release of political prisoners?

—Who could emerge as democratic leaders in Cuba and how could the United States strengthen their work?

—How can the international community be mobilized to ratchet up pressure for political change and democracy in Cuba?

—How does the U.S. government prevent other countries from adopting policies that support Raúl Castro and ensure the longevity of the regime? What can be done to undermine the Chávez-Castro alliance?

II. Responding to Instability in Cuba

The aftermath of most major political changes or natural disasters has featured internal instability or crime, as occurred also in New Orleans after Hurricane Katrina.

—What are the potential prospects for and sources of internal instability in Cuba? What would be the indicators of instability in Cuba?

—How would we expect Cuba to respond to internal instability? What institutions and forces would be relied upon to maintain order? What do we know about those institutions and their loyalty to the leadership?

—Should the United States take preemptive measures—to stabilize the country or perhaps to encourage instability? Does instability support or hurt the cause of democratic transition? What are the risks? What are the triggers for U.S. government actions and how should the United States respond?

III. Dealing with Mobilization and Mass Migration

The Director of National Intelligence reported that if Raúl sensed strong pressure from the United States, he would place security forces on high alert. Block committees would be mobilized in every town and village across Cuba. Dissidents and unemployed youths would be jailed to ensure public security and order, actions that might trigger an attempt by Cubans to leave the island. In that event the Secretary of Homeland Security would activate "Operation Vigilant Sentry," as a precautionary means to achieve the following:

—Position military and law enforcement assets to save lives and pick up migrants at sea.

—Close ports in Florida, to prevent U.S. residents from sailing to Cuba to pick up those intending to migrate.

—Prepare the necessary resources to handle large numbers of migrants intercepted at sea and temporarily detained ashore.

—Establish an interagency team ready to handle migrant processing, protection, and detention procedures.

President Bush remained committed to the Cuba policy he enunciated in his October 2007 speech at the Department of State, namely, he wanted the release of all political prisoners and free elections. "Freedom, not stability," the president said, remains the operative, or at least public, bottom line on Cuba. This of course would not preclude the administration's seeking to discourage and stop a mass migration.

—Is there anything more that the U.S. government should do to prevent repression in Cuba or a mass migration to the United States?

—Should the wet foot, dry foot policy of allowing Cubans who reach U.S. shores to stay be changed?

IV. The Reality of U.S.-Cuba Relations

—Given the long history of hostility between Cuban leaders and the United States, can the two countries begin a process of normalizing relations?

—Is there too much mistrust, especially between the Bush administration and the Castros, for a new dynamic to be established that would lead to improved understanding and eventual reconciliation?

—Does the United States government have the will and domestic support to change the relationship? Does Cuba want to change the relationship?

Abridged Minutes

Abridged minutes from the simulation are provided to enable study of the kinds of exchanges that took place among the participants.

The National Security Adviser opened the meeting by asking the Director of National Intelligence to share his assessment of the situation in Cuba. His talking points were the following:

The Immediate Situation

—In general, the situation in Cuba is quiet and the United States has not seen major military mobilization or actions by dissidents.

—The Cuban military and security forces appear to have rallied around Raúl Castro.

—The United States perceives heavy police presence on major roads as well as around embassies.

Overview

The divisions between the hard-liners who have resisted reforms that would help Raúl legitimize his government presumably continue, but it is too early to know whether Fidel's death will weaken them. Human rights activists have called for direct, transparent, and secret elections to choose the next Cuban president. Oswaldo Payá and Elizardo Sánchez, leading dissidents, have asked for the lifting of the embargo as a gesture toward easing tensions between the United States and Cuba. But another leading dissident, Martha Beatriz Roque, has rejected making any concession to the Raúl Castro government. Reports from family and friends in Cuba indicate that there have been no public celebrations and that people seem stunned by the reality that the *Comandante* who ruled Cuba for almost fifty years is dead.

—The Captain commanding the Guantánamo Bay Naval Base received a message this morning from the government of Cuba, which reported plans to proceed with prescheduled fence-line talks.

Future Trends

With Fidel's death, the United States anticipates that Raúl will have a
freer hand to undertake reforms, especially as the hard-liners in the government will no longer have Fidel's backing. Nevertheless, any reforms
Raúl carries out can be expected to be consistent with the Revolution
and preserve his power. He wants to establish his legitimacy by meeting
the expectations of the Cuban people.

—U.S. policy actions that increase pressures on Cuba would most
likely strengthen Raúl during this transition period.

—On the other hand, Raúl most likely does not have the freedom of
movement to respond to a reduction in pressure by the U.S. government.

Next, the National Security Adviser reiterated the president's commitment to current policy and asked how, within these bounds, the
United States could seize the opportunity to promote democracy and
freedom on the island.

I. Achieving the President's Objectives

IMMEDIATE ACTIONS

The Secretary of State responded by saying, "The Cuban people
deserve to be free." She urged that the principals find ways to help
Cubans gain a greater voice in their governance. At a minimum, she
said, "We must reaffirm our commitment to Cuba's freedom as well as
to human rights and democracy." The Commander of the U.S. Coast
Guard concurred but cautioned that the administration's pronounce-
ments should not be excessively confrontational. Announcements that
threatened the Cuban government if there were a mass migration could
be harmful and could potentially be seen by Cubans as implying that
the United States was prepared to welcome to our shores those fleeing a
dictatorship.

The White House Chief of Staff warned against any softening of U.S.
policy because doing so would be perceived as legitimizing the new
Cuban leadership.

Concerned about the contradiction between the administration's
commitment to freedom for the Cuban people and the desire to avoid
violence or inadvertently encourage a mass migration, the National
Security Adviser suggested that they craft a public statement to reflect
the administration's commitment to democracy without provoking

instability in Cuba or opprobrium abroad. The principals drafted the following statement, which was read by President Bush the next day:

> The Cuban people deserve to be free. This is an opportunity for the people and institutions of Cuba to move toward fully engaging their country in the international community. The USG reaffirms its current policy and is ready to work with other members of the OAS to develop relations with Cuba based on the principles of mutual respect, national self-determination, institutional democracy, and the rule of law.

The Assistant Secretary for Western Hemisphere Affairs suggested that the group decide whether to send a delegation to Fidel's funeral. The status and office of the person chosen to lead it would be seen as a sign of either the administration's continuing hostility or of its receptivity to a possible opening to Cuba. A high-level delegation might allow the United States to engage other delegations on a strategy to promote democracy in Cuba.

The Deputy Secretary of State said that in truth it has been shown that no government is prepared to buy into the U.S. policy of isolation. Latin American governments are frustrated with Washington's position, and even Europe, led by Spain, was in the process of improving relations with Cuba. The Assistant Secretary for Western Hemisphere Affairs worried that a lower-level delegation or a decision not to send a representative would be seen as disrespectful and further diminish U.S. influence with other governments on the Cuba issue; worse, the assembled leaders might use the occasion to develop a Cuba strategy without U.S. input or assent.

The USAID Administrator suggested sending former President Jimmy Carter, but the idea was rejected by the table. So, too, was the proposal to send former President George H. W. Bush or former Secretary of State Colin Powell. These former officials would be too high-profile and their presence might be seen as lending legitimacy to the Castro government. The president had made it clear that U.S. actions must be consistent with current policy. In the end, a consensus formed around naming several members of Congress who had traveled to Cuba in the past and were members of the Cuba Working Group in the House of Representatives. It was decided that Representative Jeff Flake, a Republican from Arizona, would lead the delegation.

The Coordinator for Cuban Affairs reminded the group that Cuba was not interested in improving relations with the United States. This was reflected by Fidel's disregard of overtures made by Presidents Carter and Ford. Fidel did not respond after President Carter lifted the travel ban. Again, in the late nineties, Fidel much preferred to grandstand rather than quietly work with the United States to facilitate the return of Elián González, the shipwrecked child, to his father in Cuba. This administration should not make the mistake of trying to deal straightforwardly with the Cuban government.

POSSIBLE STRATEGIES

The Coordinator for Cuban Affairs said that it had become increasingly difficult to work with the region to forge a common approach to Cuba because the rest of the hemisphere was ignoring U.S. appeals that they stand up for freedom and democracy in Cuba. Venezuela's President Hugo Chávez and other leftist presidents were allied with and propping up Cuba's Communist system. More friendly Latin governments would oppose U.S. policy for no other reason than that failure to do so could set off popular protests led by the left.

The Assistant Secretary for Western Hemisphere Affairs claimed that Brazil and Mexico were keen to improve both political and economic relations with Cuba. Their doing so would bolster the Raúl Castro government and undermine any chance for internal factions to challenge the younger Castro brother. If Mexico and Brazil were to increase their aid to Cuba, it would enhance their influence with the Cuban hierarchy and could lead to a reduction in President Chávez's influence. It would be preferable for Brazil's President Lula Da Silva to talk to Raúl than Chávez. Therefore, the principals might consider a strategy that would bolster the administration's commitment to democracy in Cuba by not objecting to moderate Latin American leaders' working with the Cuban hierarchy—even encouraging this.

The Secretary of State was concerned that there could be negative consequences because other governments might interpret U.S. actions as approval or lack of commitment to existing U.S. policy. She suggested that it would be better for the administration to concentrate on how it could publicly reinforce its commitment to freedom, human rights, and the release of political prisoners.

The Secretary of Commerce asked what could be done to further these objectives in view of the reluctance of other governments to support the United States. The USAID Administrator responded that the United States was already doing everything possible to promote groups working for change in Cuba, adding that although there was considerable public dissatisfaction, Cuban state security was effective in preventing public demonstrations. He countered the belief held by other governments that U.S. assistance to dissidents resulted in their loss of legitimacy as viable actors for change on the island. Instead, he said, the United States lacked the international support to expand civil society and press the Cuban government for a more open society. The Coordinator for Cuban Affairs praised the administration's support of human rights and civil society activists and urged its continuation, but noted that doing so would not bring about the changes sought by the administration.

II. Responding to Instability in Cuba

The Commander of U.S. Southern Command underlined the fact that the United States would intervene in Cuba under extreme circumstances only and that an intervention could be undertaken successfully only with the approval of the Organization of American States or the United Nations.

The Director of National Intelligence reported that the intelligence community assessed that widespread unrest was unlikely, despite the fact that there was considerable dissatisfaction in Cuba over the lack of opportunity for improved quality of life and greater freedoms. The Cuban government infiltrates and closely monitors dissidents and human rights groups within Cuba. Even youths, who are likely the most disaffected members of society, seem to prefer to leave Cuba illegally rather than to oppose the government.

Unfortunately, the ability of the United States Interests Section (USINT) to provide reliable information has been severely curtailed since late 2002. The tit-for-tat over travel resulted in both USINT and Cuban Interests Section (CUBINT) diplomats' being restricted to their assigned capital cities. As a result, the Director of National Intelligence was of the opinion that U.S. diplomats had limited access to information. If discontented groups exist within the military or bureaucracy or there was a buildup of tensions that could unleash spontaneous demonstrations, U.S.

diplomats would likely not be aware of the groups or even the trigger
event. "The sad fact is that we lack the intelligence to provide you with a
good basis for making decisions," the Director of National Intelligence
said. "We simply don't understand political dynamics within the Cuban
hierarchy. Although we have good contacts with dissidents and some
civil society entities in Havana, we can only tell you that there is popular
discontent. We can't tell you whether this will impact Raúl's ability to
lead or will result in organized demonstrations."

Although the Special Coordinator defended the efforts of USINT
diplomats, he admitted that the United States would be unable to identify or provide support to moderates in the Cuban government who
might be sympathetic to the prospect of a more open political system.
The risk that they would be identified and punished is just too great
to take.

According to the Chairman of the Joint Chiefs of Staff and the Secretary of Defense, the Cuban Interior Ministry would be fully capable of
quickly extinguishing popular unrest. The ministry seems to have
advance information of even small protests: before large groups can
gather leaders are picked up and the protest is aborted.

The National Intelligence Officer for Latin America pointed out that
the Cuban armed forces were not used to put down disturbances, allowing them to maintain a good image among the public and continue to
attract recruits. The military would only be used to intervene in public
unrest if the Interior Ministry were overwhelmed and unable to silence
the protest. There was little doubt about the loyalty and capacity of
both the Interior Ministry and the armed forces, he continued.

The National Security Adviser summarized the situation by saying that
there was little the United States could do to assist those working for
change without compromising them. In the past, when the Cuban government jailed dissidents, the European Union and the United States condemned the action, yet the Castro government could brand dissidents as
traitors with considerable success because they had accepted U.S. assistance through nongovernmental organizations. If the Cuban government
were to crack down on the dissident movement now, it was unclear
whether the United States would succeed in attaining a UN resolution
condemning the action. The United States was fully engaged elsewhere,
and its influence in Cuba was sadly diminished. It will be difficult to
tighten sanctions because they were already at their strictest level since

the 1962 Missile Crisis. Some naive leaders in Cuba even claimed that U.S. sanctions hurt the Cuban people more than they hurt the authoritarian Cuban government. If dissidents were jailed, the best the United States could do would be to encourage the member states of the OAS and the United Nations to agree to a declaration condemning the Cuban government for oppressive actions. Yet any such UN resolution introduced by the United States would likely be watered down before passage.

III. Dealing with a Cuban Mobilization and Mass Migration

The Chairman of the Joint Chiefs pointed out that when Fidel fell ill and turned power over to Raúl, the government organized a massive mobilization of Cuba's military reserves as a precautionary measure. Although the United States did not contemplate hostile action against Cuba, the Cuban government continued to use the presumed U.S. threat as a pretext to rally the population in times of heightened tension.

The Coast Guard Commandant considered a mass migration unlikely. Nevertheless, the Coast Guard, the Navy, and the Department of State and others put into place an operational plan to discourage and manage a migration crisis. Under the plan, U.S. residents would be prohibited from sailing out of south Florida ports, public statements urging Americans not to attempt to go to Cuba would be issued, and Coast Guard vessels would be deployed along the principal sea routes across the Florida Straits. The Coast Guard would also be alert to stopping vessels carrying militants who might attempt to launch an attack against Cuba from the Caribbean or Central America. These actions would prevent a "pull" effect that could encourage potential migrants to leave Cuba.

The Coast Guard Commandant informed the group that Castro's death had led to the activation of the Homeland Security Task Force Southeast with the Coast Guard Seventh District Commander in charge of the operation. If a mass migration appeared imminent, the president would be asked to issue a determination that such an event be considered a national security threat, which would trigger Department of Defense assistance to the Task Force.

The Assistant Secretary for Western Hemisphere Affairs cautioned that the United States should not undermine its commitment to a free Cuba by public statements that called on the Cuban regime to prevent a mass migration. He warned that doing so could be used by Raúl to justify using force to keep Cubans from leaving. The United States, not Cuba, may be blamed for abuses that Cuban security committed against Cuban citizens. The administration should be careful to avoid public pronouncement that appeared to legitimize the state's control over its citizens.

One official pointed out that the wet foot, dry foot policy itself tacitly encouraged mass migration because it allows illegal migrants who reach U.S. soil to remain. Should a mass migration ensue, the Deputy Secretary of State warned that the administration might wish to consider modifying or rescinding this policy. Another official claimed that this could only be done by an act of Congress. The National Security Adviser explained that he was undoubtedly confusing the wet foot, dry foot policy with the Cuban Adjustment Act, the latter being a law that allows Cubans who have resided in the United States for a year and a day to adjust status to permanent resident. The wet foot, dry foot policy is an executive determination announced by President Bill Clinton's attorney general, Janet Reno, which can be modified or rescinded by the president. It was formulated when Cuban Americans objected to what they feared was an agreement between the United States and Cuba in the 1994 Migration Accords to return all Cubans to Cuba, whether they were apprehended on land or at sea.

IV. The Reality of U.S.-Cuba Relations

The National Security Adviser stated that from the input he had received he feared that the administration would be unable to use the opportunity of Fidel Castro's death to promote democratic change in Cuba. The hemispheric leaders were unwilling to press Raúl Castro to enact democratic reforms, and the United States had little to no influence over Cuba. Worse, there was little the administration could do if Raúl Castro used harsh tactics against human rights activists, beyond a public campaign denouncing his actions. The United States would be condemned if it militarily intervened, and in any case its forces were fully engaged elsewhere. On the positive side, a mass migration was unlikely and the U.S. Coast Guard had a plan in place to effectively discourage such an event.

There remained the possibility that if Raúl Castro adhered to acceptable human rights guidelines, the administration might find an opportunity to establish a dialogue with Cuba. The Secretary of State said this would only be possible if Castro released political prisoners: "We cannot make concession to dictators." In any case, the chief of the Cuban Interests Section in Washington, D.C., had publicly stated that Cuba had no interest in dealing with the current administration. The Cubans would bide their time and wait for the upcoming U.S. presidential elections. The United States would stand by its principles and commitment to freedom and would not make concessions to a dictatorship.

The National Security Adviser confirmed that he would report the principals' conclusion that the United States should continue to pursue its current policy because it reflected commitment to the freedom of the Cuban people. He recognized that there was little the administration could do to further freedom in Cuba because Fidel Castro's death was unlikely to produce the unraveling of the Revolution. An internal power struggle was unlikely and so, too, was a mass migration. A moment that in the contemplation of it had seemed so pregnant with possibilities would not in fact bring significant changes in Cuba or in U.S.-Cuba relations.

CHAPTER FOUR

U.S. Policy:
A New Strategy toward Cuba

In the afternoon of February 7, 2008, following the project's first simulation exercise, which examined the scope for U.S. policy to advance the Bush administration's objectives within its historic constraints, the national security adviser convened participants to craft a new strategy toward Cuba without the constraints of ideological parameters. The group reviewed options for U.S. policy during the initial months of a new U.S. presidential administration. The purpose of the exercise was to explore policy options that would help advance prospects for the Cuban people to play a meaningful role in defining their future. Even though the group was given a free hand in developing a new policy approach, they were also told that the policy must be realistic and have an impact.

The following pivotal issues emerged from this simulation:

—How can the United States structure a policy to empower the Cuban people when the Cuban government sees this as being against its interests?

—What are the strategic implications of Cuba's nascent energy industries (oil and ethanol) for the effectiveness of current U.S. policies and future approaches?

—To what extent can external liberalization on the part of the United States encourage internal liberalization within Cuba?

—What steps can the United States take to construct a multilateral framework for conditional engagement, keeping human rights and political reform on the table?

—Can regional engagement by the United States apply effective leverage to the Cuban government, or will it reinforce the government's sense of being able to act with impunity?

The Exercise

The president tasked his national security team to develop options that would help create a new dynamic between the United States and Cuba, one that promotes political and economic change on the island by empowering the Cuban people.

Under this scenario, it was assumed that Raúl Castro was firmly at the helm of the Cuban state and that his government had taken important, if still insufficient, steps toward economic openings, including expanding the distribution of employee salaries in hard currency; issuing small loans and certificates of housing ownership; and passing new investment laws and encouraging micro-investments in tourism-related services.[1]

Simulation Exercise No. 2:
A Meeting of the National Security Council, March 15, 2009

The next U.S. administration may be dealing with a more economically viable country that has a diversified set of trading and investment partners. These developments raise important strategic questions.

Economic Realities and Timing Implications

U.S. policy must closely consider the implications of Cuba's unexploited energy resources. In 2008 Cuba produced approximately 60,000 barrels per day (bpd) and consumed more than 150,000 bpd. Venezuela made up the difference: in 2008 it provided Cuba with 92,000 bpd worth of petroleum imports, valued at US$3.2 billion, up from US$2.4 billion in 2007, as shipment size and prices increased. If the projected 4.6 billion barrels of probable oil reserves in Cuba-controlled waters off its northern coast and in the Gulf of Mexico are proven, within three to five years Cuba

1. The tourism industry is the most visible sector in which entrepreneurial activity has been authorized since the Special Period in the 1990s. For a more detailed explanation of tourism and the Cuban economy, see chapter 5, note 1.

may produce as much as 350,000 bpd.[2] The normal 60-40 split in production-sharing agreements with foreign oil companies would provide Cuba with approximately 200,000 bpd, allowing the island not only to end its energy dependence on Venezuela but potentially to export the excess in the short term, before investments are required to meet growing domestic demand for oil. Companies from Norway, Spain, India, China, Russia, and Brazil have signed exploration agreements with Cuba. A consortium led by Spain's Repsol-YPF was set to start exploratory drilling in the Gulf of Mexico in 2009, but in July 2009 it announced a delay in drilling, possibly to 2010.

Brazil is interested in helping Cuba develop not only its black gold but also its green gold, by reorienting its flagging sugarcane industry toward the production of ethanol. A two- to three-year US$2 billion recapitalization of the sugar sector could yield, conservatively estimated, 60 million tons of sugarcane. Annual ethanol revenues, at August 2009 prices of 22 cents per pound and US$2 per gallon, could reach US$1.905 billion (using a calculation of a sugar yield of 12.5 percent per ton and an ethanol yield of 18 gallons per ton of sugar).

Ethanol production is not likely to come online while Fidel is alive, but by the end of a three- to five-year development period, Cuba's future crude oil equity and sugarcane ethanol production (at US$70 per barrel and US$2 per gallon respectively) could generate revenues on the order of US$5.8 billion annually.

Thus, Cuba's economic choices will be expanding, and as Cuba's leaders consolidate power and exploit energy reserves, limited U.S. leverage with Cuba will diminish further, making unilateral sanctions even more irrelevant to the island's economic and political stability. Accordingly, participants concluded that if the United States is to play a role in Cuba's future, the time to act is now.

Raúl Castro's Economic and Political Reforms: Mikhail Gorbachev or Deng Xiao Ping?

In the expectation that Raúl Castro will continue with modest economic reforms to salvage the economy and knowing that oil and ethanol revenues are a few years off, participants concluded that a future Cuban

---

2. The U.S. Geological Survey estimates that Cuba's offshore fields contain 4.6 billion barrels of oil, comparable to Colombia's and Ecuador's oil resources, and 10 tril-

government will likely follow the model of Deng Xiao Ping's reforms rather than Mikhail Gorbachev's: like Deng, Raúl will endeavor to maintain political control while doing what his government can to provide greater opportunities and improve living conditions. Participants considered how to respond to limited economic reforms in Cuba and whether U.S. actions to modify the embargo or improve relations should be conditioned on economic or political reform on the island.

All believed that political reform and human rights must be an integral part of U.S. policy toward Cuba, but they recognized that U.S. actions to promote these or any other aspects of its policy agenda may well be rejected out of hand if they are made in isolation; also, they should not be constrained by or depend on Cuban actions. Although broader engagement—moving beyond rhetoric on human rights and democracy promotion toward a broad agenda of principled engagement—doesn't guarantee success, doing so maximizes the probability that engagement brings results. Thus, participants recommended that strategies to encourage political openings should be embedded in an indirect approach that promotes change from the bottom up, focusing on improving the livelihoods and well-being of the Cuban people and creating an environment in which citizens can increase their civic participation.

To this end, participants acknowledged that internal economic reforms—even if carried out by the Raúl Castro government to retain its power—can create greater civic and political space, making it important that U.S. policy remain flexible and perhaps even support aspects of economic liberalization on the island if they can help create such space.

How Far Should Initial Moves Go?

Deciding whether and how to modify existing policies is like dropping an anchor in unknown waters. Participants debated how far the opening moves for changes in U.S. policy should go, and how they might be sequenced in the short term. Some participants pressed for but in the end did not fully endorse ending all sanctions to the extent possible.

---

lion cubic feet of natural gas. In October 2008 Cuba's state oil company, Cubapetroleo, or Cupet, released a dramatically higher estimate: 20 billion barrels of recoverable crude, an amount comparable to resources in the United States. It must be emphasized, however, that Cuba's figure should be viewed with caution; until exploration gets under way, all such figures are speculative.

Considerable liberalization could be achieved through presidential initiatives to license particular travel-related and financial transactions, yet
certain laws and parts of others can only be repealed by congressional
vote, including the Helms-Burton and the Cuban Democracy acts, both
of which impose obstacles to establishing normal relations with Cuba.
Despite these obstacles, participants concluded that the United States
should immediately and unilaterally take steps toward external liberalization that would help create pressures on the island for greater political and economic freedoms. The purpose of such unilateral action is not
to reward Cuba but to create flexibility for the United States to determine when and how to engage with the island in order to strengthen the
capacity of Cubans to advance change from within. Participants considered it important, if the United States is to get anywhere with this
agenda, for it to take definitive action to convey that it is turning over a
new leaf in the conduct of its relationship with Cuba.

Every participant agreed that all travel and remittance restrictions currently placed on Cuban Americans should be lifted immediately. Greater
family contact, they believed, would help widen access to information, lit-
erature, and resources, all of which can help expand the horizons of the
Cuban people. Increased remittance flows not only would provide humanitarian relief for many but might also allow more Cubans to purchase
access to the Internet,[3] radios, televisions, and other forms of communications equipment. Remittances could also provide startup capital for the
development of small businesses, which would decrease Cubans' dependence on their government. To the extent that such measures opened communications, they could reduce the control of Cuba's security services over
the flow of information and provide a boost to civil society development.
For similar reasons, most participants supported moving quickly toward
ending all restrictions on travel by all U.S. citizens to Cuba as part of a
greater effort to end any and all elements of the U.S. "communications
embargo"—policies that have the unintended effect of helping Cuba's security services limit Cubans' access to alternative sources of information.

Turning to the subject of assistance to Cuba's independent civil society,
a majority of participants recognized that Bush administration policy, by

3. Prior to September 2009 Cubans could access the Internet illegally, on the black
market. In September 2009 legal access was authorized at post offices, albeit restricted
to preselected national websites and offered at the rate of US$1.62 per minute,
unaffordable for a majority of Cubans earning state salaries of US$17 per month.

narrowly focusing on dissidents, has limited its impact to bring about change on the ground and jeopardized the legitimacy of aid recipients. Thus, a majority of participants advocated that U.S. governmental and nongovernmental support should engage a broader cross-section of civil society, people who over time will work for change inside Cuba. A minority still urged that Cuban dissidents remain at the forefront of U.S. strategies to engage Cuba's independent civil society.

A majority of participants also advocated working to expand bilateral and multilateral discussions with relevant Cuban officials on a number of security issues of importance to both countries: migration, organized crime, narcotics trafficking, and environmental disasters. This agenda, pertinent for any U.S. administration at any time, would also include exchanging defense attachés, which would provide the United States with better knowledge of the inner workings of Cuba's armed forces. For some, pursuing this agenda in good faith would require sending an ambassador to Cuba—the first U.S. ambassador to Cuba in half a century. Others felt that fully normalizing diplomatic relations should remain conditioned on progress on political fronts. Other unilateral actions considered by participants as part of an opening package included removing Cuba from the State Department's list of state sponsors of international terrorism and establishing a sponsored fund to support people-to-people exchanges.

All participants counseled the president to immediately enact measures that would empower the Cuban people and engage the Cuban government on issues of vital concern. Some wished to take advantage of the opportunity available to a new administration to normalize diplomatic, political, and economic relations as much as possible through the use of executive authority. Removing all restrictions via the repeal or modification of existing legislation would require a slower, incremental process with perhaps some aspects of conditionality. Others were slightly more cautious, arguing that broader economic engagement that would require the elimination of major provisions of the trade embargo would only be appropriate if conditioned on political reform in Cuba, an engagement strategy that could be fortified by international and regional "buy-in."

A Long-Term Strategy

Participants recognized that the United States has a window of opportunity to reorient its policy and effectively engage Cuba, but they saw both up- and downsides to the development of Cuba's energy resources. On the one hand, oil wealth in the hands of the state could enhance the vulnerability of the Cuban people to a government-controlled "top-down" model of resource distribution. Thus, to the extent that Cuban authorities permit, measures should be taken to support small-enterprise development in order to create competition from the bottom up in the Cuban economy. Remittance flows can likewise help mitigate this dynamic. On the other hand, development of energy resources would reduce Venezuela's influence while potentially increasing the influence of more democratic and market-oriented governments, such as Brazil's. Thus, it may make sense for the United States to encourage regional partners to invest in Cuba's energy industries. Moreover, as Cuba's oil wealth makes the Cuban people better off and increases their economic resources, the degree of influence the Cuban government has over the populace may decrease. How could the United States effect greater economic diversification and competition to reduce the prospect that it will have to deal with a Cuban Deng Xiao Ping in the future? Participants also considered the importance of permitting the financing of U.S. agricultural exports to Cuba. Expanding the scope of this trade may provide economic relief to Cuban citizens and thus may help to empower them. Moreover, as economic openings create opportunities for micro- and small enterprises and the use of property as collateral, credit and bank loan growth can strengthen an emerging middle class, which in many countries has been a critical force in pressuring governments for political freedoms. U.S. support in these areas will be critical.

Participants attempted to reach a consensus on policies that would best promote the president's agenda and its principles (stability, democracy, economic growth, and the release of political prisoners) without reinforcing the capabilities of the Cuban government by providing new economic openings. They began by establishing the measures the United States would have to take to have a fully normalized relationship with Cuba and worked backward to devise a process of engagement. While the group recognized that the United States should have a proactive, independent policy in place, which would nevertheless reward positive actions undertaken by the Cuban government, the question of dependence versus independence highlighted tensions concerning how far U.S. policy could go if there seemed to be no progress in Cuba on human rights and political reforms.

While all agreed that a full normalization of economic relations would be dependent upon a process of engagement that resulted in further political and economic openings on the island and the resolution of issues that continue to divide the two nations (the territory of Guantánamo Bay and claims for expropriated property), differences in opinion arose over upgrading diplomatic relations to an ambassadorial appointment that might advance direct, on-the-ground dialogue and negotiations.

Creating a Regional Approach

Participants considered a number of ways the United States could encourage regional and multilateral cooperation in advancing a proactive agenda for political reform in Cuba while it recalibrates its own approach to engage the island. First, the United States might consider lifting its objections to Cuba's reinstatement as a member of the Organization of American States (OAS), as long as Cuba satisfied the purposes and principles of the organization's charters. Such a tactic would place the onus on the regional body to determine whether Cuba has met the conditions for membership, including those regarding democracy and political reform. At the April 2009 Summit of the Americas and the OAS general assembly two months later, the U.S. decision not to block lifting Cuba's exclusion from the OAS reinforced the notion that democracy should be the objective of—rather than a precondition for—Cuba's reinstatement. The U.S. position has had the beneficial outcome of improving relations with the hemisphere and redirecting the onus for Cuba's meeting hemispheric standards of democracy and transparency from United States policy to Cuba. This is discussed in greater detail in chapter 7, "Coordinating U.S. Policy with the International Community."

Several participants also advocated for the creation of a "neighborhood working group" of intermediary countries (suggestions included Canada, Brazil, Mexico, Spain, and France) to work closely with the United States to pursue a common multilateral approach to Cuba, one that promotes human rights, democracy, and equitable economic development. Given the lack of U.S. credibility on democracy promotion and human rights, this group might help foster and guarantee the mutual commitments made between Cuba and the United States. The "neighborhood working group" might also help to address the issue of reconciliation between Cubans and those in the Cuban diaspora.

A wider multilateral approach could include the carrots of integration into the Latin American community, access to international financial institutions, and participation in free trade agreements. Again, Cuban access to the U.S. market (which could someday become even more tempting as a natural destination for Cuba's own oil and ethanol exports) could be a carrot in and of itself, and within a multilateral framework, parties might work to gradually peel back elements of the embargo and the Helms-Burton legislation as other commitments are fostered. Releasing political prisoners in exchange for any number of these benefits was one possible quid pro quo proposed.

Significance and Targeting of an Assistance Package

Participants also considered the value of a targeted multilateral aid package as part of a conditional approach to advancing political and economic reforms in Cuba. They agreed on the importance of devising creative structures that are not perceived as "charity" or as threatening to Cuba's sovereignty but that nonetheless move the Cuban government forward on important economic and political fronts. For example, some participants proposed the creation of a multilateral fund to promote micro- and small-enterprise development by allowing Cubans to mortgage their homes and properties and borrow a portion of their value in hard currency. Such a multilateral and conditional approach to assistance may also advance important political reforms, particularly in areas such as the rule of law. Currently there is little beyond U.S. objections to stop a range of multilateral institutions such as the OAS and the Inter-American Development Bank (IDB) from engaging in preliminary discussions with Cuban authorities. The carrot of multilateral assistance could then be used to advance concrete programs of political and even human rights reform, such as a much-needed modification of Cuba's penal code. The fact that Cuba has agreed to a human rights peer review by the United Nations Human Rights Council undertaken in January 2009 suggests that it might be willing to entertain other forms of multilateral engagement that it has traditionally resisted.

Considerations for U.S. Policy

As this exercise demonstrated, the challenge to the United States and the international community will be to use constructively the window of opportunity opened by Fidel's death. Failure to adopt policies and measures that more effectively encourage reform in Cuba could further reduce U.S. influence on the island. As Cuba develops its energy wealth, its vulnerability to outside pressure from both the United States and Venezuela will be reduced, while its political and economic position vis-à-vis its own population will be strengthened. The Cuban government may be pressed to broaden the reform process to the degree that friendly foreign governments retain their influence in Cuba and the Cuban people are encouraged to become less dependent on the state. An isolationist policy, by contrast, prevents the United States from helping the Cuban people gain greater control over their lives and ultimately their own government.

Nonetheless, a rapid and total overhaul of all aspects of current policy poses domestic policy risks for a new administration and carries no guarantee of immediate success. Participants were united around the need for a policy of engagement and empowerment, but the two groups did not agree on how broad or how fast such an agenda should proceed. Still, there was a general consensus that combining bold unilateral actions on a number of fronts (travel, remittances, and more normal relations on the diplomatic and security fronts) with principled conditional engagement on others (full removal of trade and financial sanctions subject to improved human rights and progress on democratization) offers the greatest likelihood of a more successful policy approach toward Cuba. Embedding such an approach within a regional framework will boost its chances of success.

Whatever the exact scope or particulars of a new U.S. president's approach to Cuba, participants considered it vital that he adopt the following basic principles to guide policy action:

—The United States should make a legitimate and concerted effort to "de-Americanize" its policies toward Cuba and engage regional partners to do so, acknowledging that doing so will require compromise. U.S. policy toward Cuba must be consistent and aligned with the approach of U.S. foreign policy toward other countries facing similar circumstances around the globe. Only through a concerted regional approach can the United States hope to advance its interests and policy goals.

—U.S. policymakers should seize the initiative at this important moment in Cuba's history, rather than retain a defensive posture in which any policy change is a reaction to actions by the Cuban government.

—The United States should lift all elements of its "communications embargo" on Cuba, since prohibiting the flow of information into Cuba only reinforces the prerogatives of Cuban state security. A full lifting of the communications embargo would enable the freer movement of individuals to Cuba (all U.S. citizens, not just Cuban Americans) and uncapped remittances. U.S. regulations and policies with regard to radio, television, and the Internet, as well as those governing trade in goods and services that support media industries, would also need to be adjusted.

—To better advance the prospects of political openings and a transition to democracy in Cuba, the United States should support and engage all potential actors involved in reform, both outside and within the Cuban government, rather than identifying by name those civil society actors it believes may serve as leaders in the island's future. During this exercise, participants did not examine the particulars of current U.S. policies to support civil society activists in Cuba (for example, by USAID-supported programs), nor assess whether these programs should be reconsidered or recalibrated to advance a broader push for dialogue with reformers of all stripes. Such issues will be taken up in Chapter 6 in the project's fourth simulation exercise, focusing on Cuban civil society.

SIMULATION SCENARIO NO. 2:
CONTEXTUAL BACKGROUND OF EXERCISE

The following scenario was given to participants:

March 15, 2009. Fidel died eight months ago. The new U.S. president has asked for a review of U.S. policy toward Cuba.

Raúl Castro's close advisers organized a special session of the National Assembly in May 2008 in which Raúl was named to succeed Fidel Castro as president of the Council of State and Council of Ministers, and he also retained his post as head of Cuba's armed forces. It is anticipated that there will be a meeting of the Central Committee of the Communist Party later in the year, to name Raúl Castro to the position of first secretary of the Communist Party.

In a move made to appease the hard-liners, Ramiro Valdés Menéndez was named vice president of the Council of State and is continuing in his position as minister of information science and communications. Moderates within the Cuban government and the Cuban people were encouraged by the selection of Carlos Lage Dávila as first vice president. Francisco Soberón Valdés remained as minister president of the Central Bank.

Raúl Castro has consolidated his power in the months since Fidel's death in July 2008. The attempt by hard-liners to block economic reforms has been discouraged by Raúl's decision, only days after Fidel's funeral, to announce a Cuban Bill of Rights guaranteeing to every Cuban the right to healthcare, housing, and employment. He also promised to improve economic opportunity and increase freedoms. Economic reforms announced by Raúl include the following:

—Measures to meet the most urgent concerns expressed during the national discussion–food, housing and salaries. Access to food has improved; China is building several large housing projects in Havana, Santiago de Cuba, and Camagüey; and the number of companies paying Cuban employees in hard currency has increased.

—New investment laws to facilitate the opening of businesses has resulted in over 100,000 new micro-investments in tourist-related services, including *paladares* (private restaurants), bed and breakfasts, transportation, and handicrafts. The tourist sector represents the sole opportunity for small entrepreneurship; many of these businesses receive informal "investments" via remittances from Cuban Americans.

—The issuance of over 20,000 certificates of ownership for apartments and houses occupied by Cuban families, resulting in home improvements and private sales. Despite some conflicts between Cubans and Cuban Americans over expropriated property, many Cuban Americans have provided funds to upgrade property owned by friends and relatives in exchange for future ownership. The quid pro quo for current owners is basic upgrades of their living quarters such as fresh paint and new appliances.

—The creation of a National Civic Corps to reduce youth unemployment in which young men and women serve their country in lieu of mandatory military service.

The contradiction between improved economic conditions, for which many Cubans are giving Raúl's government credit, and the government's simultaneous desire to keep control over the reform process and its potential to unleash political dissent is generating tensions. Raúl has not loosened state control over the political system: he and the rest of the Cuban hierarchy serve indefinitely, and the Communist Party remains the dominant political force in Cuba. The indirect system of elections, in which nominations for office are made by women, youths, and workers' groups affiliated with the Cuban Communist Party, has not been changed. There is more tolerance for free speech, and dissident movements have been allowed to form political parties. However, after an initial jump in the popularity of dissidents, their numbers have declined, as Cuban security forces have increased surveillance and harassment. Street demonstrations are prohibited, and meetings in excess of ten participants are illegal unless preapproved by State Security.

Cuba joined the UN Human Rights Council and agreed to allow UN officials to monitor its human rights activities beginning in 2009. In January 2009, a United Nations representative reviewed the human rights situation in Cuba and commended the government for the provision of shelter, food, and healthcare. He praised reforms that have allowed enhanced access to information and loosened restrictions on private investment, but he remained critical of the government's suppression of the opposition and its refusal to release political prisoners.

The number of political prisoners has declined to approximately one hundred. Dr. Oscar Elías Biscet, a human rights advocate, remains jailed, but the noted author Raúl Rivero and the independent trade union leader Pedro Pablo Alvarez Ramos have been released and sent into exile in Spain. Student and youth protests were swiftly suppressed by Cuban authorities. Leaders were detained for several days and, upon release, were warned that the next time the prison sentences would last years.

Hugo Chávez's relationship with Raúl Castro has not been as warm as Chávez's relationship with Fidel Castro, for Chávez aspires to be the ideological heir to Fidel's Revolution. The Cuba-Venezuela connection continues to be reinforced by Venezuela's largesse in the form of three billion of dollars' worth of annual oil donations in exchange for Cuban doctors and teachers. The European Union has begun a dialogue with Cuba and quietly dropped the sanctions imposed on the country in 2003.

In the final months of the Bush administration, United States policy toward Cuba was based on rhetoric. The president and members of his administration refused to make any changes in policy until Cuba underwent a democratic transition. At the same time, one of two Cuban American candidates for office, both Florida Democrats, won a seat in the U.S. House of Representatives, and more Cuban Americans were considered to be violating limits on travel and remittances than in the past, indicating that they were determined to maintain contacts with the island. The number of Cuban Americans supporting unrestricted travel and remittances to Cuba and legalization of the sale and donation of humanitarian and agricultural goods also continues to rise. Many Cuban Americans fear that their community will be excluded from participating in shaping Cuba's future and participating in the developing economy. Cuban American businesspeople are actively lobbying for exceptions to the embargo that would make it possible for them to support micro- and family enterprises in Cuba. Support to upgrade U.S.-Cuban diplomatic representation to the ambassadorial level and to open a dialogue with the Cuban government is also gaining ground. No proposals, or action, to resolve the issue of expropriated property have been made, however.

Domestically, the new U.S. administration is dealing with a recession. Oil prices have become a major drag on ending the recession, and healthcare reform remains a top priority. Internationally, the administration continues to focus on the Middle East and Afghanistan and Pakistan, and the Israeli-Palestinian conflict is an additional foreign policy challenge.

In an attempt to restore damaged relations with the other countries in the hemisphere, the president has scheduled a "listening tour" of major allies; he plans to visit Mexico City and Brasilia, where Cuba will be a major topic on the agenda.

Role-Play No. 2: "A Meeting of the National Security Council"

Characters in the Role-Play–

National Security Adviser (Chair)	USAID Administrator
Secretary of State	Deputy Secretary of State
Secretary of Defense	Deputy Secretary of Defense
Secretary of Treasury	Deputy Secretary of Commerce
Secretary of Commerce	Assistant Secretary for Western
Secretary of Homeland	Hemisphere Affairs
Security	Coordinator, Office of Cuban Affairs
Director of National	National Intelligence Officer for
Intelligence	Latin America
White House Chief of Staff	Commandant, U.S. Coast Guard
Chairman of the Joint	Combatant Commander, U.S.
Chiefs of Staff	Southern Command

Instructions: Background and Meeting Agenda

The president asked for a strategy review to craft a comprehensive new policy toward Cuba that would promote the U.S. objectives of having a friendly, democratic, and stable neighbor. No deadline was given for announcing the new policy, but the president and the principals hoped to make Cuba one of their first foreign policy success stories. In the week prior to the meeting, the president discussed strategic alternatives with the National Security Adviser and several cabinet secretaries but came to no final decision. The principals now need to decide among the following strategic approaches:

—Engage the Cuban government on issues of mutual interest and ease sanctions without waiting for Cuban reforms.

—Demand a qui pro quo for U.S. easing of sanctions and other improvements in relations.

—Move toward a complete normalization of relations with Cuba, including seeking executive and legislative action to end the embargo.

I. Strategic Considerations

The National Security Adviser informed the principals that the president believed the administration's objectives in Cuba should be the same as its objectives in the hemisphere: to support representative democracies, promote economic development, and increase regional cooperation. He sought their recommendations on establishing a long-range strategic policy that would engage Cuba and the Cuban people.

—How far and how deep should the United States go in modifying its policies toward Cuba?

—Would major reforms result in changed Cuban behavior? Would they encourage the Cuban people to become agents for change in Cuba?

II. Changing the Terms of the U.S. Embargo against Cuba

The 1996 Helms-Burton Act codified the embargo regulations and set conditions for its removal. Two years later President Clinton, after consultations with Congress, substantially modified the embargo by announcing "new measures" that permitted the licensing of travel and the transfer of financial and other resources to Cuba. New regulations were written to reflect these modifications. Subsequently, President Bush announced a further set of regulations to curtail several of the Clinton measures. In addition, the traditionally exempt fully hosted travel, in which no financial transactions between Americans and Cubans took place, was also prohibited.

Although the Helms-Burton legislation codified all sanctions regulations, these regulations included provisions for the secretary of the treasury to license any prohibited activity. Thus, the president can direct the secretary to license prohibited activities and thereby modify and rescind many embargo regulations—but not all. The regulations that he is unable to change are those that were codified in other legislation. The 2000 legislation that permitted food sales to Cuba codified the travel regulations then in force without giving the secretary the authority to modify them. The Cuban Democracy Act of 1992 codified licensing procedures for telecommunication that must also be observed by the secretary and the Office of Foreign Assets Control. These circumstances led to the questions:

—Does the president retain significant authority to modify the embargo?
—What initiatives might he undertake?

III. The Importance of the Cuban Government's Response

The traditional U.S. approach to Cuba mandated that any easing of the embargo required a quid pro quo from the Cuban government: it would have to guarantee greater freedoms for the Cuban people.
—Should the administration publicly state that the precondition for an easing of the embargo is Cuba's release of political prisoners or other actions?
—Or would there be value in proceeding with a long-range strategy of normalizing relations regardless of Cuban actions?

IV. Reducing Cuba's Dependence on Venezuela

As long as Cuba is dependent on Venezuelan oil subsidies, the Cuban government is unlikely to remove itself from the influence of President Chávez.
—What strategies might the United States employ to lessen Cuba's dependency on Venezuela?

V. Reintegrating Cuba into the Hemisphere

—What should be the criteria for lifting Cuba's suspension from the OAS? (On June 4, 2009, the OAS passed a resolution calling for Cuba's participation in the OAS to be based on a "process of dialogue initiated at the request of the Government of Cuba and in accordance with the practices, purposes and principles of the OAS.")

VI. A New U.S. Approach to Cuba

The principals were asked to draw up a list of specific actions for the president's consideration.

Abridged Minutes

Abridged minutes from the simulation are provided to enable study of the kinds of exchanges that took place among the participants.

A National Security Council policy review was under way. Principal policymakers dealing with Cuba considered how the new administration could press for representative government, economic openness, and improved human rights in Cuba.

I. Strategic Considerations

The National Security Adviser asked the principals whether and how the administration should engage Cuba and probed the degree to which doing so would result in increased space for civic participation by Cuba's citizens.

The Secretary of State stated that engaging Cuba would increase the likelihood that the Cuban government would not object to assistance from NGOs. Nevertheless, private Cuban groups might still refuse U.S. government assistance for fear of being labeled and marginalized, as the dissident movement was. A change in regulations to allow travel by American religious, cultural, and humanitarian groups would support like-minded organizations in Cuba. She said that historically, when more liberal travel and remittance regulations were in effect, from 1999 to 2002, Cuban civil society and the dissident movement expanded as a result of exchanges and enhanced support provided. Proof of this was that a major dissident initiative, Project Varela, led by a Christian Democrat, Oswaldo Payá, succeeded in collecting 35,000 signatures on a petition requesting a referendum on the Cuban constitution. This period of greater openness became known as the Cuban Spring. It ended with the jailing of dissidents in 2003, after a tightening of U.S. travel and other regulations.

The National Security Adviser agreed with these observations but cautioned that it remained extremely difficult to determine how fast the administration should proceed and whether and what might be expected from Cuba in return. He said, "Deciding how far to go in reducing sanctions and reaching out to the Cuban government is rather like dropping an anchor in unknown waters." The anchor should not simply be thrown into shallow water, where it would accomplish little. On the other hand, placing it in deep waters—for example, by permitting a range of economic and commercial transactions—could provoke negative reactions at home, seen as rewarding of the Cuban government without reciprocal action, as well as from the Cuban government. The Secretary of State concurred, saying that it would be impossible to know how the Cuban government would react to U.S. actions: many experts have concluded that, in fact, Cuba's leaders prefer the status quo, able to blame its economic shortcomings on the U.S. embargo.

Those around the table would have to decide on a new approach to Cuba that was grounded in the administration's belief that the time had come to replace the failed policy of isolation and regime change. In the end, the United States should gauge its actions by the degree to which they promote U.S. national interests and strengthen the Cuban people's ability to increase their independence from their government.

The Assistant Secretary for Western Hemisphere Affairs pointed out that Cuba might welcome lifting the travel ban or even restoring people-to-people travel because of the revenues that U.S. travel would generate. On the other hand, the United States should not be surprised if the Cuban government did not respond positively to its initiatives. The Cuban hierarchy's reaction would be based on its ability to manage changes brought about by U.S. policy; the Cuban leadership does not like surprises and would not welcome unexpected actions that could challenge its control over the Cuban people.

The Cuban government's priority would continue to be to remain in power and preserve the Revolution. Ironically, however, many in the United States would see American changes in policy as "concessions" and would anticipate and even demand that Cuba respond to these "concessions" by giving Cubans more freedoms. If Cuba were to react negatively or fail to release political prisoners, many would call on the administration to stop making concessions. Thus, it would be best to avoid raising expectations by linking U.S. actions to Cuban reactions, since doing so would in effect give Raúl Castro a veto over U.S. policy. Raúl might well want to avoid an influx of U.S. citizens, especially those working with NGOs, that would strengthen the ability of Cuban organizations to expand the provision of services to their communities.

The USAID Administrator suggested that the criterium for deciding on how far to go in revising the embargo might be the degree to which doing so would improve the lives of the Cuban people. Greater access to information and resources would reduce their dependence on the Cuban government: if Cubans had wider access to information, they would begin to develop the knowledge, and possibly strengthen their desire, to insist on reforms within their own system.

The Coordinator of the Office of Cuban Affairs believed that enhanced U.S. contact would empower the Cuban people through increased information about reform processes and building civil society. If there were a better relationship between the two governments it would encourage Cuban civil society entities to accept assistance from NGOs that were funded by USAID. In Eastern Europe change was fostered through the Helsinki Accords, which authorized human contact and exchanges. The same might occur in Cuba if the administration were to end the travel ban.

The Secretary of Commerce asked whether the United States should move ahead with significant easing of the embargo if the authoritarian Cuban government was unwilling to end human rights abuses, permit free and fair elections, and open up its economy. The Secretary of Defense responded that in his view it would be in the interest of the United States to move ahead with greater contact with the Cuban government, regardless of Cuba's response. Doing so would provide the administration with better contacts and information about the Cuban government and promote cooperation to reduce the possibility of a mass migration and the movement of illegal narcotics.

The White House Chief of Staff pointed out that the nations of Latin America were becoming increasingly vocal in their condemnation of the embargo. Many Latin American presidents who in the past had avoided Cuba were paying visits to the island and engaging Cuban leaders in regional forums. The United States could significantly improve its image in the region by easing or lifting the embargo and in ceasing to oppose OAS engagement of the island.

II. Revising the U.S. Embargo on Cuba

To this end many principals pressed the National Security Adviser to recommend that the president act boldly within his first one hundred days and end all sanctions. The Secretary of the Treasury pointed out that it was not possible for the president to completely lift the embargo because certain regulations were U.S. law. The Helms-Burton Act of 1996 codified the embargo, making ending it contingent on the removal from power of both Castro brothers. The Cuban Democracy Act of 1992 banned trade with Cuba by foreign subsidiaries of U.S. companies. Still, the president has the power to modify embargo regulations through the Secretary of the Treasury's licensing authority. President Clinton did so in 1998, when he put in place more liberal travel and remittance regulations. After initially leaving in place the Clinton regulations, President

Bush restricted travel and remittances after Cuba jailed human rights activists in the spring of 2003. Moving beyond family travel, the Secretary of the Treasury recommended that the president now reinstate people-to-people travel for religious, professional, humanitarian, and cultural purposes. But a majority of those around the table were not satisfied and felt that this did not go far enough; they argued that the president should lift the travel ban and the embargo in his first one hundred days.

The Secretary of the Treasury said that, if authorized, he would hope to also instruct the Office of Foreign Assets Control (OFAC) to lift restrictions on certain categories of exports, such as on the sale and donation of radios, TVs, and Internet service provision, and on the imports of medicines produced in Cuba. The Coordinator of the Office of Cuban Affairs wondered how the Secretary of the Treasury could proceed with these measures while the Helms-Burton Act was in force, since it stipulated that Cuba would have to be undergoing a process of democratic transition before the embargo could be lifted.

The Secretary of the Treasury said he doubted that Congress would repeal either the Helms-Burton Act or the Cuban Democracy Act, but that the president had the authority to modify embargo regulations by using his executive authorities and foreign policy prerogatives. Nevertheless, he urged the administration to consult and gain the support of key members of Congress before acting unilaterally.

III. Possible Policy Initiatives

The Assistant Secretary for Western Hemisphere Affairs suggested that the president open up two-way travel to and from Cuba by lifting the travel ban and easing travel restrictions on Cubans who wished to visit the United States. Allowing increased numbers of Cuban family members, academics, and artists, among others, to visit the United States would allow them to gain an insight into a free society and build important contacts that could stimulate change in Cuba. In addition, the administration should expand the flow of information to Cuba. Cuba has some of the world's lowest cell phone and Internet access coverage in the world. Very few newspapers and magazines are available to the public; few radios and TVs can receive frequencies from off the island; access to the Internet is monitored and restricted to domestic websites, and most electronic communication equipment, including cell phones, is too expensive for Cubans to purchase. If change is to occur in Cuba, the Cuban people need access to much more information. The administration should encourage communications with Cuba by licensing satellite and other hookups to telecommunications as well as the sale and donation of radios, TVs, computers, and cell phones.

The Director of National Intelligence audaciously pointed out that the United States was inadvertently assisting Cuban security by prohibiting access to the Internet and the sale of communications equipment. The Cuban government had consistently banned books and newspapers and restricted access to information via radio, television, and the Internet in order to prevent citizens from gaining knowledge and contacts that might lead them to seek greater freedoms. Measures that opened communications would reduce the control of Cuba's security services over the Cuban people, he continued. "The United States should lift the communications embargo on Cuba."

The USAID Administrator suggested that a targeted aid package be a part of a multilateral approach to Cuba. Care would have to be taken that assistance not be perceived as "tied" or "charity" or as a threat to Cuba's sovereignty. One principal proposed the creation of a multilateral fund to promote micro-enterprise development and to assist civil society groups. Others wanted to ensure that if the United States provided resources, further multilateral assistance would be tied to the release of political prisoners, democratic elections, and a much-needed modification of Cuba's penal code. Others cautioned that Cuba would reject such conditionalities.

All cabinet members advocated expanding bilateral and multilateral discussions with relevant Cuban officials on a number of security issues of importance to both countries: migration, organized crime, counternarcotics strategies, and the environment. This bilateral diplomatic agenda, pertinent for any U.S. administration at any point in time, would also include exchanging defense attachés, to provide better knowledge of the inner workings of Cuba's armed forces. Restoring the reciprocal ability of diplomats to travel in Cuba and the United States would also be essential. The majority of the principals agreed that now is the time for the president to name the first U.S. ambassador to Cuba in half a century. A minority of the principals felt that this step toward fully normalizing diplomatic relations should come later.

IV. The Cuban Government's Response

The principals agreed with the Secretary of State's observation that a future Cuban government is likely to follow cues from Deng Xiao Ping rather than Mikhail Gorbachev. Raúl Castro is likely to continue making modest economic reforms designed to salvage the economy and satisfy public demand. He will move cautiously, wishing to maintain political control while doing what he could to provide greater opportunities and improve living conditions. He will attempt to buy time in the expectation that if Cuba can develop its offshore oil and production of ethanol from sugarcane, the state would have additional revenues that would permit it to enhance social services and allow the regime to consolidate its power.

The National Security Adviser personally believed that political reform and human rights must be an integral part of U.S. policy toward Cuba. However, U.S. actions to promote these or any aspect of the policy agenda should not be constrained by or dependent on Cuban actions. U.S. policy should be completely independent and based solely on U.S. interests and values.

The Coordinator of the Office of Cuban Affairs said it was probably true that Cuba prefers the status quo and fears a more open U.S. approach. Nevertheless, she urged the principals to acknowledge that if Cuba offered no responses it would make it difficult and even impossible for the administration to successfully continue its long-range strategy of easing sanctions. She believed it would be key for the administration to remain flexible in its approach—stopping when needed but maintaining the forward motion and retaining its long-term focus on reducing sanctions and improving relations.

V. Reducing Cuba's Dependence on Venezuelan Oil

The Secretary of Commerce reported that Venezuelan subsidies amounted to approximately US$3.5 billion annually. According to the United States Geological Survey, Cuba's unproven offshore oil reserves, near its north coast and in the Gulf of Mexico, were estimated at over 4.6 billion barrels of probable oil reserves and close to over 10 billion metric yards of natural gas. Within three to five years, Cuba could be producing as much as 350,000 barrels per day (bpd), sufficient to meet its growing energy requirements. Today, Cuba receives roughly 90,000 bpd from Venezuela and consumes a total of 145,000 bpd per day. The normal 60-40 split in production-sharing agreements with foreign oil companies would provide Cuba with roughly 200,000 bpd, allowing the island to end its energy dependence on Venezuela. Cuba could export the excess production in the short term, but domestic demand could rise rapidly if the Cuban government began to permit market-based reforms.

Cuba could increase its energy production further if it decided to undertake a joint venture for sugarcane ethanol production with Brazil. Cuba has the capacity to reclaim one million hectares of sugarcane land within a two- to three-year period, which could generate upwards of US$2.3 billion of annual revenue in ethanol. If both the ethanol and the oil industries become fully operational, the Cuban government can expect additional revenues of US$3 billion to 5 billion per year.

The Secretaries of State, Commerce, and the Treasury agreed that the president should seek to lessen Cuba's dependence on Venezuelan subsidies by encouraging Brazil to become involved in both Cuban ethanol and offshore oil production. Some advisers urged the administration to allow U.S. companies to develop Cuba's offshore oil. The USAID Administrator disagreed with the idea of helping Cuba develop its offshore oil wealth, concerned that if Cuba were to do so it would strengthen the government, making Cubans even more vulnerable to government control. The Secretary of Commerce suggested that with or without U.S. companies, Cuba would develop its oil and some of the drilling would take place very close to the Florida coast.

The Deputy Secretary of State took the opportunity to point out that if the Cuban state were to increase its wealth as a result of its energy reserves, there was even more reason for loosening restrictions on transfers of resources to the Cuban people. If the population had access to private resources its vulnerability to an oppressive government would be lowered. The administration should therefore not restrict financial remittances and gifts to the Cuban people.

VI. Reintegrating Cuba into the Hemisphere

The National Security Adviser reported that the president had asked for the principals' recommendations as to whether the United States should drop its objections to Cuba's reinstatement as a member of the Organization of American States. The White House Chief of Staff responded that if the majority of OAS members agreed that Cuba met the criteria for membership, it should be reinstated. In any case, doing so would provide an incentive to Cuba to meet the conditions for membership, including those regarding democracy and political reform. Some principals were less certain and suggested a gradual, principled approach. One suggested the creation of a "neighborhood working group," possibly including Canada, Brazil, Mexico, Spain, and France, that would reach out to the Cuban government regarding membership criteria. The Coordinator of the Office of Cuban Affairs reminded participants that not only had the Cuban hierarchy professed profound disinterest in being reinstated in the OAS, Cuba would likely be insulted by the idea of a committee passing judgment on its conduct.

The Assistant Secretary of State believed that the OAS and other multilateral institutions should decide how to manage Cuba's potential participation without U.S. involvement. If Cuba decided to join multilateral financial institutions, it would have to undertake reforms that would be beneficial to the Cuban people, and its refusal to release all political prisoners would be a major stumbling block. The bottom line, said the Deputy Secretary of the Treasury, should be that if Cuba met the membership standards of these organizations, it should be permitted to join.

VII. A New U.S. Approach toward Cuba

All principals agreed that the administration should jettison the policy of isolation and regime change. It was deemed time to accept the Cuban government as a reality; the Revolution cannot be undone, but over time it can evolve, as all governments can. Some cited the case of Mexico's evolution under the Institutional Revolutionary Party (PRI).

Most participants believed that as the administration began to frame a new policy toward Cuba, it should seize the initiative rather than retain a defensive posture in which any policy change would be dependent on actions by the Cuban government. A new approach in policy would be needed to put the responsibility for reform on Cuba, rather than allowing Cuba's leaders to shift the blame for its failures to the "threat" from the United States. Further, the United States should "de-Americanize" its approach and align its policy with the nations of the region and the international community. U.S. policy should reflect U.S. national interests and principles, and should have the result of improving the U.S. image in the region and beyond. Finally, the United States should also engage the Cuban government and seek a constructive relationship on issues of mutual importance. This would likely lead to enhanced contact for the U.S. government and nongovernmental organizations with Cuban citizens. In sum, the administration should promote the well-being of the Cuban people and the growth of civil society. U.S. public and private assistance should be available to all groups seeking peaceful change in Cuba, not just those that embody U.S. policy.

The following measures, which could be carried out immediately or over time, were recommended by the National Security Adviser to the president:

—The president should immediately and unilaterally take definitive actions that would convey its desire to establish an improved relationship with Cuba.

—Two-way travel and interaction that promotes the well-being of the Cuban people should be authorized because it would help create pressures on the island for greater political and economic freedoms.

—The new administration should lift all travel and remittance restrictions currently placed on Cuban Americans. Many but not all participants advocated removing all restrictions on travel.

—The administration should take measures through licensing that would remove the "communications embargo."

—The administration should engage the Cuban government on issues of mutual concern such as migration, health, environment, and interdiction of illegal narcotics trade.

—The administration's goal should be to normalize diplomatic relations to the degree possible using the president's executive powers.

—The Secretary of the Treasury should use his powers to rescind major provisions of the trade embargo.

CHAPTER FIVE

Understanding the Cuban Leadership

The third simulation exercise, held on March 4, 2008, focused on the internal dynamics, motivations, and decisionmaking processes of the Cuban hierarchy. Following on the heels of Fidel Castro's decision to step down and temporarily hand over power to his brother, Brookings project advisers and special guests assessed the objectives and incentives of members of Cuba's political and military leadership. By seeking to understand the possible political and economic strategies that the Raúl Castro government might adopt in the immediate future, the exercise helped the project advisers develop a better sense of the interplay between U.S. policy and Cuba's political dynamics. The exercise also highlighted major gaps in knowledge about Cuban actors and their motivations.

In this simulation the participants took on the roles of advisers to Raúl Castro. Their goal was to replicate the strategies that the Cuban hierarchy might employ to sustain its rule. The key concerns that emerged in those deliberations help indicate the ways the Cuban government might set its priorities in this transitional period and generated the following central questions.

—How will the government of Raúl Castro deal with Cuban citizens' rising expectations for economic improvement? Will economic changes undermine or reinforce the authority of the state?

—How far can Cuban authorities liberalize economically without threatening to undermine the social achievements of the Revolution (pensions, health, education) and its key support base?

—Should Raúl Castro seek to include a broader spectrum of voices within the Communist Party and use the Party to institutionalize his vision? Can Raúl or any future leader match Fidel's political dominance?

—Can Cuba successfully reduce its overwhelming dependence on Venezuela without jeopardizing short-term supplies of crude oil?

—Will economic reforms end up serving to let off steam and take off the pressure for genuine political change? Or will partial economic liberalization create pressures for broader and more rapid political change inside Cuba, possibly forcing the Cuban hierarchy to move beyond its comfort zone?

—What measures will the Cuban government need to take to convince U.S. policymakers and the international community that they should provide incentives to encourage reform?

—Will growing energy revenues provide Cuban leaders with enough increased credibility and popularity to decrease their fear of greater political competition? And will higher revenues bolster the hierarchy's confidence in its ability to maintain control?

The Exercise

Participants were called upon to put themselves in the shoes of an inner circle of advisers to Raúl Castro as they meet to discuss where they want to take Cuba over the next five years, and how to get there.

By attempting to view Cuba's complex political, economic, and social challenges through the eyes of key members of the Cuban leadership, participants sought to better understand several important issues. Lacking insights into the dynamics of decisionmaking within the Cuban hierarchy, the group sought to understand, first, how an uncharismatic Raúl Castro might consolidate his leadership and what institutional capacity he will draw on to do so. What role would these institutions play in opening up a new chapter in the Revolution? Next, participants sought to examine the extent to which the Raúl Castro government would endeavor to meet the Cuban population's demands for improved economic conditions. Would the leadership's survival be contingent upon continuing the initial reforms undertaken by Raúl during his interim presidency? Finally, participants assessed how the Raúl Castro government will approach the international community, and how it might manage strategic partnerships

---

B O X 5 - 1 .   Raúl's Consolidation of Power: Recent Developments

On March 2, 2009, almost one year to the day after the date of the simulation recreated in exercise 3, the Cuban hierarchy announced a major reshuffle in the Council of State and the Council of Ministers that included the removal of some of Cuba's most prominent politicians. The most visible individuals replaced were those the outside world knew best as Cuba's international face: Foreign Minister Felipe Pérez Roque and Secretary of the Council of Ministers Carlos Lage Dávila.

The reshuffle completed Raúl's consolidation of power. Politics and decisionmaking are likely to remain as centralized and tightly controlled as they were under Fidel. The dismissals came in advance of a Cuban Communist Party Congress announced for 2009, but indefinitely postponed in the summer, avoiding what would have been the first since 1997 at which a Cuban leader would have had to gather support for his plans.

The new appointments suggest no new directions in policy but rather a reaffirmation of loyalty, stability, and control. They include several members of the military who are loyal to Raúl and on whom he may rely in times characterized by expanding reforms or internal dissent. The new appointments comprise both military loyalists—those involved in managing big economic portfolios in state-owned enterprises—and Party loyalists who rose through the Party, a cohort of unknowns who share a history of cracking down on inefficiency and running a tight ship. The reshuffle heralds two new trends in governance.

1. Reasserting control over decisionmaking. Raúl appears to have wanted, via the dismissals and the subsequent postponement of the Communist Party Congress, to maintain his control over decisionmaking as he navigates the uncertain waters of economic reforms and manages policy toward the Obama administration, which has hinted at

---

and prepare for uncertainty in order to ensure its longevity. Through these three interrelated challenges—politics, economics, foreign affairs— what vulnerabilities will a Raúl-led government encounter as it embarks upon the various components of its strategy? Could Raúl and his closest advisers map a way to govern Cuba and ensure the continuity of the Revolution beyond Fidel and Raúl's lifetimes?

Simulation Exercise No. 3: A Meeting of Raúl Castro and His Advisers, March 4, 2008

Raúl's close group of advisers unanimously agreed that their top priority would be to preserve power and continue the Cuban Revolution. They

seeking an expanded dialogue with Cuba. Shaping a more institutionalized Communist Party, as discussed in this chapter's simulation exercise, may have been moved to the back burner, to be pursued in a time of greater stability.

Consolidating his leadership may also have become a priority for Raúl as a result of tensions between the two brothers over the decisionmaking process since Raúl's accession to the presidency. Although tensions between the brothers continue, the dismissals and their replacements neutralized two factions loyal to Fidel: the "Havana Talibans" and the technocrats. The intransigent Havana Talibans, young, ardent defenders of the Revolution who resolutely support Fidel, had been led by Foreign Minister Pérez Roque and Otto Rivero Torres. Several members have been demoted since the fall of 2008, including Carlos Manuel Valenciaga Díaz, a member of the Council of State and Fidel Castro's personal secretary and chief of staff. The technocrats had been led by Carlos Lage, who championed Cuba's economic openings during the Special Period. The dismissal of Lage and Pérez Roque thus signals a stifling of debate on foreign and economic policy within the councils and eliminates the two most prominent candidates previously touted to succeed Fidel.

2. Halting Cuba's economic freefall. The changes in the Council of Ministers affected the ministers of foreign trade, foreign investment, the food industry, finance and prices, domestic trade, and the iron and steel industry. Raúl's calls for a "more compact and functional structure, with fewer agencies under the Central State Administration and a better distribution of their duties" most likely are intended to streamline and bring discipline to the ministries connected to economic performance, with a particular emphasis on food production.

advised Cuba's new president that to succeed without the charismatic and domineering power of Fidel Castro, he had to build on his reputation as a consensus seeker, a pragmatist, and a "doer" rather than a "talker." They urged him to pursue creative solutions that would address the Cuban people's desires for improved material well being. Advisers considered the results of government-sponsored forums for discussion held across the island over the past year. During these meetings, citizens stridently and publicly criticized the stagnant economy and even spoke out against some limitations that may be considered more political than economic, such as tight restrictions on citizens' freedom to travel abroad. The forums have also had the effect of raising citizens' expectations for change to a dangerous level, according to several participants. It may not be enough to simply increase the availability of consumer goods. On the contrary, Cubans are in search of more fundamental changes in their society; some hope to build their own lives independent of government interference or influence. As a result, Raúl's advisers concluded that the fundamental challenge for the Raúl Castro government will be meeting these demands for improved conditions without seriously undercutting the authority of the state.

Advisers commended Raúl for his deep loyalty to Fidel, despite the differences of opinion they have had in the past over matters of political and economic strategy. They praised his decision to continue seeking Fidel's counsel on matters of urgent national importance, as articulated by Raúl during a speech on February 24, 2008, to Cuba's National Assembly. Nonetheless, they anticipated that Raúl, while similar to Fidel in his strong support of the core principles of Communist ideology, would have to establish his own credentials and credibility as Cuba's leader in order to overcome pent-up popular aspirations for change.

Noting that Raúl had shunned the spotlight when he was the minister of defense, seldom meeting with Western ambassadors or high-level visitors, Raúl's advisers recommended that Cuba's new head of state more enthusiastically assume some of these ceremonial duties. To use an analogy from the world of film, in the past Fidel served as the consummate director of the Cuban saga, while Raúl always felt more comfortable serving as the producer behind the scenes, ensuring stability, maintaining order, and implementing key policies. Now these roles have been reversed, and Raúl, his advisers noted, will have to assume the public mantle of power, yet in a way different from Fidel's style of wielding power. The advisers noted that no individual could fill Fidel's role as leader of the Revolution. Indeed, because Raúl needs a wider base to exert influence, institutional "buy-in" from the Cuban Communist Party (Partido Comunista de Cuba, or PCC) and the Cuban military, the Revolutionary Armed Forces (Fuerzas Armadas Revolucionarias, or FAR), will be critical.

Raúl's advisers expressed their full confidence in the loyalty of officials from the top ranks of government, the Communist Party, and the military: First Vice President José Ramón Machado Ventura, Minister of the Interior General Abelardo Colomé Ibarra; and new Minister of Defense General Julio Casas Regueiro. After widespread speculation abroad that Carlos Lage Dávila would be promoted to first vice president and usher in an era of rapid change, the advisers applauded the appointment of José

Ramón Machado Ventura to this position as an important signal of Raúl's intent to preserve control and order even as his government tentatively undertakes reforms. Nevertheless, their faith in Lage's loyalty to the Revolution remained unwavering. Indeed, each of Raúl's closest advisers was confident that what unites them is far greater than what would potentially divide them.

The Institutions of Government

Moving to a discussion of institutional capacities, Raúl's inner circle of advisers conceded that the Council of State holds mostly symbolic power. Advisers recommended that in order to further consolidate his rule, Raúl should mobilize the Communist Party and the Revolutionary Armed Forces, Cuba's two strongest government institutions, as vehicles to disseminate, explain, and enforce the decisions of the Cuban hierarchy. This imperative is all the more important, they argued, in the absence of Fidel's charismatic authority and in an environment where reforms that permit greater economic openness may create new, unpredictable challenges to the status quo.

THE CUBAN COMMUNIST PARTY

Participants emphasized the importance of the Cuban Communist Party as the key channel for carrying out policies at the local level. Particularly because Raúl is not a towering leadership figure, reinforcing and strengthening the profile of the Party's role, the advisers believed, will help validate and solidify a post-Fidel, perhaps less personality-driven, model of Cuban revolutionary governance. A majority of the Brookings participants role-playing Raúl's advisers suggested that the Party might evolve into a more open forum for discussion and an umbrella for relatively diverse opinions. For them, mimicking the Chinese model, in which leadership passed from a highly charismatic individual to a more firmly institutionalized ruling party, seemed an appropriate strategy to help ensure the longevity of the Revolution after the departure from the scene of its current cast of elderly leaders. Others, however, noted that thus far Raúl seems to be following Fidel's example, perhaps consulting more earnestly with his intimate circle of confidants, but still for the most part serving as the sole source of the state's vision.

Regardless, all advisers agreed that the next full Communist Party Congress is long overdue. In the past, Party Congresses have served as venues for authorities to unveil and seek the endorsement of strategic plans at critical moments. As Cuba is again approaching a turning point, Raúl's advisers viewed a Party Congress as the ideal setting for Raúl to more clearly enunciate his government's broader plans for reforms and subordinate his own role as head of state within the context of the Party's renewed importance.

In late April 2008, Cuban authorities announced that they would be holding their next Party Congress, the first since 1997, in the second half of 2009, suggesting that the basic contours of a road map for the way forward in the post-Fidel period possibly had already been agreed upon. In August 2009, however, the Party announced that the congress would be postponed indefinitely, indicating a need for additional preparations before what would presumably be the last congress led by the "historic leadership of the Revolution" could be held.

THE REVOLUTIONARY ARMED FORCES

Whatever the future role or structure of the Party turns out to be, all of Raúl's advisers agreed that the military will remain the backbone of the state. Despite limited resources and some evidence of corruption, the FAR is a disciplined, professional, hierarchically organized, and comparatively well-run institution. Few advisers worried about the possibility of disloyalty within military ranks, although it was noted that some lower-ranking officers remain disenchanted because of their low salaries and the lingering legacy of the Ochoa affair. (Arnaldo Ochoa was a well-known, popular general within the FAR who had served on numerous international missions, notably in Angola and Ethiopia. In 1989 he and several other military leaders were accused of numerous acts of corruption. Convicted, Ochoa was executed by firing squad. Many Cubans thought that Ochoa was innocent, the victim of a politically motivated conspiracy.) On balance, the advisers were quite generous in their praise of the Cuban military's proven track record of adapting, rationalizing, and carrying out the government's objectives. For example, they pointed to the nationwide military mobilization following Fidel's illness and temporary handover of power in July 2006, which involved over 200,000 soldiers. This impressive show of force has helped ensure a smooth succession to Raúl Castro's leadership, demonstrating once again that the FAR has always played an important role when the Revolution's survival was at stake.

The armed forces, with the Ministry of the Interior, will continue to be the guardian of the Cuban Revolution from internal and external enemies, just as Raúl groomed them to be during his long tenure as minister of defense. Advisers praised the Ministry of the Interior's ongoing work as first responder to domestic disturbances or popular discontent. This arrangement allows the armed forces to maintain their distance from the dirty work of policing and internal surveillance, preserving their credibility among the Cuban people. The police and security services that make up the Ministry of the Interior have proved to be particularly effective at preventive policing, and the ministry's capacity to anticipate trouble, infiltrate opposition groups, and curtail potential disorder is impressive. Advisers feared that, in the event of prolonged unrest, some soldiers of the armed forces might refuse orders to confront the population. Yet as long as the Ministry of the Interior continues its excellent work as first responder, and as long as the government can convince citizens that it intends to improve economic conditions, these worrisome circumstances should not come to pass.

Raúl's advisers also recommended preserving the Revolutionary Armed Forces' dual role as a "think tank" and a bureaucracy able to operate large state enterprises. Through its involvement in key productive sectors, the military remains an important tool for devising and carrying out creative economic policies, including successful strategies for managing the tourism industry. More to the point, the advisers considered the military crucial to the survival of the Cuban Revolution because it carries out the economic programs needed to fill state coffers. At the same time, it is responsible for public mobilizations necessary to deal with hurricanes, droughts, and other emergencies.

The Economy

Moving beyond instrumentalities and institutions, the group considered the important question of Cuba's economy. Advisers noted Raúl's willingness to broaden Cubans' economic freedoms to some degree, yet it remained unclear how fast reforms could be safely carried out, as well as what types of reforms would be most appropriate in light of the leadership's desire to preserve the fundamentally socialist character of Cuban society. Reforms that remove some onerous restrictions on economic and social activity without dramatically altering economic relationships were deemed to be relatively safe. Possible reform measures included both more concrete and symbolic steps.

In the weeks following this simulation exercise, the Cuban government seemed to follow this path by pursuing both "cosmetic" reforms and those with important real-life implications. As officials remove restrictions on the purchase of several high-tech devices (cell phones, computers), raise wage caps for certain professions, and grant Cubans equal access to tourist and hotel facilities, citizens' access to communication, exchange, and resources increases. (See box 5-2 for reforms enacted by the Raúl Castro government.)

Advisers considered agriculture to be a prime target for early reforms. At the time of this simulation exercise, Raúl had already given several indications that his government would make increasing agricultural output and reducing the island's dependence on imported food products a priority. This was all the more important as global food prices had reached alarming highs. Possible steps that participants considered included the leasing of idle state lands to private farmers and the decentralization of distribution channels. Indeed, since the date of the simulation, Cuban officials have undertaken these very measures while also reducing restrictions on access to agricultural implements, allowing producers to sell directly to major consumers. There may also be ongoing discussions about reducing the percentage of their harvest farmers are required to sell to the state.

Several advisers felt that a logical next step would be to revive and strengthen reforms from the early 1990s that permitted farmers' markets, certain small businesses, and other forms of private economic activity, especially in urban areas.[1] They argued that these measures are a proven way forward that can provide Cubans with the necessary short-term economic breathing room to quell the prospect of political unrest. Others

---

1. A status labeled "self-employment" was authorized in 1993, during the Special Period, when 117 licensed categories of home-based professions were created, including food service, hairdressing, and mechanic shops. These measures improved livelihoods in times of large-scale layoffs in state-owned enterprises, but also perpetuated the problems associated with the dual-currency system, since by design all transactions occurred in U.S. dollars and were taxed to bring significant revenues into state coffers. As the economy recovered, self-employment was scaled back: licenses were curtailed and license holders were subject to increasing taxes and restrictions. The tourism industry is the most resilient industry in which entrepreneurial activity has been sustained over time. Licenses continued to be issued to cater to unmet demand in the tourism industry for private taxis, restaurants, and bed-and-breakfast establishments. The expansion of self-employment today could serve as a valve for Cubans seeking more entrepreneurial freedoms and would relieve pressure to institute deeper reforms. It would also project a more open Cuba to foreign visitors and the international community.

were more cautious, pointing out that these reforms, if taken too far, could lead to a slippery slope of rising expectations and burgeoning private economic clout, with somewhat unpredictable consequences.

This discussion highlighted the difficulty of expanding and continuing the reform process. In agriculture, for example, truly improving output may require eliminating supply and demand bottlenecks created by artificial pricing, controlled markets, and limited access to fertilizers and transport—all basic structural issues that seem, for now at least, to be beyond the scope of proposed reforms. More broadly, some worried that the government could only deliver upon its promise for economic improvements and sustain the loyalty of the Cuban people if it were prepared to undertake major structural reforms such as liberalizing foreign investment regulations and devaluing and unifying the dual currency.[2] Sooner or later, some advisers felt, the Revolution would have to face the facts and address its fundamental economic flaws—the lack of salary incentives, few opportunities for advancement, and restrictive price controls—all of which severely hamper Cuba's economic growth.

Others, however, cautioned that it was preferable to move slowly with incremental reforms at the margins of the economy, so as not to arouse fear, anxiety, or instability among the citizenry. The aim of such a strategy would be to improve conditions slightly, increase the government's popularity, and buy time. Advisers further warned that any reform process should be designed so as not to threaten or disrupt the ability of the state to provide for those most loyal to the Revolution, such as members of the military bureaucracies, citizens from naturally conservative rural areas, members of state-organized labor unions, and Cuba's significant and growing pensioner class.

2. Cuba has two currencies, the nonconvertible peso, worth US$0.05, and the Cuban convertible peso, called the CUC, which is pegged to the dollar and is worth US$1.08. ("CUC" doesn't actually stand for anything but is just a common term used to distinguish the convertible from the nonconvertible peso.) The dual-currency system creates a social divide between two groups, those with access to remittances or jobs in the tourist sector, who earn CUCs, and those who receive pensions and state salaries, which are paid in pesos. The latter group accounts for the vast majority of salaries in Cuba; the monthly average salary is the equivalent of US$17. Many basic goods are sold at nonconvertible-peso stores, but imported luxury goods and also some basics such as meat and powdered milk must be paid for in CUCs at tourist-targeted "dollar stores" or must be obtained on the flourishing black market.

BOX 5-2. Tentative Economic Reforms under Raúl Castro

Building on a series of public discussions where Raúl Castro offered stark assessments of the performance of the Cuban economy, between March and June 2008 the Cuban government called for a series of structural changes to deal with inefficiency and low productivity, insufficient work incentives, a dual currency that distorts prices and incomes and limits purchasing power, soaring imports, and an aging population. Comprehensive reforms to address these shortcomings and to allow greater private or market-based activity have not, however, been pursued, except in agriculture. Tentative reforms that have been implemented seem inadequate to spur growth across the board, much needed in light of a soaring trade deficit driven by a 41 percent increase in imports, attributable to a rise in global oil and food prices and a decline in nickel exports. Furthermore, the three hurricanes that hit Cuba in the summer of 2008 took an enormous toll on the momentum of the reform process; hurricane damage amounted to $10 billion or 20 percent of Cuba's GDP.

Agricultural reform. The value of Cuba's food and livestock imports exceeded $2.2 billion in 2008, up from $1.5 billion in 2007. Between September 2008 and June 2009, in a comprehensive reform aimed at increasing domestic production, the government turned over almost half of the 1.7 million hectares of idle state lands to independent farmers and cooperatives, paid off state debt owed to farmers and cooperatives, and increased prices paid to producers. The Agriculture Ministry is also making headway in decentralizing decisionmaking: offices have been established at the municipal level, and a pilot project in Havana is enabling financially independent state enterprises to enter into contracts with producers for the harvesting, transportation, and sale of food.

Decentralizing state-owned enterprises. In March 2009, Raúl had a regulation lifted that required the Central Bank to approve expenditures by state-owned enterprises in excess of $10,000. This measure is granting more authority to managers and speeding up the flow of supplies to agriculture and tourism, sectors that require particular agility. This measure is in line with Raúl's emphasis on perfeccionamiento empresarial (enterprise optimization in the context of state ownership), a system based on modern management and accounting techniques that forms the backbone of economic reforms in Cuba, starting with the tourism industry in 1987. Although the perfeccionamiento empresarial framework is not new, lifting the regulation gives punch to a law—enacted in 1998 to facilitate greater efficiency and productivity in Cuba's state-owned enterprises—that had not gained traction

---

The currency question brought these concerns into stark relief. One adviser audaciously pointed out the government maintains the nonconvertible peso because it lacks sufficient foreign reserves to back and circulate only CUCs, convertible pesos. Since Cuban monetary authorities have far overvalued the island's GDP, any attempt to unify the convertible and

under Fidel. This is a first step in decentralizing decisionmaking, but deeper reforms will be needed to create efficiency and profitability in the state enterprise system while simultaneously avoiding official corruption from becoming more widespread.

Salary reform. In 2007 a policy was announced that wage caps would be eliminated across all sectors and salaries would be tied to productivity. In his first address to Cuba's parliament, in July 2008, Raúl grounded the policy within the context that equality would no longer mean egalitarianism, affirming, "Socialism means social justice and quality, but equality of rights, of opportunities, not of income." Although these plans have been put on hold while the Cuban government weathers the economic downturn, intermediate measures were announced in May 2009 to double the minimum wage in state-owned enterprises, raise salaries in the education sector, and grant permission to hold more than one job, including a part-time job. To counter the effects of an aging population on the workforce—the ratio of workers to retirees reached 3:1 in 2008, one of the highest in Latin America—the government also raised the retirement age by five years, to sixty for women and sixty-five for men.

Currency reform. In September 2007, Raúl Castro stated that a unification of exchange rates, though necessary, was not likely to take place before 2012.

Foreign investment. Despite Raúl's call for more foreign investment in Cuba, results have been meager. Plans for the offshore drilling project by a consortium led by Spain's Repsol have been delayed until at least 2010, and in real estate and tourism, port development, and other energy projects, plans have not progressed to the stage of committing funds or implementation.

Consumer freedoms. The most visible reforms that have been implemented have not focused on major economic policies, but rather on the removal of "excessive prohibitions" on Cubans' everyday lives, including permitting Cubans to purchase cell phones, electronics and home appliances and enter hotels previously reserved for tourists. While removing restrictions on consumer freedoms, most Cubans cannot afford the purchases of these goods and services.

Source: Oficina Nacional de Estadísticas (National Statistics Office), Anuario estadístico de Cuba, 2008 (Annual Statistical Profile, 2008) (Havana: 2009).

nonconvertible peso would result in a single currency of less value than the current convertible peso, prompting a corresponding drop in real GDP and inhibiting the government's ability to finance education, healthcare, and food distribution. Thus, while all the advisers agreed that unifying the currency would resolve one of Cuban citizens' chief economic grievances, many demanded assurances that such a policy would not further under-mine living standards or threaten state-provided social services. Advisers believed Cuba could potentially benefit from the assistance of interna-tional actors or financial institutions before the country undertakes the risks associated with a dramatic currency reform, let alone the adoption of other major macroeconomic reforms. However, U.S. opposition to Cuba's participation in these institutions—not to mention the advisers' own reser-vations about receiving external financing from organizations that are per-ceived as "neoliberal" in their economic approach—presents a formidable obstacle. In September 2007, Raúl announced that it would be overly opti-mistic to imagine that currency reform would be achieved before 2012.

Meanwhile, all the advisers were comfortable urging that Cuba's export-oriented industries, particularly in primary products such as oil and nickel, but also tourism, be diversified and opened up to foreign investment. Many hoped that with proper management and an appropri-ate investment climate, Cuba would develop enough offshore oil and sug-arcane ethanol resources to become energy self-sufficient. Economic growth in these non-labor-intensive sectors would help reinforce state power by bolstering top-down revenue-distribution mechanisms.

Participants also considered the ideological implications of these eco-nomic reforms. Will the government be seen as abandoning its historic commitment to egalitarian socialism if greater consumerism becomes per-missible, and if officials endeavor to incentivize production, whether by reducing wage caps, decentralizing agricultural production, or through more fundamental structural reforms? To the extent that Raúl moves for-ward with economic reform and those reforms create inequalities, how can he articulate a reform project within the historic tenets of the Cuban Revolution? Advisers viewed this difficult question as an area of potential vulnerability.

In the end, the majority of participants, role-playing Raúl's trusted inner circle, were not inclined to recommend radical market reforms for fear of provoking instability. Most felt it would be better to expand economic opportunity and productivity slowly without inviting strong economic dis-locations or undermining the social achievements of the Revolution. Nonetheless, all agreed that managing the at times countervailing expecta-tions of the Cuban people (pro-growth and in favor of greater economic opportunity, but resistant to increases in economic inequalities, such as those produced by Cuba's dual currency system) will by no means be easy.

The International Community

Despite policies of continuing economic and political isolation by the United States, Raúl Castro's close advisers felt confident that Cuba enjoys a generally favorable international position at this point in time. Thanks to generous oil subsidies from Venezuela, high commodity prices in recent years, and the prospect of developing its own oil resources, not to mention rising anti-Americanism around the world, Cuba has not been forced to make concessions in response to foreign demands, whether by the United States or other actors. That said, new statistics reveal that Cuba's export-oriented industries have taken a hit in 2008. Nickel prices were down by as much as 40 percent over 2007; and Cuba's food and livestock imports exceeded US$2.2 billion in 2008, up from US$1.5 billion in 2007—hence Raúl's focus on expanding domestic food production.

Participants advised Raúl Castro to proceed cautiously in modifying Cuba's relationship with the United States. Of course, by improving relations with the United States, Cuba ultimately stands to gain access to the all-important U.S. market. But the potential costs of such a monumental diplomatic shift—open flows of communication and people—could weaken the government's control. Likewise, some advisers feared that a strong easing or the lifting of the U.S. embargo would deprive Cuba's leaders of the pretext they have used for so long as an explanation of their own economic policy failures.

The status of the island's energy resources will form the basis of a critical calculation in Cuba's foreign (and domestic) policy choices (explored in detail in chapter 4). Major new energy flows, from both fossil and biofuels, would clearly give Cuba new foreign policy choices, namely the prospect of eliminating the island's dependence on Venezuela.

While agreeing that this is an important goal, especially in light of Venezuela's own economic uncertainties, all the advisers urged Cuba to proceed cautiously. As long as Cuba maintains only a seventeen-day supply of crude oil in reserve, Cuba must do nothing to jeopardize its ties to Venezuela. Although Venezuela certainly gains substantially from its relationship with Cuba, gaining both credibility with the world's political left and Cuban assistance in providing education and health care to its population, their mutual dependence is asymmetrical, Cuba's dependence on Caracas to ensure short-term stability being far more acute. To begin breaking the island's continuing cycle of external dependence—on Spain, the United States, the former Soviet Union, and now Venezuela—advisers recommended that the Cuban government strengthen trade relations with the major economic forces in Latin America, especially Brazil, Argentina, and Mexico. Perhaps Cuba's most sensitive medium-term foreign policy challenge is carefully reducing its dependence on Venezuela while not jeopardizing the flows of Venezuelan subsidies.

Advisers also positively noted the considerable sympathy of many international partners towards Raúl Castro's reform efforts. Several governments have even strengthened their relations with Cuba at this critical moment. Advisers expressed support for Cuba's expanding political ties with Russia, Mexico, and Brazil while also praising Spain's efforts to convince the European Union to restore normal relations.

Considerations for U.S. Policy

A number of important insights surfaced in the course of this simulation exercise. First, participants did not find that domestic or international conditions credibly threaten Raúl Castro's hold on power in the short run. Despite grassroots demands for economic improvement, the international community will be tolerant of Raúl's government and openly receptive to some measures toward economic liberalization. Cuba's loyal security services maintain a tight grip on domestic politics. Putting this in a "real-world" policy context, it is unlikely that Raúl will feel pressure for democratization during his first years of rule beyond a call for broadening voices and perspectives within the Communist Party. In the coming years, the Raúl Castro government may be willing to "liberalize within bounds" as long as doing so does not risk its losing control. For U.S. policymakers, then, the question is whether there is sufficient confidence in the power of even partial economic liberalization to create pressures for change in other arenas of Cuban society. If so, that could provide an opportunity to take Raúl's government at its word by offering to support key areas of economic liberalization. The international community already seems prepared to take up this gamble and engage with the Raúl Castro government, especially in the development of energy resources, even if there is no up-front commitment to fundamental political reform. Personal freedom has undoubtedly been expanded to some degree already by the liberalization of the sale of cell phones, computers, and other communication devices.

The group quickly came to two important conclusions concerning changing institutional arrangements in Cuba. First, Raúl Castro clearly needs to establish his own credentials, and he cannot hope to compete with Fidel's charismatic leadership style. As a result, Cuban officials may look to a stronger, more institutionalized Communist Party to replace Fidel as the long-term political face of the Revolution. To be credible in such a scheme, the Party would need to change its image and demonstrate that it has become more responsive to the needs of the people. This leads to the possibility that individual Cuban politicians might assume a lower-profile role within less personality-driven government structures.

Second, all participants agreed that the Cuban armed forces represent the most competent government entity within Cuba. The military's continued strength, unity, and influence over economic affairs will all be needed to guarantee whatever agenda is undertaken by the Party and Raúl. In other words, both the armed forces and the Party will be critical to putting Raúl Castro's vision for Cuba into place. The fusion of leadership at the highest levels of the Council of State, the military, and the Party facilitates this process.

In their roles as "Raúl's advisers," simulation participants struggled most with trade-offs on economic policy. Participants felt that the Raúl Castro government recognizes that if it is to retain power, it must meet the profound need to address Cubans' demands for improved economic conditions. Raúl even allowed such demands to enter public discourse through government-sponsored forums and other means. Preliminary measures to energize the agricultural sector and remove other consumer limitations should provide a degree of relief for Cuban citizens. Yet there was significant uncertainty about how the Cuban government would seek to solve this problem beyond such short-term measures, let alone how successful they would be at managing Cuban citizens' expectations for change. Earnings from natural resource exploitation could provide a big boost in the future, yet the pace of development in these sectors remains unknown. Further, if oil and ethanol provide significant injections into Cuba's macro accounts before other structural reforms are undertaken or contemplated, such a resource boost might simply entrench central control over the economy and diminish pressure for grassroots reforms. Moreover, the development of energy resources will reduce Cuba's dependence on Venezuela, while limiting the ability of the U.S. government to use economic sanctions to influence developments on the island.

In the end, the quality and quantity of further reforms will be directly related to the Cuban hierarchy's confidence in the ability of state institutions—the Communist Party, the armed forces, the Ministry of the Interior, and the Council of State—to successfully manage whatever rising expectations result. Many participants had difficulty conceiving how anything short of a massive overhaul of the economy would truly put Cuba on a long-term path to growth and stability. Others cautioned the group to not expect abrupt change. In the short run, further liberalization could increase Raúl's popularity, setting him apart from Fidel as a more practical leader.

On balance, participants saw Cuba under Raúl moving toward a model of patrimonial authoritarianism, where economic opportunity expands but political power and critical economic decisionmaking authority remains concentrated in the hands of the state (patrimonial authoritarianism has been described as a political system based on holding power in order to create, access, and distribute rents). As a result, participants felt that the Raúl Castro government is likely to proceed in a stop-and-go fashion, announcing reforms and then assessing their impact before considering deeper and broader measures, all with an eye to ensuring that any changes do not endanger the state's ability to maintain political and social control.

For U.S. policymakers, a key lesson from the exercise was not to expect consistency in Cuba's policy. Raúl will govern from an institutional rather than a personal base, and his operating mode will be calculated pragmatism to keep this base in power. An important decision for U.S. policymakers will be how to view limited reforms: as an easing of pressure that blunts demands for deeper change, or as an unleashing of a process that Raúl cannot control once it begins? Even if Raúl weathers the transition period and benefits from significant energy inflows in five to seven years, change in the future may be more difficult. Furthermore, Raúl himself is old and another transition will be in the offing in the short or medium term. This perhaps argues for U.S. policymakers to act on the likely but sporadic openings Raúl will offer in the meantime, in effect testing—as Raúl himself will be doing—whether some economic freedom can indeed build pressure for deeper reforms and greater freedoms.

SIMULATION SCENARIO NO. 3
CONTEXTUAL BACKGROUND OF EXERCISE

The following scenario was given to participants:

March 4, 2008. On February 24, 2008, Raúl Castro was named president of the Council of Ministers and José Ramón Machado Ventura was named the first vice president.

There had been widespread rumors among Cuba watchers that Carlos Lage Dávila, a reformer and technocrat, would move up to first vice president, so when he didn't, those hoping for greater change were disappointed. The promotion of those in the council to higher positions underlined the conservative and cautious nature of the Cuban hierarchy.

Nineteen months had passed since Fidel Castro fell ill and turned power over to his brother, on July 31, 2006. The transfer of power had been remarkably smooth. The mobilization of 200,000 military reserves ensured order, and the opening of an islandwide public discussion provided avenues for Cubans to express their hopes for change.

Raúl maintained a low profile during his interim presidency, and it is anticipated that he will continue to avoid the spotlight as he ascends to the presidency. Raúl will have to convince the Cuban people that he is fully in charge—not always an easy task when Fidel continues to influence decisionmaking through his regularly appearing "Reflections," widely published in- and outside Cuba.

Raúl's priority is to remain in power and ensure the continuation of the Revolution. He and his advisers, concerned about rising expectations on the part of Cuba's citizens, must decide on a strategy that will reinforce their authority and legitimacy.

Cuba's younger generation did not experience the Revolution, and they are not dedicated to its survival. They are restless and demanding and seem to long only for material goods; they are envious of their peers who have defected to the good life in Miami. Cuban youths want better lives that are only possible if they can get jobs that pay in convertible pesos.

Raúl has responded to these frustrations by instituting reforms that have given the Cuban people access to the perquisites of modern life in convertible pesos—if they can afford them. For example, Cubans may purchase cell phones and other communications devices and stay in tourist hotels that were formerly off-limits.

Most of Raúl's close advisers supported the reforms, but those close to Fidel did not. A minority of the advisers believe that the long-term viability of the Cuban economy depends on the government's undertaking deep and broad structural reforms that would unify the two currencies, the nonconvertible and convertible pesos, and begin a process that would lead to a market–based economy. Others are fearful, preferring a process of minor reforms carried out over time.

Raúl has convened the meeting to develop a consensus with his closest advisers on how to consolidate their government and manage popular expectations of further reforms. He has invited those on whom he has relied throughout his career—most of them comrades from the years in the Sierra Maestra—and has kept the informal meeting secret.

Although his first question concerns their assessment of internal and external conditions, his true reason for calling them together is because he trusts them to advise him on how to consolidate his power and maintain the Revolution. He hopes they will help him decide how far to go with economic reforms. Broad reforms are more risky because of their unpredictable effects on the body politic. But limited "cosmetic" reforms may not be an adequate response to the frustrations of broad segments of the Cuban population, including youths and Afro-Cubans.

Cuba's current international standing is high. The European Union and Latin American leaders trust that internal reform will follow Raúl's formal assumption of power. Russia and China plan to increase assistance to Cuba, and the United States is seen as unlikely to change policy or create any unexpected difficulties in the final year of the Bush presidency. Raúl's first responsibility will be to ensure the continued flow of subsidized oil by reassuring Venezuela's president, Hugo Chávez, that Cuba remains a loyal friend.

Role-Play No. 3: "A Meeting of Raúl Castro and His Advisers"

Characters in the Role-Play—
President Raúl Castro
First Vice President José Ramón Machado Ventura
Vice President and Minister of the Interior General Abelardo Colomé Ibarra
Vice President and Minister of Defense General Julio Casas Regueiro
Minister of Communications Ramiro Valdés Menéndez

President of the National Assembly Ricardo Alarcón
President of the Central Bank Francisco Soberón Valdés

Instructions: Background and Meeting Agenda

These men are Raúl's trusted friends and confidants. For some time he has conversed with them individually about the economy, external relations, and his plans to lead Cuba. As president he has now brought them together to map out a strategy that will ensure the success of his government and the continuation of the Revolution.

Raúl would like to discuss a broad strategy that will guide him over the next five years. He proclaims that the test of his rule will be whether Cuba remains independent, grows economically, and earns increasing respect as a member of the international community. He believes that the decisions they come to today and how well they rule together will determine whether the Revolution—and indeed they as a ruling group—will be able to set Cuba on a successful path for the next fifty years.

I. The Quality of Raúl's Leadership

Raúl tells his advisers that he wants "Fidel's legacy to endure and the Revolution to be stronger than ever. I count on you to give me your best advice on how to proceed. Shall we continue and increase reforms or slow them down? Can we allow expectations to rise while preserving the Revolution and our ability to rule now and in the future? Failure is not an option. The Revolution is our common legacy to the Cuban people." Everyone present understands that their plans must be broadly acceptable to the Cuban armed forces and the Cuban Communist Party, and must not alienate the Cuban people. They also understand that Raúl is both helped and hindered by the continuing commentary and interference of his brother, Fidel. Fidel's charisma has given Cuba a leadership role in the international arena that Raúl may not be able to sustain. The meeting opens with a discussion of how Raúl can effectively consolidate power and ensure loyalty.

II. Dealing with the Faltering Economy

Raúl asks for advice on an economic strategy that will meet Cubans' desire for change without creating any serious challenges to his power. "The question is how far and how fast?" he clarifies to his advisers.

—What are the major components of the economic package? Who are the intended beneficiaries, what sectors will be targeted, and should the package be rolled out sequentially or as a more comprehensive effort?

—Which are the power groups that must accept it and what incentives can be offered?

—What are the package's prospects of success and what are its vulnerabilities?

III. Cuba's Institutions: Their Loyalty and Role

Raúl asks his advisers for advice on supporting the interests of the following groups:

—*The Communist Party.* Bearing in mind divisions among women, youth, labor, and Party hard-liners, what kind of strategy would bring the interests of these groups together?

—*The armed forces.* What are the important factions, and how are they likely to react?

IV. Dealing with the International Community

Raúl is well aware that he must skillfully manage international perceptions as well as Cuba's foreign relations. Cuba has many friends and allies, but he welcomes the group's advice on how to diversify Cuba's energy dependence and deal with the United States and the Hemisphere.

—*Venezuela and Latin America.* What should be the strategy for dealing with Venezuela? Raúl must ensure that Cuba does not forgo Hugo Chávez's largesse for any reason, Cuba's own or Venezuela's political situation.

—*The United States.* Raúl wants to discuss how to deal with a new Democratic administration in Washington. How should Cuba respond, should the United States lift travel restrictions on Cuban Americans or even completely lift the ban on travel to Cuba for all Americans? Should Cuba seek an improved relationship with the United States, or would it prove destabilizing?

—*The European Union.* How can Cuba advance its relationship with the EU and obtain European investment and trade as well as political support while preserving the Revolution?

Implications for the United States

Following the simulation, Brookings advisers and special guest would review the implications of the discussion for U.S. policy.

Abridged Minutes

Abridged minutes from the simulation are provided to enable study of the kinds of exchanges that took place among the participants.

March 4, 2008. President Raúl Castro met informally with First Vice President José Ramón Machado Ventura, Minister of the Interior General Abelardo Colomé Ibarra, the new minister of Defense, General Julio Casas Regueiro, Central Bank President Francisco Soberón Valdés, Minister of Communications and Information Ramiro Valdés Menéndez, and President of the National Assembly Ricardo Alarcón.

Over the preceding year, Raúl proved his competence and gained greater acceptance among the Cuban people. He told those assembled that they had been invited because they are the men he trusts most. He wanted their view on how to map out a strategy that would allow the group to successfully govern Cuba over the next five years. He didn't want to hear platitudes and anticipated receiving indispensable advice on how to govern.

I. The Quality of Raúl's Leadership

Raúl's advisers responded to Raúl Castro's initiative by pledging their loyalty and continuing commitment to the Revolution. They unanimously agreed that their top priority was to ensure that Raúl consolidated power and support to preserve and strengthen the Cuban Revolution. First Vice President Machado Ventura acknowledged that Raúl's leadership style, distinct from Fidel's, must reflect his own strengths, not Fidel's. To succeed without the charismatic and domineering Fidel Castro, Raúl would have to build on his reputation as a consensus seeker, a pragmatist, and a "doer" rather than a "talker." He would have to pursue creative solutions that address the Cuban people's desires for improved material lives without undermining his authority. But they must also be alert to any challenge to his rule emanating from within or

outside the government. The Raúl-inspired forums convoked throughout the island over the past year provided a needed release for Cubans
to publicly criticize the stagnant economy and political restrictions.
Nevertheless, Machado Ventura urged Raúl to phase them out to avoid
raising expectations.

Vice President and Minister of Defense General Julio Casas Regueiro
responded that the public forums served the dual purpose of allowing
Cubans to let off steam and providing the Ministry of the Interior with
a valuable gauge of popular support for the government as well as critical information on sources of disloyalty. The discussions illustrated the
extent to which broad sections of the population desired deep changes.
Meeting those desires would, however, be extremely difficult. Fidel and
others were worried that reforms would create inequalities and possibly
give rise to an economic elite. General Regueiro said that although he
would support Raúl's decisions entirely, he hoped that Raúl would
avoid raising expectations that could result in certain factions and
groups within and outside the government going too far. He concluded
that he preferred less rather than more innovation, to avoid undercutting Raúl's authority.

First Vice President Machado Ventura urged agreement on measures
that would establish Raúl's credibility among the population and put
his own stamp on the government, a difficult feat to accomplish while
simultaneously assuring Fidel Castro that the government would retain
strict control. Raúl's decision to continue seeking Fidel's counsel on
matters of urgent national importance, as he promised in a speech on
February 24, 2008, to Cuba's National Assembly, was deemed very
wise. In some cases, Fidel's criticisms could provide useful cover for not
proceeding rapidly with reforms that could ignite unrest. Nonetheless,
the group should help Raúl establish his own credentials by devising a
strategy that would allow him to respond to popular aspirations for
change while maintaining the core values of the Revolution.

President of the National Assembly Ricardo Alarcón urged Raúl to
assume a more public profile than he had as minister of defense. He
should begin meeting with some of the key ambassadors as well as
attend international conferences. Some whom Raúl might court are
Latin American leaders, key among them President Hugo Chávez of
Venezuela, as well as traditional friends such as Chinese and Russian
leaders. To use an analogy from the world of film, in the past Fidel

served as the consummate director of the Cuban saga, while Raúl served as the producer behind the scenes, ensuring stability, maintaining order, and implementing key policies. Now, as Raúl assumed the public mantle of power, these roles have been reversed.

Vice President and Minister of the Interior General Abelardo Colomé Ibarra argued that circumstances demand that Raúl not attempt to personify the Revolution as Fidel had done. Rather, he should use the institutions of power built over the past five decades as a platform from which to govern. No one can really fill Fidel's shoes as a world leader. In any case, the cold war is over, with the result for Cuba that its position in the world is diminished: Raúl's priority should be to become Cuba's leader, not a world leader. He should seek institutional "buy-in" from the Cuban Communist Party and the Revolutionary Armed Forces. "As everyone knows," Colomé declared, "What unites us is far greater than what might potentially divide us."

II. Dealing with the Faltering Economy

First Vice President Machado Ventura reminded the group that most of those present had approved Raúl's reform package. The package proved successful in reducing resentment that arose out of restrictions placed on Cubans vis-à-vis foreign visitors. Cubans now had access to first-class tourist establishments, even if most could not afford them. Allowing Cubans to purchase cell phones and other electronics had been very popular with youths. Raúl gained in popularity as a result of these measures, but they were only the tip of the iceberg in terms of Cubans' demands. Young Cubans are now demanding unrestricted access to the Internet and well-paying jobs. Minister of Communications Ramiro Valdés Menéndez concluded that this posed a danger: state security would have to remain vigilant because the socialist character of Cuban society could be corrupted by anti-revolutionary ideas on the Internet and television.

Central Bank President Francisco Soberón Valdés advised the government to proceed with its plan to modify restrictions on private landholdings, which would stimulate increased agricultural production and reduce Cuba's reliance on food imports. He thought it would benefit those most loyal to the Revolution: the rural population. He urged the government to design an agricultural strategy whereby idle state land could be leased to individuals and cooperatives and distribution channels could be decentralized, to reduce Cuba's reliance on food and energy imports in the medium term.

Minister of Communications Ramiro Valdés Menéndez warned that balance must be maintained between private producers and those in cooperatives. The military's control over rural Cuba should not be jeopardized, as agricultural reform could create a ripple effect that could necessitate changes in other areas of the economy. For example, improving output would at some point require dealing with supply-and-demand bottlenecks created by artificial pricing, controlled markets, and limited access to fertilizers and transport. Therefore, the Party and the armed forces would have to be consulted before instituting reforms even in the agricultural sector, since their buy-in was essential.

Machado Ventura spoke for the group when he said that Raúl's first order of business should be to consolidate power, so as to make sure that he would have absolute loyalty for whatever strategies the government adopted. In any event, incremental reforms on the margins of the economy were the tried and true modus operandi of the past and would work best now. Such a strategy would improve conditions, increase the government's popularity, and buy time. The reform process should not threaten the ability of the state to provide for those most loyal to the Revolution, such as members of the military, employees of the state bureaucracies, citizens from naturally conservative rural areas, members of state-organized labor unions, and Cuba's significant and growing group of pensioners.

Central Bank President Soberón proposed introducing the market reforms that were popular in the early 1990s. Licensing small family businesses had provided Cubans with economic breathing room and quelled potential political unrest. Providing young people and their families with jobs and better remuneration would keep them productively engaged.

Although this might not be the right time for major changes, Soberón continued, at some point the government will have to take more dramatic action if it is to keep the loyalty of the Cuban people. Many were urging the adoption of a single exchange rate by devaluing the convertible peso and revaluing the nonconvertible peso—and doing so should be on Raúl's agenda—but uniting the currencies in this fashion would have consequences. It would reduce the government's ability to purchase imported food and other items, perhaps resulting in the deterioration of government subsidies. It would also mean that Cuba's actual wealth would diminish and there would be a decline in real GDP.

If Cuba is to align its economy with that of the rest of the world and one day join international financial institutions, painful monetary and fiscal reforms will have to be undertaken. But implementing these hard reforms without access to the financial assistance of these international institutions did not make sense; doing so without access to their funds would prove even more destabilizing. These measures will have to wait until Cuba has access to international funding and can freely purchase dollars on the open market.

Raúl's advisers agreed that Cuba could improve relations with foreign investors without inviting significant additional risks. Cuba's export-oriented services and extractive industries, particularly in primary products such as oil and nickel, but also in tourism, would be more attractive to investors if some of the regulations on local hiring and other government regulations were removed or reduced. The government should, however, be aware that the more foreign investors there are, the more difficult it is for the state to prevent them from corrupting Cuba's citizens. Already Cuba was moving aggressively to attract foreign governments and private companies, including U.S. firms, to develop its offshore oil and gas. If Raúl could neutralize Fidel's objections to the idea, Cuba could partner with Brazil to develop its production of sugarcane ethanol. Foreign investment was more attractive and safer than Cuban investment because it allowed revenues to flow directly to the state, thereby providing additional sources of revenue for the Party and the security forces.

Raúl's advisers suggested that he should expand economic opportunity for Cubans slowly without inviting economic dislocations or undermining the social achievements of the Revolution. He could move more rapidly with outside investors, especially those from countries whose governments are friendly to Cuba and the Revolution, who would not demand substantial changes but would still invest and provide jobs for Cubans and revenues for the state. Over the next five years, Raúl might concentrate on broader agricultural reforms, expanding domestic investment in micro-enterprises, and eliminating bottlenecks that prevent economic growth. It is hoped that revenues from energy development will allow a slower pace for economic reforms.

III. The Loyalty and Role of Cuba's Institutions

Raúl's inner circle conceded that the Council of State holds mostly symbolic power. To further consolidate his rule, Raúl will have to mobilize Cuba's two strongest government institutions, the Communist Party and armed forces, to be the vehicles to disseminate, explain, and enforce the decisions of the Cuban hierarchy. Cuba will undoubtedly face new and unpredictable challenges to the status quo, making it imperative that any potential divisions or disloyalty within the leadership of the government, Party, and military be dealt with sooner rather than later. In this way Raúl can prepare for his own succession.

THE CUBAN COMMUNIST PARTY

Machado Ventura said that the Party was the key channel for carrying out policies at the local level. The Party would validate and solidify a post-Fidel, and even a post-Raúl, model of Cuban revolutionary governance. The Party would serve as a forum for discussion and then implementation of reforms agreed upon by the inner circle. Machado Ventura pointed to the Chinese model in which leadership passed from a highly charismatic individual to a more firmly institutionalized ruling party as a possible strategy for ensuring the success of the Revolution beyond Raúl's lifetime. Valdés Menéndez noted that thus far Raúl was following Fidel's example wisely: although consulting more earnestly with his intimate circle of confidants, he remained the single source of the state's and Party's vision.

Raúl was advised to articulate his vision for Cuba's future at the next Party Congress. Already long overdue, the congress would validate Raúl's strategic plans and his leadership. All present in the room would be involved, not only in drafting proposals for Raúl's consideration but in ensuring that, once approved, those proposals are enthusiastically backed by key Party leaders at the local level. (In late April 2008 Cuban authorities announced that they would hold their next Party Congress, the first since 1997, during the second half of 2009, suggesting that they expect to get agreement on the basic principles that will guide Raúl's government. As noted in box 5-1, the congress was postponed indefinitely in the summer of 2009.)

THE REVOLUTIONARY ARMED FORCES

Whatever the role or structure of the Party, all the advisers agreed that the military would remain the backbone of the Cuban State. Despite limited resources and some evidence of corruption, the Cuban military is a disciplined, professional, hierarchically organized, and comparatively well-run institution. General Casas Regueiro observed that there was no potential for disloyalty within military ranks, although it was noted that some lower-ranking officers remained disenchanted by their low salaries and the lingering disillusionment generated by the June 12, 1989, execution of General Arnaldo Ochoa Sanchez, a hero of the Revolution and of Cuba's military victories in Angola. Raúl pointed out that the Cuban military has a proven track record of adapting, rationalizing, and carrying out the government's programs. The military not only ensured the success of the Revolution but has proved to be the critical factor in the survival of the Revolution at every crisis. Its ability to turn itself into an effective agent for building and managing a tourism infrastructure allowed Cuba to adapt to the withdrawal of the Soviet Union and the ensuing loss of five billion dollars' worth of annual subsidies. On the political side, the nationwide military mobilization of over 200,000 active and reserve troops at the time of Fidel's illness ensured the smooth transition of power to Raúl Castro.

Together with the Ministry of the Interior, the Cuban armed forces will continue to be the guardian of the Cuban Revolution from internal and external enemies, as it was when Raúl led the military during his long tenure as minister of defense. The Ministry of the Interior has been effective in detecting and responding to internal threats. Although the two ministries work together closely, Interior's provision of policing and internal surveillance had allowed the armed forces to avoid confrontation with the pubic. The ministry's impressive capacity to anticipate trouble, infiltrate opposition groups, and head off potential disorder will continue to provide a strong foundation for the survival of the Revolution.

Raúl suggested that the government meet minimal public expectations for reform in order to ensure that the Ministry of the Interior remains the primary guarantor of the country's stability. He said that it is essential to avoid the use of the military in the case of a public disturbance. If the armed forces were called in to confront Cuban civilians, its reputation would be destroyed and the Revolution tainted. Valdés Menendez asked Casas Regueiro whether troops would fire on the public if ordered to do so in the event the military were called to assist the Ministry of the Interior in suppressing a demonstration. Casas Regueiro responded that Cuba's armed forces had been loyal to Raúl, their commander in chief, for half a century, and that he had no doubt that they would follow orders.

Raúl's advisers urged him to continue to expand the military's dual role as a "think tank" and manager of large state enterprises. The military's involvement in the key productive sectors of tourism and agriculture would provide the state with revenues critical to its survival, but action by the armed forces had been less successful in the agricultural sector, where farmers seemed to respond best if they had some sort of land tenure or ownership.

Raúl summed up the discussion by saying that they must never forget that the military is crucial to the survival of the Cuban Revolution. It is the backbone of the Revolution—the Cuban state's inspiration, defense, and source of funding. It is the organization that he and Fidel created and that ensured their success. In times of stress, crisis, or transition, Cuba's Revolution would be safe if the military charted the way forward.

IV. Dealing with the International Community

Alarcón stated that one of the brightest hopes for Cuba would be its excellent relations with the international community. Venezuela continued to provide generous oil subsidies worth an estimated three billion dollars annually. Brazil supplied a one-billion-dollar line of credit and showed interest in developing Cuba's production capacity for sugarcane-based ethanol and its offshore oil and gas reserves. Relations with Mexico and the hemisphere have warmed, and Spain has succeeded in restoring the European Union's relations with Cuba. Cuba was continuing to reinforce its relationships with China, Russia, and other countries whose governments might provide an alternative source of oil should Venezuelan subsidies be reduced. The United Nations continues to vote overwhelmingly in support of Cuba's annual resolution condemning the U.S. embargo. Raúl should nurture and expand these relationships to minimize Cuba's economic vulnerabilities from the decline in revenues from nickel exports and an increase in expenditures on food imports.

Cuba will undoubtedly need to continue to improve its image, particularly with the Europeans, if it hoped to forge closer ties with them. Ending the death penalty, ratifying the UN Human Rights Conventions, and releasing political prisoners would solidify their friendship and possibly bring new investments. An important point made was that if the EU refused to support the isolationist policy of the United States, it would further discredit the Bush administration.

Although Hugo Chávez gained credibility with the left from his close association with Fidel and the Revolution, Raúl must begin to diversify Cuba's dependence on Caracas for two thirds of its oil requirements. "We learned the lesson of dependence when the Soviet Union abruptly abandoned us," Valdés Menéndez said. Soberón replied that breaking the island's cycle of external dependence—on Spain, the United States, the former Soviet Union, and now Venezuela—was difficult because these serial dependencies had enabled Fidel to become a world leader and all Cubans to enjoy a high level of health care and education. Advisers agreed that Cuba would seek to retain Venezuelan subsidies while diversifying potential energy sources and developing its own energy reserves.

Relations with the United States are at a historical nadir, but improving them is not a priority, Alarcón said. In fact, Cuba would be challenged to come up with a good strategy if the next U.S. administration were inclined to improve relations. Raúl should carefully weigh whether and to what degree Cuba should seek better relations with the Americans or respond to a new administration's decision to permit increased travel to Cuba. Although Cuba ultimately stands to gain access to the U.S. market from a normal bilateral relationship, the potential costs in terms of open flows of communication and people could weaken the government's control over its population. Weaker U.S. sanctions and a more cordial relationship would also make it harder to scapegoat the United States and would shift the onus for economic and political reform to the Cuban leadership. More critical to Cuba than improved relations with the United States is for it to strengthen its relations with the major developing nations, especially Russia, Mexico, and Brazil.

Speaking for all those present, Machado Ventura thanked Raúl for his confidence in them and assured him of their absolute loyalty. Raúl could be confident because it was highly unlikely that domestic or international conditions would threaten his hold on power, but in any case he should seek to establish his credibility as a leader on his own terms. One way to do so would be to reinforce the fusion of leadership at the highest levels of the Council of State, the Revolutionary Armed Forces, and the Cuban Communist Party. As for the international community, Cuba could count on Venezuelan oil subsidies in the short term, and in the longer term would have access to substantial new energy reserves from offshore oil and gas and the production of sugarcane ethanol. Raúl should concentrate his international efforts on promoting and diversifying Cuba's economic relationships.

Raúl's greatest challenge will be the rise in expectations for further reforms among the Cuban population, which could be worsened if the new U.S. administration decides to loosen restrictions on travel and remittances. More contact with relatives and friends will result in demands for better jobs and increased freedoms. Remittances are already creating disparities among Cubans with and without access to hard currency. Since Cuba cannot move quickly or undertake broad reforms, it should attempt to limit expectations. Raúl has been skillful in allowing some social reforms; additional reforms, however, should be undertaken cautiously and with the full support of the Party and the armed forces.

CHAPTER SIX

Transforming Disparate Voices into a Dynamic Civil Society Coalition

On April 16, 2008, the Brookings Institution, in conjunction with the University of Miami, held its fourth simulation exercise on the dynamics, motivations, and decisionmaking processes of Cuban civil society groups. As Cuba moves toward an uncertain future, participants sought to examine and better understand the interests, capabilities, and weaknesses of four key but overlapping sectors of Cuban civil society:

—Religious groups, especially the Catholic Church
—Youth
—The Afro-Cuban community
—Organized opposition and pro-democracy groups

Recognizing that the viability and sustainability of a successful transition in Cuba will depend on internal actors who seek change, in order to develop more effective policy U.S. policymakers must understand the nature of Cuban movements for change: their strengths and weaknesses, the risks they face, their ability to take proactive positions and not merely to stand in unified opposition.

The following pivotal issues emerged from this simulation:

—If the objective of U.S. policy is that Cuban democracy must be sustained by Cuban actors, to what extent can Cuban opposition groups and civic organizations unite to create a positive movement for change?

—If the Cuban state accelerates its own reform process, will Cuban civic organizations use this space to coalesce and promote change, or will such incremental reforms dampen the impetus for deeper democratic change?

—To what extent can the Catholic Church's leadership and lower-level clergy in Cuba infuse legitimacy into a broad-based civil society movement for change in Cuba? Conversely, to what extent would a civil society with strong strains of secularism be willing to grant religion, and the Catholic Church in particular, a substantial leadership role?

—How can nascent civil society networks constructively engage disaffected youths and channel their frustration into a push for reform rather than letting it dissipate in apathy?

—Do Afro-Cubans remain the loyal "foot soldiers" of the Revolution, as commonly described? Does the continued exclusion they face motivate a desire to push for greater reforms or reinforce a fear of economic and political uncertainty in an environment of transition?

—Can emerging civil society actors in Cuba create a broad-based umbrella movement for change? What cultural strategies can be used to increase the mass appeal of concrete economic and political demands?

—What are the pros and cons of civil society actors' accepting foreign support and what forms should such support take?

The Exercise

The day was divided into two parts. Before beginning the simulation, project advisers and special guests assessed the motivations, visions for change, and obstacles confronting the four sectors of Cuban civil society. Then they put themselves in the shoes of a fictional list of civil society activists representing a variety of actors and strategies to discuss possible means for collaboration in order to mobilize membership, build horizontal and vertical linkages, and formulate a common agenda for change that has mass appeal. Participants assessed and evaluated the capacity of civil society groups to mobilize, their rationales for action, and their converging or diverging interests. Finally, the day's proceedings ended with a teleconference with the Cuban activist Oswaldo Payá, widely considered to be among the most successful opposition actors within Cuba for his well-known Varela Project (which in 1998 circulated a petition advocating civil rights reforms in Cuba) and associated initiatives.

Raúl Castro has raised the bar of expectations for reform and has taken symbolic actions such as lifting restrictions on access to cell phones, personal computers, and admission to tourist hotels. Importantly, he has also discussed measures to improve productivity, such as gradually removing wage caps on certain state salaries and allowing for productivity bonuses; such reforms effectively redefine Cuban socialism as a system of equality of rights and opportunities, not of egalitarianism.[1]

Raúl's rationale in undertaking such reforms is likely to relieve tensions within Cuban society and to consolidate control by improving basic productivity and elevating living standards, rather than to create civic and political spaces or the emergence of civic organizations. A key question for these civic groups is whether such incremental reforms will give space and impetus for political mobilization, or whether they will diminish motivation for civic engagement. In the short term, despite some increased space for criticism resulting from the national debate authorized by Raúl Castro, dissidents and human rights activists and others who may think outside of a socialist framework continue to be marginalized.[2] The simulation thus sought to test whether Cuban civic organizations would unite in pursuit of common objectives, and to examine potential motivating factors or points of divisions that might drive or hinder

1. Raúl Castro's speech to the National Assembly, July 11, 2008.
2. The Cuban government likely considers the organized opposition to be an increased threat to its stability now as it begins a reform process. News from Cuba frequently suggests that the nationwide crackdown has indeed increased since Raúl Castro assumed power in 2006. Raúl Castro's government enforces political conformity through beatings, short-term detentions, public acts of repudiation, and the denial of work, among other tactics. Short-term detentions, routinely timed to prevent individuals from peaceful assembly, are particularly prevalent under Raúl, a tactic likely aimed at diverting international attention from Cuba's human rights record at the same time that it releases a few prominent dissidents imprisoned since the 2003 crackdown. The Cuban Commission for Human Rights and National Reconciliation documented 325 arbitrary detentions by security forces in 2007. ("El Gobierno de Cuba Continúa Violando el Derecho de los Ciudadanos a las Libertades Civiles, Políticas y Económicas," 2008 [www.cubasource.org/pdf/elizardo_informe_08.pdf]). In the first half of 2009 alone, it documented 532 detentions. See Cuban Commission for Human Rights and National Reconciliation, "The Human Rights Situation in Cuba after Three Years of Changes in the Highest Levels of the Government," August 10, 2009 (www.lexingtoninstitute.org/library/resources/documents/cuba/otherresources/ CubaCCHRNR ReportISemester2009.pdf). To counter "antisocial" behavior beyond dissidence among the wider population, the Raúl Castro government has relied on the "dangerousness" provision of the Cuban Criminal Code, which allows the state to imprison individuals before they have committed a crime on suspicion that they might

groups as they aim to establish a common reform agenda. Such analyses of the potential for action will be essential to crafting more effective U.S. strategies to support a peaceful transition in Cuba, with Cubans at the helm, determining the island's future.

Cuban Civil Society Today

Although the four aspects of Cuban civil society under examination—religious groups; youths; the Afro-Cuban community; and opposition and pro-democracy movements—do not represent all relevant actors or groupings within Cuban civil society, they were identified by the project organizers as sectors that deserved particularly close attention and study. Before assessing in the simulation exercise how representatives of each sector might attempt or struggle to collaborate with one another, it was important to first discuss each group's own position and generalized point of view. Participants also probed the extent to which each of these four "groups" could be thought of as separate and distinct. Overlap clearly exists; it may present conceptual difficulties, but does not prevent making broader evaluations of each group's interests.[3] Having a clear understanding of these primary motivations would help participants more thoroughly analyze the constraints to transforming disparate desires for change into unified civic participation.

Religious Groups

There was wide agreement among participants that the Catholic Church could play a major role among civil society groups to lend broad-based

---

do so in the future. The overtly political provision defines as "dangerous" any behavior that contradicts socialist norms, including failure to attend pro-government rallies, belonging to official party organizations, and unemployment. See Human Rights Watch, "New Castro, Same Cuba: Political Prisoners in the Post-Fidel Era" (www. hrw.org/sites/default/files/reports/cuba1109web_0.pdf).

3. Much academic inquiry has targeted civil society in the Cuban context. In particular, Cuban academics such as Rafael Hernández have challenged the often-held assumption that "civil society" in all cases connotes groups or activities that are separate or independent from government. A strong case can be made that institutions affiliated with the Cuban government—such as the Confederation of Cuban Workers, the Federation of Cuban Women, the Union of Cuban Writers and Artists, and some academic circles—do maintain dialogue with those in higher levels of government and

legitimacy to a future transition process. The Church would bring to this process an extensive semiformal national network; relatively safe, protected spaces of expression; and human and material resources to train young activists and leaders. Indeed, today the Catholic Church represents the largest single civil society network on the island, with connections to youths, Afro-Cubans, women, and human rights groups, as well as to the international community. In recent years, as the state has found it increasingly difficult to provide basic services, operationally independent grassroots sectors of the Cuban Catholic community have stepped in to provide humanitarian relief. Cuba's branch of the Catholic charity Caritas, with 12,000 volunteers, can be considered one of the first national nongovernmental institutions in post-Revolution Cuba. Baptist, Methodist, and other Protestant churches are also increasingly engaged in the provision of social services. The Reflecciones group in Cárdenas cultivates farmland and prepares and delivers meals to the elderly and poor. Participants pointed out that despite the capacity for religious organizations to provide services formerly exclusively provided by the state, none had developed a cohesive vision for change.

Likewise, lower-level clergy have on a more limited but still significant basis helped to organize youth-oriented, cultural, and educational activities. Father Dagoberto Valdés's well-known Centro de Formación Cívica y Religiosa (Center for Civil and Religious Formation) in Pinar del Río is one example of such activities, along with his publication of the magazine *Vitral* and the online forum Convivencia.

Despite these positive developments, questions arose concerning the Catholic Church's non-monolithic structure and its lack of a cohesive vision for change. Participants cited internal divisions between the Church's organized hierarchy and some portions of the lower clergy. The Church hierarchy seems hesitant to express open sympathy for the organized opposition or for dramatic political reforms, or simply does not consider doing this to be in its best interest, lest such a position provoke the state and threaten the Church's hard-earned organizational independence. Participants noted that the Church's low-key strategy of coexistence with the

---

do influence the political process, even if with clear ideological limitations. In this exercise, however, we focused on the chosen actors because of their perceived importance as sources of mobilization for change. See Rafael Hernández, *Looking at Cuba: Essays on Culture and Civil Society* (Gainesville: University Press of Florida, 2003).

Cuban government had resulted in the restoration of its position in Cuban society, following decades of persecution that saw churches closed and priests expelled in the 1960s and '70s. Today, churches have been reopened and the state does not interfere in matters of dogma or religious practice. The leadership's priority therefore appears to be not to reach an accommodation with the state per se, but to protect the Church's ability to fulfill its fundamental mission: sharing the gospel in a safe, protected space of expression.

Lower-level clergy are more inclined to take activist postures, while still for the most part remaining somewhat wary of openly affiliating themselves with the established opposition. Given the broad spectrum of opinions within the religious sector over the nature of the transition and the extent of the restructuring to be undertaken, participants wondered whether there could be a consensus inside the Church's hierarchy to recognize and advocate for some greater political or economic reform process.

Similar questions informed the group's analysis of Protestant and other faith groups on the island, including practitioners of Santeria, a syncretic religion that grew out of the slave trade and combines the worship of traditional Yoruban deities with the worship of Roman Catholic saints. Participants considered whether religious groups could facilitate the development of a common vision of change by activation of broader horizontal links and interaction among citizens and associations. Some efforts by various religions to provide humanitarian services and train community leaders, professionals, and youths to take a more active role in civil society are occurring, but there has been no coalescing of such individuals around a consensual agenda. With such forums still limited in size and scope, the potential for Cubans to acquire leadership skills within a religiously oriented civil society framework remains weak in comparison to the strong influence of government-affiliated mass organizations.

Finally, while taking note of the increase in the number of those searching for a moral compass in faith, participants highlighted the need to distinguish between nominal institutional religious adherence and the lack of traditional loyalty to organized faith groups. For example, although 60 percent of the population is baptized, only 1 to 3 percent of Cubans are practicing Roman Catholics, in contrast to 75 to 85 percent who state that they believe in the "divine."

Looking forward, questions about the ability of religious groups to provide an impetus for change revolved around the key issues relating to their relevance in light of low religious adherence and the prospect of improved living conditions and the willingness of the Church hierarchy and other religious leaders to step up to the plate to support a political reform agenda and lead cooperation between religious groups. Will a civil society that in practice is strongly secular look to religious groups, and the Catholic Church in particular, to play a leadership role in a political transition? Will the Church take on such a role, or will the Church hierarchy block the Church's formal engagement in political reform? Is there sufficient understanding and cooperation among religious groups to bring cohesion to a process of political transition? As Cuba's macroeconomic situation improves (a possibility examined in chapter 5), are religious groups likely to retain their social relevance and influence?

Youths

Of a total population of 11.4 million, approximately 8 million Cubans were born after the 1959 Revolution. Of this group, the 2.2 million born after 1992 have only experienced Cuban Communism under the austere conditions of the so-called Special Period ushered in by the collapse of the Soviet Union. As such, youths may be far less likely to harbor much enduring loyalty to Cuba's revolutionary heyday, may be more prone to disillusionment, and may be more willing to push for greater openness.

Participants highlighted the crucial divide between youths not associated with government organizations and those working for or within the government or government-affiliated institutions. Youths within the government or government-affiliated institutions may uphold basic principles of revolutionary ideology but, feeling little nostalgia for the past, may also be the single most important force for change today and in the future. But the majority of youths on the island today are disconnected and disenchanted, posing a significant challenge for the government's efforts to inject hope and revolutionary pride into a younger generation. Yet at the same time, nascent civil society networks also face significant difficulties in finding ways to constructively engage youths and channel their frustration into a push for political as well as economic change.

In contrast to older generations, for whom "change" may be more precarious and associated with a loss of stability, disconnected youths are less predisposed to behaving "inside the box," focusing instead on seeking immediate gratification, working in the informal sector and the tourist economy to generate greater material well-being. Participants agreed that students in particular are more prone to disillusionment and restlessness: the incentive for getting a good education is falling as youths see no connection between the educational opportunities offered by the Cuban state and career prospects. University enrollment has declined 30 percent since 2005 across the island, as work in the informal sector or the tourism industry increasingly has promised higher wages than jobs requiring a university education. Likewise, migratory outflows, perhaps the clearest indicator of youth disillusionment, are growing.

Project advisers considered the problematic aspect of Cuban youth in light of their discussions during the third simulation (chapter 5) of the effects of Raúl Castro's recent and future reform efforts on rising expectations. All agreed that recent changes may have elicited some hope among disaffected youths. But again, with generalized frustration among youths well entrenched and skepticism high, the costs of failing to meet expectations could be even more far-reaching among the young than within the wider population. The margin of error could be low, and a "tipping point" could be reached, pushing youths' frustration into bold mobilization.

Whether that mobilization leads to destructive behavior or whether it can be channeled into peaceful movements for change will likely depend on the readiness of existing civil society networks to focus on this demographic group. On the other hand, participants considered the possibility that not only disaffection but also apathy are both widespread, which may lead youths to simply stand aside, expecting the state or other actors to fulfill their needs without seeking their own participatory role in a reform process. Or, given the chance, many may simply opt to vote with their feet and take to the seas in search of better opportunities elsewhere, as is currently occurring.

Afro-Cubans

Afro-Cubans, 62 percent of the Cuban population, comprise those of black (11 percent) or mulatto ancestry (51 percent of the population).[4] Cuba is an extensively integrated society, and equitable access to housing, healthcare, and education makes it misleading to speak of a single Afro-

4. "Afro-Cubans: Powerless Majority in Their Own Country," *Cuba Facts*, no. 46, March 2009 (http://ctp.iccas.miami.edu/FACTS_Web/Cuba%20Facts%20Issue%2046%20March.htm).

Cuban "perspective." Still, several important general trends, motivations, and dynamics can be observed. First, all participants agreed that racial discrimination has limited Afro-Cubans' access to employment compensated in convertible currency. In the tourism sector, the highest-paying industry, Afro-Cubans hold 5 percent of jobs, whereas Caucasians hold 80 percent. Second, because most of those who have left the country are Caucasian, relatively few Afro-Cubans enjoy access to foreign remittances. Thus, the economic hardship of the Special Period has been disproportionately borne by the Afro-Cuban population.

Afro-Cubans have been traditionally thought of as stalwart supporters of the Revolution for the concrete benefits it bestowed in terms of access to education, healthcare, material goods, and training. Yet the resurgence of racism in the Special Period and beyond, coupled with the degree to which Afro-Cubans have faced economic difficulties, has likely substantially weakened this link, resulting in increasing popular disaffection. Nevertheless, participants felt that many Afro-Cubans, as key historic beneficiaries of the Revolution's social welfare policies, might understandably fear the consequences of rapid change and the strengthening of economic inequalities under a capitalist transition. In addition, regional differences play into Cuba's racial politics, with higher portions of Afro-Cuban citizens residing in Cuba's eastern provinces. There, material difficulties over the past fifteen years have been particularly acute, and the government has stringently clamped down on any form of dissent emerging from these areas.

In light of these dynamics, participants concluded that Afro-Cuban disaffection may perhaps represent as great a challenge to the government as the estrangement of youth, requiring deep structural and institutional changes. Interlinked causes of disaffection are manifest in the intersection of racism with inequality, youth, and crime. Government-affiliated institutions seem to have recognized this problem and are paying more attention publicly to the Afro-Cuban issue. For example, one participant noted, in April 2008 a discussion of race was featured on the agenda of the annual congress of the National Union of Cuban Artists and Writers. The new Academy of Sciences, too, is incorporating the subject into its focus on youth, social disaffection, and crime. The bottom line, however, is that low living standards form the crux of Afro-Cuban disaffection. Consequently, the Cuban government may focus on short-term solutions to address immediate needs and concerns, hoping thereby to put off the need to make more far-reaching structural and institutional reforms, to assert political control, and ultimately to render pressure from civic groups representing the Afro-Cuban community obsolete. Raúl's July 26, 2008, speech on the fifty-fifth anniversary of the attack on the Moncada and Manuel de Céspedes Barracks in Santiago—which highlighted the renovation of aqueducts to provide, by 2010, a daily supply of water across the mostly Afro-Cuban eastern provinces of Santiago, Holguín, Baracoa, Las Tunas, and Camagüey—may serve this purpose well.

Participants examined the long tradition of horizontal civil society linkages among Afro-Cubans, who combine religious identities with ties of community, culture, and common experience. They concluded that such linkages are not heavily formalized and remain embodied in loose organizations such as Santeria. Participants agreed on the limitations inherent to these networks, which lack organization and structure. Vertical linkages are a work in progress, and the recent appointment of high-level Afro-Cubans to the National Assembly and Politburo, including three women, may assist in promoting affirmative social policies (access to welfare and economic opportunities) and antidiscrimination measures. So far, however, few Afro-Cuban civil society organizations possess the adequate organizational capacity to make demands on and communicate with the state in an organized fashion. While some Afro-Cuban voices have permeated the leadership ranks of the opposition movement—including the prominent imprisoned human rights advocate Oscar Elías Biscet, the activist Antúnez family, Félix Bonne Carcassés, and Vladimiro Roca—their reach to wider Afro-Cuban communities remains limited. Overall, few Afro-Cubans have obtained positions of leadership with sufficient organizational capacity and a clear alternate political trajectory in the government sphere, religious groups, or the opposition movement. Participants concluded that this reflects the diffusion of the Afro-Cuban population across a wide range of competing occupations, positions, interests, and points of view.

It remains to be seen whether the Afro-Cuban community will cross a threshold and begin to operate as a distinct civil society actor in the public sphere. Since the 1990s some Afro-Cuban musicians and artists have more forcefully articulated a sense of "black" identity, but such expressions, despite their political overtones, remain in the cultural realm; although they may give voice to frustration, including to youths of all races, they do not seem to have inspired a strong desire for collective political action. Participants debated whether there were any "signs" that might signal whether Afro-Cubans will remain resistant to broad change (for fear of a loss of privileges under a transition scenario that sees the largely Caucasian Cuban American community exerting significant influence) or whether they, too, can find common ground with other sectors of civil society to push for sweeping reforms.

The Organized Opposition: Democrats, Dissidents, and Activists

Participants considered the wide range of actors that constitute the "established opposition" within Cuba today and debated whether these diverse groups could coalesce around a common denominator or vision. Despite the signing of several declarations of unity among leading opposition activists, for the most part the three traditional political fronts—Liberals, Social Democrats, and Christian Democrats—being shaped by the most prominent dissident groups continue to pursue their own uncoordinated and often conflicting visions of change.[5] The question of leadership remains a problem, with most opposition groups known for their individual leaders rather than the movements they represent. Such personality-driven activism has had the tendency, many believe, to keep the opposition fractured.

Significant efforts have been undertaken to mobilize political opinion, the most well-known being the Varela Project—started in 1998 by Oswaldo Payá of the Christian Liberation Movement and named after Felix Varela, a Cuban religious leader—and its continuation, the Todos Cubanos (All Cubans) program. The Varela Project relied upon Article 88 of the Cuban Constitution of 1976, which provides for citizens to introduce legislation by petition containing at least 10,000 signatures. The principles of the Varela petition, demanding the rights to free expression and association, amnesty for nonviolent political prisoners, free enterprise, and electoral reforms, were seen as the first steps to create the necessary space for all Cubans to be able to freely participate in economic and political life on the island. The petition was an unprecedented example of successful political organizing and was presented to the National Assembly with a total of 25,404 signatures in 2002 and 2003. The Cuban legislature rejected the petition, and the Assembly's Constitution and Legal Affairs

5. For example, on the political front Oswaldo Payá represents Christian Democrats; Hector Palacios and Martha Beatriz Roque, Liberals; and Vladimiro Roca, Social Democrats.

Committee responded with its own counterinitiative: to amend the Cuban constitution to make the socialist nature of the Cuban state permanent. The government claimed that its own petition met with 99 percent voter approval. To further crush the Varela Project and the dissident movement at large, beginning on March 18, 2003, the Cuban government arrested, summarily tried, and jailed seventy-five civil society leaders, including independent journalists, librarians, and trade unionists.

In spite of the continued existence of mobilizations such as the Varela Project, participants disagreed in their assessment of the dissident movement's level of impact within Cuba today. Most agreed that because of the opposition's lack of access to the mass media and their constant vilification in the state press, few Cubans are likely to recognize the dissident movement as a true symbolic or practical alternative. Some participants felt that international support may be the only thread propping the movement up. Others saw the opposition as a weak but nonetheless substantive movement with significant roots.

The key issue confronting participants was whether a dissident-based opposition culture could provide the foundation for an opposition movement, or whether dissident groups in their current form would become less relevant in light of changing political and economic dynamics. In the end, a common concern emerged: with greater economic openings in the offing, more is now at stake for the dissident movement than at perhaps any other moment in its history.

Participants debated whether sufficient political space for engagement and dialogue among opposition leaders would be able to arise to allow a "movement" to emerge, and whether leaders would be able to refocus their attention from "opposing" to creating a positive message that promoted unity. To avoid fading into irrelevance, opposition groups would have to move out of their comfort zone and speed up their processes of mobilization.

Simulation Exercise No. 4:
A Meeting of Cuban Grassroots Activists, July 26, 2010

Concluding this broad discussion, participants moved on to the simulation exercise itself. Organizers asked participants to put themselves in the shoes of a fictional list of civil society activists as they meet to discuss common objectives and possible means for collaboration. Individuals representing the religious community, youths, Afro–Cubans, and dissidents were called together by a Methodist minister in Santiago de Cuba. It is assumed that they meet in 2010 in a Cuba characterized by significantly greater openness and potential for reform than when Raúl assumed the presidency. Fidel and First Vice President Machado Ventura have passed away, and Carlos Lage Dávila has ascended to the first vice presidency, raising hopes that further economic reforms will help open greater political space. Travel and remittance revenues are up after a new U.S. president has removed some restrictions. Uncertainty prevails, and even though an increasingly wide array of civil society actors believe greater change is necessary, they are divided between those preferring to adopt a wait-and-see approach and those who believe that the time to push aggressively for reform is now. Members of the group meet to discuss the viability of formulating a declaration of unity and to begin exploring means to collaborate and mobilize peaceful civic action. They hope that the diversity within their own ranks will allow their movement to transcend the framework of established opposition groups, allowing them to appeal to a broader segment of the population.

Rather than simulate a meeting of established members of the democratic opposition, the aim of the exercise was to gather together fictional personalities who for a variety of reasons have come to the conclusion that greater changes in Cuban society are needed but do not necessarily affiliate themselves with the existing dissident movement. Although members of the existing dissident movement might possibly participate in such a meeting, no individual is identified as such. More fundamentally, the exercise sought to explore how civil society actors would respond to the Cuban government's incremental reforms. Would elements of civil society press for more political as well as economic openings, and if so, what might be the tools to do so successfully? Conversely, might such reforms diminish the impetus to search for deeper political openings and democratization?

Declaration of Principles

In their respective roles as members of diverse Church-affiliated, Afro-Cuban, youth, and other civil society groups, simulation participants immediately set out to establish consensus around a clear set of basic principles. Nevertheless, as discussions got under way, significant differences in perspective emerged. Some participants stressed the need to keep any consensual agenda strictly tied to political reforms and political themes:

democracy, rule of law, and freedom for political prisoners. Others were more wary of such a focus, as it would seem to ally their actions with the same basic tenets of the established dissident movement, thereby threatening their legitimacy as "new voices." Some lobbied for a strong focus on economic themes, connecting the idea of economic difficulties to the need for greater economic freedoms, which are in many ways inherently political. Once again, differences emerged, with those representing the perspective of Afro-Cuban activists expressing significant concern for any kind of economic platform that would endanger their access to state-provided welfare services.

To the extent that any consensus did emerge, it was around general principles of patriotism, family, and justice, which would resonate even with the Raúl Castro government. Such principles included declarations on equal rights, a call on the government to be held accountable to the people, support for the "family," and the rule of law. The purpose of such principles would be to reflect that there is a widening base of Cubans who seek change, and the first steps toward change would be to press the state for accountability, and to make "advancing the family" a goal of equal importance to advancing the interests of the state.

Strategies for Civic Action

Simulation participants then began to explore how civic action could demonstrate or advance such basic principles, to begin to create confidence for public discourse and engagement. Participants considered a wide range of possibilities, from a proactive political campaign to popular public events around music or cultural themes. As participants tested the alternatives, they found consensus only around the latter.

Some participants emphasized that the time to act is now, as civil society had been unwittingly granted some space that should be seized to press concrete demands on the Cuban government. One participant proposed finding ways to bring greater pressure to bear on government channels in order to push concrete political or economic demands such as freedom for political prisoners. Another strongly suggested convening a national non-violent strike of civil disobedience to symbolically commemorate the "Cry of Yara."[6] Yet in addition to the fear that such an action would provoke

6. Yara is a small town and municipality in Cuba's Granma Province, located halfway between the cities of Bayamo and Manzanillo, in the Gulf of Guacanayabo.

wide reprisals and sacrifice the space that civil society had already earned, serious questions about capacity emerged. Representatives at the table were forced to confront the fact that the organizations they represented did not have either the resources or the networking capability to pull off such a feat in the near future.

Broader, more sweeping proposals emerged, including building a wide national coalition of civil society groups to call for a constitutional assembly or a transitional government within one year. Alternatively, one participant suggested replicating Oswaldo Payá's petition strategy, but depoliticizing its content to garner broader appeal. Basic demands could be as simple as nonviolence, respect for human rights, respect for free enterprise, and the establishment of a truth and reconciliation commission. Issues of sequencing arose among the group, with some arguing that before calling for any such measures, key members of the National Assembly or Central Committee should be approached, perhaps with an open letter, to start a dialogue about representative government and subsequently lay out a course for a peaceful transition.

After extensive debate, the one course where consensus emerged was to host a series of events focused on music and culture. A celebration would draw a wide turnout and could be focused on a positive message about what Cubans seek—the benign, but uniting principles the group formulated at the outset of the simulation. For example, a national day of prayer to honor the upcoming beatification of Brother José López Piteira, the first native Cuban to receive this honor, would be a powerful and "Cuban" means to demonstrate public awareness. Celebratory cultural events conducted in different parts of the country could become their own mobilizing force, and this mobilization would in effect become the political message—perhaps as much to the Cuban people as to the government. For the Cuban people, the purpose would be to show that many are united in a common and positive pro-Cuban agenda that calls for more opportunity for the family, and greater respect for the law, including accountability for politicians. For the Cuban government, the message would be the breadth of desire for change, where the same calls would

---

The Great War (1868–78), the first war of independence Cuba fought against Spain, began in Yara on October 10, 1868, with the "Cry of Yara," when Carlos Manuel de Céspedes, a sugar-mill owner, and his followers proclaimed Cuba's independence from Spain.

demonstrate that reforms cannot stop at cosmetic change. Stifling the emergence of such a wide-based movement founded on "Cuban values" would be highly problematic for a government redefining its socialist base and support among the populace.[7]

Creating a Cultural Umbrella Movement

After assessing their own limited capacities as representatives of small movements and reviewing the plausibility of several strategies of civic action, participants gradually converged around two more fundamental conclusions: (1) Cuba requires a larger "umbrella" movement to unite forces for change, and (2) that movement will only succeed if it can promote cultural strategies that cut across social cleavages.

Participants discussed the challenges and practicality of creating, leading, directing, and managing an umbrella movement. Great concern emerged about the inherent challenge of creating a truly social movement not centered necessarily around one individual leader (replicating the *caudillismo* in Cuba's past) but nonetheless with a clear leadership structure and organizing capacity. Could Cuban civil society seek to build a series of interlocking networks that come together around a broader general agenda?

In particular, participants discussed how to engage Cuban youth. On the one hand, the disaffection felt by youth offers a vast potential to be tapped as a resource for change. Yet citing the general lack of a defined, nuanced long-term vision for political reform among this sector and, more important, disaffected youths' general rejection of any campaign that seems overtly "political," participants again highlighted the need to articulate a platform of political and economic change through culturally appealing slogans and strategies. To this end, civil society leaders will have to find means to bring together frustrated and apolitical youth, who may be difficult to turn into agents of change, with those who make high demands for change but may be difficult to manage.

To successfully engage the Afro-Cuban community and deal with potential anxieties regarding change, participants recommended that an umbrella civil society movement strongly emphasize an integrated approach, perhaps drawing on the nationalist legacy of the Revolution itself

---

7. The issue of the Revolutionary Armed Forces being called upon to suppress widespread unrest was discussed and discounted during the project's third simulation exercise, on the Cuban hierarchy, detailed in chapter 5.

in order to avoid any racial tensions. Fears of change could also be averted by emphasizing a politically savvy and bridge-building social justice discourse alongside calls for political liberties. Thus, an umbrella movement might pledge its commitment to guaranteeing a safety net and welfare measures (particularly pensions) during a transitional period while also prioritizing the improvement of standards of living (including those gained from access to convertible currency).

Building on this discussion, some participants highlighted the importance of not defining a broad umbrella movement as being "opposed" to the Revolution per se, because the nationalist symbolism and concrete benefits bestowed under the Revolution remain important to Afro-Cubans and many other sectors of the population. Rather, an umbrella movement might position itself as a natural evolution, combining the rhetoric of the Revolution's commitment to equality and social justice with a more pragmatic economic framework and political liberties. However, a few participants saw such a strategy as problematic because it might isolate more traditional dissident activists who hoped for a cleaner break with the symbols and legacy of the Communist system.

A number of participants stressed the importance of avoiding the danger of being labeled agents of outside actors. The new umbrella organization should maintain a certain degree of distance from the rhetoric and activities of established dissident movements and move beyond a framework of politicized dissidence as conceived today. Direct collaboration with the dissidents was also seen as problematic, given the fragmentation of existing opposition movements.

Despite these challenges, participants recognized the potential benefits of incorporating dissidents and their traditional focus on human rights into a broader overarching agenda for change, not least because such a movement could draw on these groups' demonstrated capacity to organize networks, project coherent political messages, and mobilize citizens. If dissident leaders could agree to seek ways to reduce conflict between competing platforms, they might be able to craft common proposals with a broad set of civil society actors. Thus, a new umbrella movement might provide a unifying forum for a fragmented dissident leadership.

Foreign Support

Another key point of discussion involved the willingness of activists in any future umbrella group to receive foreign support if it were available—

particularly U.S. financial support. Although opinions differed on the value of accepting direct funding from foreign sources, all participants agreed that any movement accepting overt U.S. support risks its perceived legitimacy in a Cuban context where nationalism remains a prominent and vigorously defended principle. Under such circumstances, multilateral aid would perhaps be more constructive and less threatening.

Although U.S. financial support for opposition groups was deemed a problem, participants agreed that NGO funding, including from U.S. NGOs, for humanitarian aid and for the support of human rights activists' families should be continued. Such funding should be accompanied by new nongovernmental efforts to increase person-to-person contacts. To this end the United States might support exchange programs bringing Cubans to the United States and vice versa and permit U.S. civil society groups to travel to the island, which would enable such groups to engage their Cuban counterparts and would effectively move away from current U.S. micromanagement of dissident actors on the island.

A proposal was made to create a regional civil society fund, managed by the Organization of American States, through which the United States, in the short and medium terms, could channel funds to support existing regional or international nongovernmental organizations that provide public goods and services, offer technical training, and support grassroots media and education projects. Greater civil society involvement may also be directed through the activities of international networks that already have a significant presence in Cuba, such as the Freemasons. Finally, participants also proposed that international organizations such as the Inter-American Commission for Human Rights and the European Commission for Democracy through Law (known as the Venice Commission) be approached through relevant embassies in Havana to provide consultative opinions to Cuban civil society actors on a broad range of technical expertise. To this end, the United States might work with its partners and allies in the Western Hemisphere and Europe to make embassies a repository of information and contacts for Cuban civil society entities.

Of course, the possibility of such initiatives largely depends on the Cuban government's openness to their existence, surely not an easy prospect. Nonetheless, in the medium term, financial assistance for such schemes would perhaps be best managed by means of regional or multilateral cooperation, whether through the OAS or through special partnerships with other regional institutions and allies.

Considerations for U.S. Policy

The underlying premise of this simulation exercise was that successful democratic change in Cuba must by carried forward by Cuban actors. This analysis and the dynamics of the discussions demonstrated the complexity of that proposition, and hence the complications for U.S. policy. U.S. policymakers might simultaneously explore three areas in their push to open up increased political and economic spaces in Cuba: engaging civil society actors, engaging the Cuban government, and taking advantage of the momentum created by economic reforms.

Civil Society Actors

In their engagement of Cuban civil society actors, U.S. policymakers should recognize that fostering cohesion is a general Cuban value—not part of the Revolutionary political, cultural, or economic agenda—and therefore U.S. policy should encourage elements that strengthen cohesion. Drawing on the lessons learned from this exercise about the strengths and limitations of religious groups, youths, Afro-Cubans, and dissident groups to mobilize movements advocating change that enjoy widespread appeal, U.S. policy will need to maximize the number of civil society actors and widen the base of society it engages in order to assist these actors to diffuse their principles, develop cohesive messages for change, and build capacity and networks.

To date, U.S. engagement of Cuban civil society hinges on USAID-supported programs that directly benefit key dissident leaders. Yet such a narrow focus jeopardizes the perceived legitimacy of these individuals and provides cannon fodder to the Cuban government's nationalist reflex. But even more important, as the simulation exercise highlighted, financial support directed toward the organized opposition can be perceived as a liability by other civil society groups who might otherwise collaborate with dissident leaders and offer more broad-based support and access to networks. Ensuring that U.S. support is more widely disseminated will avoid the risks that targeted support could prove counterproductive.

The group's struggle to reach a consensus on what kinds of concrete strategies and actions with true practical potential might be taken up by an emerging umbrella group, coupled with the importance all participants gave to building movements of mass appeal, reinforced the point that civil society groups and networks must first grow and develop the skills

and capacities to engage with each other before they can coalesce into
larger movements presenting a viable alternative and platform for change.
To better advance the prospects of political opening and a democratic
transition brought about by Cuban actors, the United States should avoid
micromanaging civil society actors and pursue means to support and
engage all potential actors involved in reform both outside and within the
Cuban government.

The Cuban Hierarchy

The Cuban government can cut off the space for political movements to
emerge, making multilateral strategies necessary to maximize both access
and political reach to press the Cuban government to allow spaces for
civic engagement. The United States government, possessing little leverage
over the Cuban political process, should engage other actors—the Organization of American States, the European Union, Brazil and other Latin
American states, and the Vatican—to exert such diplomatic pressure on
the Cuban government. Once again, participants emphasized the importance of the United States' working constructively to engage the Cuban
government on issues of bilateral interest such as counternarcotics, migration, public health, and disaster management. Such relations, as well as
contacts with government-affiliated civil society organizations, would generate information flows about the decisionmaking mechanisms of the
Cuban government and would help to develop trust among government
officials from both countries, providing a bridge to the Cuban government
at all levels.

Economic Openings

Finally, the United States should consider how it could best act to help
open civic spaces in an economically increasingly viable Cuba. As explored in greater detail in chapter 5, if the Cuban government consoli-
dates revenue growth from productivity and energy reforms in the short
and medium terms, this will likely bolster the government's credibility
and its confidence in its ability to maintain political control. This is
because the non-labor-intensive nature of the new economic activity
would help reinforce state power by generating cash inflows that will not
have to be paid out in wages. Instead, the Cuban government could use
it to reinforce top-down revenue distribution mechanisms. The United
States might exploit the dichotomy between such discernible growth in

revenue and fiscal stability for the Cuban state and the lack of wealth reaching the wider population. Policymakers should take creative steps to encourage the wider dissemination of wealth across the island, including supporting micro-finance institutions through regional or multilateral collaboration, engaging multilateral actors to form small- and medium-size enterprise development funds, and lifting U.S. caps on remittances. Such measures should assist in preventing the possibility that incremental reforms diminish incentives for civic engagement.

SIMULATION SCENARIO NO. 4
CONTEXTUAL BACKGROUND OF EXERCISE

The following scenario was given to participants:

July 26, 2010. After formally assuming Cuba's presidency in February 2008, Raúl Castro announces additional measures to improve agricultural output and allow an expansion in family businesses. Cuba and Brazil signed a joint venture agreement for the development of ethanol from sugarcane. A test well off the north coast of Cuba confirms substantial exploitable offshore oil and gas. The economy continues to grow at an annual rate of 5 percent.

Even though many Cubans have seen marginal economic gains, most, especially youths, remain disillusioned. During the first year of Raúl's rule, income has just barely kept pace with inflation. The government hasn't unified the unpopular dual currency or restructured the economy to permit and encourage private investment and entrepreneurship. Illegal emigration to the United States continues at record levels, providing a way out of Cuba for those willing to risk their lives at sea.

Tensions increase with Fidel Castro's death in August 2009. Following an elaborate state funeral, significant but sporadic protests erupt that reflect some political but mainly economic grievances. Cuban officials manage to quell the disturbances with short-term detentions of suspected ringleaders. Though the government is firmly in control of the situation, the older leaders within the Communist Party and the Cuban armed forces believe that Raúl must move slowly with economic reforms or risk undoing the Revolution.

Indeed, Raúl has been moving slowly. He has continued to carry out reforms cautiously and sporadically, including issuing licenses for 100,000 small family businesses, for which remittances from Cuban Americans have provided the seed capital. There is a certain degree of optimism among the Cuban people, possibly due to greater contact with and assistance from Cuban Americans. Average monthly household income has increased from US$17 in 2007 to US$30 in 2010, and more Cubans possess the means to purchase luxury items, including televisions, radios, and computers. But the government still restricts open access to the Internet.

Although most Cubans are satisfied to "wait and see" how the government will continue the reform process, leaders of religious and cultural groups are demanding a greater voice in government and also expanded civil rights, such as the right to assembly and to speak out publicly and in print, without being treated as "dissidents." They do not consider themselves dissidents. They provide community services such as medicine distribution and a forum for discussion for their members.

Although youths and Afro-Cubans are dissatisfied, they are not openly challenging the government and prefer to form informal groups for discussions and to listen to music and to engage in other cultural activities.

Traditional dissident groups such as Oswaldo Payá's Christian Democrats and Martha Beatriz Roque's more conservative Assembly to Promote Civil Society (Asamblea para Promover la Sociedad Civil en Cuba, a coalition of independent civil society groups) continue to oppose and openly criticize the government. Their membership has not grown significantly because the government continues to suppress their activities. Independent artists, journalists, and doctors who provide their services either free or on the black market are often members of like-minded dissident groups, such as the independent librarians and journalists.

Dissidents such as human rights activists, independent journalists, and librarians differ from other members of civil society as they repre-sent a direct challenge to the government, whereas religious and cultural groups primarily provide community services.

Role-Play No. 4:
"A Meeting of Representatives of Cuban Civil Society"

Characters in the Role-Play–
Pastor Emiliano García (Afro-Cuban), 35, presiding, Methodist Church
    of Santiago de Cuba (300 congregants)
Padre Félix Castañeda, 43, Catholic Church of Santa Maria
    (200 regular congregants)
Lisandra Carvallo, 23, Catholic Youth for Social Action (100 members)
Francisco Pelaez, 26, Presbyterian "Reflection" Youth Group
    (100 members)
Esmeralda Martinez, 35, Freemason Lodge of Holguin (100 members)
Eliana Gómez, 26, Independent Bloggers Association of Santiago
    (25 members)

Liset Pérez, 27, Independent Journalists of Santiago de Cuba
(50 members)
Dr. Jorge Ramírez, 32, Santiago Doctors for Change (50 members)
Jesús Salazar (Afro-Cuban), 30, Santiago Network of Independent
Farmers (100 members)
Marcos Valle, 35, Independent Union of Tourist Industry Workers
(100 members)
Yuniel Iglesias, 21, Federation of Independent Students, Oriente
University (100 members)
Michel Hermida, 25, El Cartel, an underground rap music collective
(40 members)
Mariela Espinosa (Afro-Cuban), 32, Felix Varela Artists Collective
(30 members)
Cristián Ávila (observer), 45, Santiago representative of the Christian
Liberation Movement
Liliana Torrejón (observer), 38, Assembly to Promote Civil Society
Liliana Rosa (observer), 30, Women in White and Independent Libraries

Instructions: Background and Meeting Agenda

*Participants received instructions in the form of a description of the
background and the meeting agenda. Knowing these instructions helps
readers interpret the course of the dialogue.*

Emiliano García, a well-respected Afro-Cuban Methodist pastor in Santiago de Cuba, has convened a meeting of representatives of independent civil society entities. Participants include Catholic clergy and lay
people, Baptists, Presbyterians, and Methodists as well as Freemasons
and small community-based groups. Afro-Cuban, Caucasian, and
mulatto youths have joined independent activists, including journalists,
librarians, doctors, and trade union leaders.

They share the view that they can no longer "wait and see" what
actions the Raúl Castro government might take next. They fear that if
they continue to wait they may fade into irrelevance within their communities. They aspire to unite around a common cause: by acting
together they believe they can persuade the government to recognize the
important role they play in their communities throughout the island.

Tensions and uncertainty abound. Church officials and lay people privately admire the work of the dissidents but remain wary of formal alliances that could invite greater repression and endanger the religious freedom they have worked so hard to regain. Dissidents, however, urge the religious and cultural groups to openly speak out against state repression.

Afro-Cubans and youths aspire to more freedom, choice, and opportunity in their lives. Young people are very aware of the lack of opportunity for enhanced well-being and their inability to enjoy life the way they see their friends and relatives in Miami doing. Afro-Cubans would like greater opportunities for advancement, and some are resentful about the growing gulf between those with access to remittances or jobs that pay in convertible pesos and those—many of them Afro-Cubans—who must survive on their peso salaries and government subsidies.

I. Declaration of Principles

Pastor García asks the group to consider what basic ideas they would incorporate into a declaration of principles:
—Should the declaration request the release of political prisoners or demand basic rights?
—Or should it focus on economic and social rights for the individual?
—What themes can their diverse group agree on?

II. Coalition Activities

The group considers what activities would be appropriate and useful in building their reputation and membership:
—Should activities reflect the declaration of principles and be apolitical or nonpartisan?
—Should the coalition support political activities of member human rights and dissident groups?
—What activities can be carried out without interference by the state security apparatus?

III. Coalition Leadership and Organization

Should they appoint a strong leader to guide the organization or is there a means to decentralize power, while simultaneously empowering the diverse civil society groups that will make up the coalition's membership?

IV. The Role of Foreign Support

The coalition's members do not have the resources to organize its activities, so they must decide whether and from whom it might accept financing. Although U.S. government financing is available, it is also the most suspect to the Cuban authorities.

—From whom should the coalition accept funding?

V. The Coalition's Action Plan

On the basis of their discussions, Pastor Garcia lays out the coalition's action plan.

Abridged Minutes

Abridged minutes from the simulation are provided to enable detailed study of the kinds of exchanges that took place among the participants.

Pastor Emiliano García thanked the representatives for coming, especially those who had made long journeys from Pinar del Río and Havana. He opened the meeting by urging participants to find ways to work together to have a voice in the evolution of Cuban civil society. The time is right for civil society to play a larger role in individual communities and in a broader national agenda. Only by forming a coalition will civil society groups across the island have sufficient reach and standing to expand their networks and membership and carry out their work. García went on to say that he hoped that by the end of the day participants would draw up a declaration of unity to serve as the founding document for a coalition of civil society groups. He urged them to agree to carry out activities to demonstrate their collective purpose. But he warned that it would not be easy to find common ground and themes that would allow them to appeal to a broad and diverse public. Nevertheless, since they had all taken substantial risks to attend the meeting, this indicates their readiness to take some proactive action to allow them to become effective agents for change.

I. Declaration of Principles

Uncertainty prevailed. Although most of those present agreed that change was necessary, they were divided between those preferring to go slow and those who believed that the time to push aggressively for reform was now. However, everyone present agreed that the first step to explore was whether consensus around basic principles could be reached.

The discussion brought to the fore significant differences in perspective. Some participants stressed that their agenda would have to be tied to political reforms, since any declaration of principles should reflect the long struggle of Cuba's human rights activists. Most important, a declaration of principles would have to demand democracy, rule of law, and freedom for political prisoners. A failure to reiterate these goals and carry on the crusade to achieve them would be a betrayal of those who had dedicated their lives to the cause of human rights.

Consensus was blocked by those supporting a political declaration, until an independent journalist warned that binding the various groups to a political agenda would surely fail. Religious groups would refrain from joining for fear that their fate would be that of the dissident movement and they would become targets of state security. This in turn would jeopardize their provision of community services. Moreover, state security would be very suspicious of any coalition, particularly one that appeared overtly political.

A youth representative suggested that the new coalition should move away from making well-known complaints, such as the lack of basic freedoms, and instead become a "new voice," one that represents all Cubans. The declaration should reflect themes common to all such as the desire for material and social improvements in their lives. One Afro-Cuban suggested that there be a strong focus on the need for better jobs, higher remuneration, and the right of Cubans to invest in their own country. Another Afro-Cuban worried that removing or diminishing the influence of the state in the economy would threaten state-provided welfare services, affecting those most vulnerable to the withdrawal of subsidized health, food, and education: Afro-Cubans and pensioners.

A consensus emerged that the declaration should reinforce patriotism, family, and justice, which would resonate even with the government. The representatives agreed that the coalition's declaration of principles would speak to the shared desire for equal rights and opportunities for all Cubans; the government's responsibility to provide basic necessities to its citizens; the importance of "Cuban values," and the obligation of all citizens to obey the law. The purpose of such principles would be to show that there is a widening base of Cubans seeking change and that the first steps toward change will be to press the Cuban government for accountability and to make "advancing the family" a goal comparable to advancing the interests of the state.

II. Coalition Activities

Esmeralda Martinez, of the Freemasons, suggested that the new civil society coalition should try to attract members by carrying out activities of benefit to the community. A number of pastors agreed, arguing that helping others would also prepare Cubans to play a larger role in their communities. An independent librarian suggested that if the coalition was to be truly broad-based, it would have to carry out activities that reflected the ideals of the dissident movement as well as those of the religious community. At a minimum, the organization would have to support projects promoting basic freedoms. For example, it might endorse a petition for the release of political prisoners. Continuing with this idea, the representative from the unrecognized union movement suggested convening a national nonviolent day of civil disobedience to symbolically commemorate a historic event such the "Cry of Yara."

A youth representative suggested that the coalition organize, within a year, a constitutional assembly or a transitional government. Many objected to this, stating that such actions were illegal. A human rights activist agreed that the coalition should not engage in illegal or provocative action, but that it should support peaceful and legitimate initiatives by dissident groups such as an effort to establish a truth and reconciliation commission.

This led to a discussion about whether the coalition's initial activities should reinforce and reflect or go beyond the nonpolitical themes identified in the declaration of principles. Pastor García suggested that initial activities should reflect the ideas expressed in the declaration. He urged that their first priority be the coalition's survival: nothing would be gained if their members were jailed and the movement died before it could begin to build a durable structure. It would therefore be best to begin with apolitical activities that would expand networks and support the aspiration for improved well-being. As the movement strengthened, it would consider how to support the work of human rights activists and dissidents. Religious leaders agreed with García, adding that they were obliged to protect the space that they had carved out over the last ten years.

An Afro-Cuban representative proposed that the coalition host a series of musical and cultural events. Such a celebration would draw a wide turnout, and local authorities may be inclined to permit a popular cultural event to take place, even if it was not state-sponsored. Coalition representatives could organize the event at which performers could present positive ideas, promote cohesion across communities, and facilitate a good reception for the coalition's activities. Events conducted in different parts of the country could become a mobilizing force, and this mobilization would in effect become the political message, perhaps as much to the Cuban people as to the government. For the Cuban people, the purpose would be to show that many are united in a common and positive pro-Cuba agenda that calls for more opportunity for the family and greater respect for the law, including accountability for politicians. For the Cuban government, the message would be the breadth of desire for change, where consistency of the message would demonstrate that reforms cannot stop at cosmetic change. Stifling the emergence of such a wide-based movement founded on "Cuban values" would be highly problematic for a government redefining its socialist base and support among the populace.

A priest suggested, in a similar vein, that a national day of prayer be organized to honor the upcoming beatification of Brother José López Piteira, the first native Cuban to be declared a saint. This action would express Cuban traditions and be a force for understanding.

Pastor García agreed that the first activity of the new umbrella group would be a nationwide musical event. Member groups would organize events in their own towns and obtain permission from the local authorities to do so. This type of activity would be an inducement to young people to participate—hopefully without encountering problems with local authorities.

III. Coalition Leadership and Organization

Pastor García commended the group for the progress made so far. There would continue to be risks as independent organizations attempted to organize events around the island. Permits for musical events would have to be obtained from local authorities, and whether they were forthcoming would depend on whether the government considered the concerts benign or provocative.[1]

A prominent dissident said that if the coalition was to become an umbrella group for numerous small groups around the island, a decision would have to be made about its leadership and management. Some representatives felt that the coalition should find ways of avoiding vesting too much power in one individual.

Various representatives thought that there should be different divisions within the coalition. The youth representatives agreed, pointing out that young people yearn for change but have no long-term vision. If the coalition had a youth wing, it could devise slogans and strategies that would bring together frustrated youths willing to work for change. An Afro-Cuban said that the message to her community should draw on the nationalist legacy of the Revolution in order to avoid any racial tensions. Fear of change or retribution might be averted by emphasizing the importance of maintaining the social benefits of the Revolution while advocating actions to try to gain a greater voice in Cuba's government.

Religious representatives highlighted the importance of not defining their coalition in opposition to the Revolution because they wished to avoid losing the nationalist symbolism and concrete benefits associated with it throughout its history. Rather, they urged that the movement reinforce and expand the scope of community services provided by their churches. If they were successful, Cuba's leaders would see that independent organizations could ease the growing burden on government without threatening the Revolution's commitment to equality and social justice.

An independent journalist responded that it would be practical to create subdivisions within the coalition to cater to the specific interests of youths, Afro-Cubans, religious and cultural groups, and dissidents. Creating divisions would also allow the coalition to maintain a certain

1. On September 20, 2009, a "Concert for Peace" was held in Havana by Juanes, a Colombian rocker who has won numerous music industry awards. The concert attracted an estimated one million Cubans to Revolution Square in Havana. Reuters (www. reuters.com/article/worldNews/idUSTRE58J0YT20090920) reported that Juanes's Peace without Borders concert was not about politics but reconciliation between the people of the United States and Cuba. The event was met with mixed emotions in Miami, where views within the Cuban American community ranged from those criticizing the concert for "legitimizing" the Castro government to enthusiasm among younger members of the community—second-generation Cuban Americans as well as more recent émigrés.

distance from the rhetoric and activities of the various groups under its "umbrella." Dissidents would not feel constrained by the coalition and the coalition could distance itself from ideas and activities of some member groups that some other member groups found objectionable.

Pastor García agreed that the coalition would benefit enormously from the demonstrated ability of the human rights movement to organize networks, project coherent political messages, and mobilize citizens. At the same time, the coalition clearly needed to base its activities on community work rather than dissent if it was to survive. In the end, success was ultimately bound up in finding ways to work together. Each representative and each group would have a better chance of success if they built on their own specific strengths. Ideally, the coalition would provide a bridge between dissidents and the apolitical civil society groups.

IV. The Role of Foreign Support

All the participants acknowledged that without outside funding the coalition would be limited in its ability to spread its message or carry through on a program of activities. The only realistic source of funding was foreign entities, but foreign funding attracts government scrutiny, and in some case limits the ability of the organization to act freely. One priest pointed out that foreign NGOs would be the best source of financing that avoided political pitfalls. Several other participants suggested that support from the European Union and multilateral institutions would also be beneficial to civil society and would be acceptable to the Cuban government.

Several dissidents suggested that the coalition request assistance from nongovernmental organizations funded by the U.S. government, but others feared that doing so would place their legitimacy in question and provide the Cuban government with an excuse to take repressive measures against them. Members of the religious community suggested that they accept funds from private U.S. organizations but not those directly funded by the U.S. government; religious denominations had been very generous in providing assistance to individual churches. The consensus was to accept funding from U.S. private religious and cultural organizations that do not accept U.S. government financing.

The majority of attendees noted that because relations between the United States and Cuba were improving, the government might be more tolerant of the coalition's activities because the general level of tension

and paranoia was reduced. Cubans were less fearful to join and participate in community activities when external and internal tensions were
reduced. Pastor García responded that the coalition would likely have a
greater chance of success if relations between Cuba and the United
States were advanced. In the early years of the new century, improved
bilateral relations and enhanced travel by groups and individuals from
the United States had proved to be a major source of inspiration, ideas,
and financing for civil society groups in Cuba. All participants were
hopeful that this might again become the case and might provide a fer-
tile environment for their efforts.

V. The Coalition's Action Plan

The following points were established for future planning:

—The declaration of principles will be based on promoting the well-
being of the family, community, and nation.

—The coalition will be essentially apolitical, which will be reflected
in both its declaration and in its activities.

—The coalition will sponsor cultural events throughout Cuba as
occasions to announce its formation and its declaration of principles.

—The coalition leadership will be decentralized, with a division for
each of the four types of civil society groups: religious-cultural, youth,
Afro-Cuban, and dissidents.

—Each division will seek to reinforce the activities of its member
groups and support the activities of the other divisions and the broader
coalition.

— Financial support from private and public sources other than the
U.S. government will be gratefully accepted.

—The coalition will have the best chance of success if the Cuban
government does not consider it a threat and if relations between Cuba
and the United States improve.

CHAPTER SEVEN

Coordinating U.S. Policy with the International Community

On October 9, 2008, in advance of the U.S. presidential election, Brookings Institution advisers and guests met to explore the opportunities and constraints facing policymakers as they seek to coordinate U.S. policy with international partners and allies. Democratic governance and the robust rule of law in Cuba are goals the United States shares with the European Union and most of the countries of the Western Hemisphere. What has divided the United States from its allies is the means to arrive at those goals: U.S. policy has been rooted in isolating Cuba to pressure its government to change, with occasional modifications to allow greater travel and remittance flows from the United States. Since the 1970s, most other countries have sought normal relations with Cuba, but without a clear and coordinated international effort to move the Cuban government toward allowing greater space for Cubans to play a more direct role in the politics and economics of their country.

The aim of the meeting was to assess how a new U.S. policy of engagement toward Cuba, with the goal of creating an environment that enables Cuban actors to bring about change, could advance common objectives with the international community. Participants tested the readiness of international actors not just to engage with Cuba, as they are already doing, but also to encourage Cuba to uphold democratic norms critical to allowing Cuban actors the political space needed to advance change from within. They explored how the United States, other key nations, and international organizations might cooperate in a meaningful way across an array of policy tools: direct diplomacy, security, trade, and the promotion of democracy, human rights, and civil society. Participants also explored political and policy changes inside and outside Cuba that could potentially divide international actors, an exercise that provided some perspective on unproductive political approaches.

The following pivotal issues emerged from this simulation:

—How can the United States and its partners manage a shift in U.S. policy from isolation to critical and constructive engagement without appearing to reward the Cuban government?

—How can the international community ensure that strategies that engage the Cuban government do not end up helping the government's authoritarian structures to become even more entrenched?

—How can Cuba's membership in the Organization of American States be restored in a manner consistent with the purposes, principles, and practices of the organization?

—Given that the United States and its allies lack contacts and the critical insight into the inner dynamics of the Cuban government, how might a coordinated policy effectively increase the stake for reform-minded leaders inside Cuba to press for political change, engage the Cuban government to open spaces for civic activity, and support a broad base of civil society actors?

—Would instability cause fractures in the leadership or the military, and if so, would this empower civil society? On the basis of these assessments, what should the response of the international community be to instability on the island?

The Exercise

The exercise consisted of three parts. The first helped to define the parameters of international policy toward Cuba. Representatives of the diplomatic community shared their perceptions of Cuba's internal dynamics, their governments' policies toward Cuba, and their perspectives on what the next U.S. president's approach toward Cuba might be. The insights gained in this part set the context for potential points of convergence and divergence among these organizations and governments and the United States.

This discussion was followed by a simulation exercise set in October 14, 2010.[1] The secretary of state asked key partners to discuss how they might coordinate approaches toward Cuba in order to promote political openings on the island. Specifically, advisers role-playing the simulation examined how the United States might promote democracy and human rights and provide civil society assistance in Cuba while furthering trade and security interests. They also discussed Cuba's reintegration into the OAS and other multilateral bodies. Although traditionally the United States has isolated Cuba, the secretary was now prepared to consider changes in U.S. policy that would facilitate a common approach toward the island. The challenge facing the governments attending the meeting was to determine whether they could put aside historical differences and craft common approaches toward Cuba that would be both complementary to new U.S. strategies and mutually reinforcing.

Finally, the players were confronted with a scenario involving the breakdown of internal order in Cuba and were asked to design a common response by the international community. The crisis was injected into the simulation exercise to test whether an emergency would break down the nascent steps that had recently been coordinated among governments or whether this newfound unity might serve as a foundation for dealing with crises in Cuba.

International Perspectives on Cuba

A new dynamic to engage a Raúl Castro–led government has emerged across the Western Hemisphere. Since Raúl assumed the presidency in February 2008, a record number of Latin American leaders, many of whom had been hesitant to visit the island because of fears that doing so could endanger relations with Washington, have attended highly publicized meetings with both Castro brothers.[2] The Rio Group, comprising

1. Representatives of foreign governments and the international community who participated in the opening discussion did not participate in the simulation.

2. Since formally assuming the presidency until mid-2009, Raúl Castro has received visits from the following presidents of Latin American countries: Michelle Bachelet of Chile; Luiz Inácio Lula da Silva of Brazil; Cristina Fernández de Kirchner of Argentina; Evo Morales of Bolivia; Rafael Correa of Ecuador; Hugo Chávez of Venezuela; Martín Torrijos of Panama; Álvaro Colóm of Guatemala; Manuel Zelaya of Honduras; Daniel Ortega of Nicaragua; Leonel Fernández of the Dominican Republic; and several other Caribbean heads of state.

all of the Latin American countries except for French Guiana and the English-speaking Caribbean, admitted Cuba to its ranks in November 2008, stating that the organization would be more representative and inclusive through its expanded membership. (Founded in 1986, Grupo do Rio is a regional organization whose fundamental position and principles include democracy and human rights, as reaffirmed under the Veracruz Act of 1999.) This desire to integrate the island into the hemispheric architecture has, however, obscured and superseded specific policies to promote democracy, human rights, and the rule of law.

Ironically, the U.S. policy of isolating Cuba has left the United States itself isolated from the rest of the international community and has jeopardized U.S. standing in the hemisphere. In the course of the discussion, participants agreed that a critical element of a new U.S. policy toward Cuba would have to be to reorient this dynamic by redirecting the focus of the international community from changes in U.S. policy to change in Cuba. Participants discussed individual country positions and policies toward Cuba so as to assess their priorities and objectives in engaging the island and to frame approaches toward international partners that reflect these concerns and priorities.

Relations of Hemispheric Nations with Cuba

Canada and Mexico are the only two countries in the hemisphere to have maintained uninterrupted diplomatic relations with Cuba since 1959. Since 1994 Canada has engaged the Cuban government in a dialogue on issues of mutual interest, including human rights. Canada is the island's single largest source of tourists, and its second largest investor, after Spain, with investments in mining, power generation, and food production, as well as participation in an offshore oil drilling consortium led by Spain's Repsol.

Mexico's loss of territory to the United States has made it especially wary of outside interference and protective of its sovereignty, factors that have made it traditionally sympathetic to the Cuban Revolution. Increasing cooperation between the United States and Mexico in the late twentieth century highlighted Mexico's position in the "strategic triangle" of Mexico-U.S.-Cuba relations: maintaining close relations with both countries provides Mexico with the potential to become a broker in U.S.-Cuba relations. Under the Calderón administration, bilateral Mexico-Cuba relations were significantly strengthened, and dialogues were opened on migration, healthcare, debt restructuring, and expanding trade. Nevertheless, the triangular relationship presents difficulties for Mexico: since the United States' wet foot, dry foot policy came into effect in 1995, Mexico has become an alternate route for Cubans to enter the United States. Although a Mexican-Cuban migration accord signed in October 2008, whereby Mexico would return undocumented Cuban migrants to Cuba, appears to have reduced the flows, Cuban migration continues to impact Mexico's relations with the United States in the areas of security, migration, and border enforcement.

Brazil, under President Luiz Inácio Lula da Silva, has forged close personal and political links with Raúl Castro, especially growing out of Brazil's focus on economic cooperation in oil and gas exploration and production, agriculture, biotechnology, medicine, information technology, the environment, and mining. Brazil has also championed Cuba's reintegration into the hemispheric architecture, leading the development of a framework for Cuba to become a regular affiliated member of the Mercosur (Common Market of the South), Unasur (Union of South American Nations), and the Rio Group.

The Cuba-Venezuela political and economic alliance has continued virtually unchanged since Raúl assumed the presidency and includes exchanging crude oil (92,000 barrels per day) at highly subsidized rates for Cuban teachers and medical personnel (24,000 Cuban health professionals are currently in Venezuela). Venezuela is Cuba's largest source of imports; it grants preferential tariffs for over one hundred Cuban products and is investing in Cuba's oil industry. Hugo Chávez and Fidel Castro were also the driving forces behind the founding of the Bolivarian Alternative for the Americas (Alternativa Bolivariana para las Americas, or ALBA) in 2005 as a project to link Latin America and the Caribbean Basin in political, economic, and security cooperation initiatives.

Other Partners

The European Union's relationship with Cuba, dating back to the provision of humanitarian aid in 1993, has been characterized by "constant swings between periods of honeymoon and disharmony," one participant said. As a bloc, the EU is Cuba's largest trading and investment partner (one third of all trade, one half of joint ventures) and a major source of tourists. Since applying diplomatic sanctions (reducing diplomatic ties, particularly by limiting high-level visits) in the aftermath of the Cuban government's crackdown on dissidents in 2003, internal EU debate on how to structure policy toward Cuba has fluctuated between the position of Spain, which has promoted normalized relations since 2007, and that of the new democracies of Central and Eastern Europe, which advocate closer ties with dissidents and the continuation of diplomatic sanctions on the Cuban government. In June 2008, the Spanish position won out: the EU fully lifted restrictions on Cuba, allowing European nations and the EU collectively to reengage with Havana in a dialogue on human rights, the environment, science, and technology and to intensify cooperation on issues of mutual interest. Despite continued concerns over the lack of progress on human rights and Cuba's statement that human rights were not on the table, in June 2009 the EU decided to expand dialogue with the Cuban government.

Within the EU, Spain is spearheading engagement at the national level, with wide-reaching cooperation agreements and assistance on environmental stewardship, disaster relief, small-business development, and food security, as well as joint efforts in regional disaster relief, including in Haiti. Spain is Cuba's third most important trading partner, accounting for 62 percent of total EU exports to Cuba, and is the leading source of foreign investment in Cuba, in the tourism, tobacco, and banking industries. The Spanish company Repsol leads an international consortium for oil exploration. The United Kingdom, too, maintains strong cooperation with Cuba on counternarcotics and anti-money-laundering efforts, and also provides aid for environmental stewardship, sustainable energy, and development. France, too, maintains close relations and is especially active in cultural exchanges.

China, reviving historic contact, has repeatedly stated that modern bilateral relations with Cuba are grounded in mutual economic, not political, interests. China is Cuba's second most important trading partner in imports and third in exports, and also has invested strongly in Cuba's nickel, oil, biotech, transport, and electricity sectors. Russia, too, has been edging closer to Cuba under Prime Minister Vladimir Putin. Russia seeks to regain influence in Cuba and has sent several high-level delegations to reestablish commercial and security cooperation, but there has been no indication that Russia would reopen closed military bases, particularly in light of the thaw in Washington-Moscow relations under the Obama administration.

How Can the United States Build on Its Partners' Ties to Cuba?

The United States lacks critical insight into the Cuban government's key decisionmakers and decisionmaking mechanisms and the dynamics among civil society groups. To gain such insight at this decisive moment in Cuba's history, the United States might build on its partners' deeper contacts with the Cuban government and civil society to help inform a new U.S. policy of engagement with Cuba. Cuba will be inclined to improve its contacts with the United States and others, in order to diversify its relations and develop more partners for importing and developing oil and gas, as suggested by Raúl Castro's visit to major oil producers in February 2009, including Angola, Algeria, and Russia.

Cuba's traditional trading partners—Mexico, Brazil, Canada, China and the European Union—and new partners will expect Cuba to meet international economic standards, including the repayment of debts and observance of human rights. None, however, are likely to condition their relations with Cuba on its making a democratic transition and holding free and fair elections.

Since the advent of the Obama administration, the United States has demonstrated a more creative approach to managing the hemisphere's desire to reinstate Cuba into the hemispheric community. At the April 2009 Summit of the Americas and the OAS General Assembly two months later, the president and secretary of state demonstrated that multilateralism and democracy can be reinforcing. The U.S. decision not to block lifting Cuba's exclusion from the OAS reinforced the notion that democracy should be the objective of rather than a precondition for Cuba's reinstatement. This position has had the beneficial outcome of improving U.S. relations with the hemisphere and redirecting the onus for Cuba's meeting hemispheric standards of democracy and transparency from United States policy to Cuba.

Simulation Exercise No. 5, Part I: A Meeting of Foreign Ministers Convened by the U.S. Secretary of State in Washington, D.C., October 14, 2010

Participants were confronted with a scenario, set in October 2010, in which Raúl has experienced a medical crisis and his departure from the political scene is imminent. Fidel already passed away the previous year. Without a clear succession, it is speculated that power will pass to one of the vice presidents during the next meeting of the National Assembly in six months. But it is unclear whether a high-profile leader or a trusted, less-known member of the Revolutionary Armed Forces or the Cuban Communist Party will be named president and Party leader. The environment in Cuba is characterized by increased uncertainty and unease over a future reform process. Raúl's recent unification of the currency has lowered the value of the peso, drawn sharper divisions between economic winners and losers, and caused further deterioration of public services. Other reforms designed to improve the well-being of the Cuban people have not been carried out, causing widespread disaffection and apathy. Despite the end of the U.S. wet foot, dry foot policy, annual out-migration continues at 40,000.

Within the context of the final days of the Castro government, participants role-played a scenario in which the U.S. secretary of state convenes a meeting with the foreign ministers of Spain, Mexico, Canada, Brazil, Chile, and the United Kingdom, the EU foreign affairs chief, and the secretaries general of the OAS and of the United Nations. The U.S. secretaries of the treasury and of commerce and other State Department officials also attend. In light of increased contact between Cuban and U.S. diplomats and the exchange of military attachés, speculation is rife that after Raúl's departure from the political scene a full normalization of U.S.-Cuba relations may follow.

To the regret of U.S. allies around the table, the secretary of state cites certain limitations to a new U.S. policy. First, the United States is not yet ready to make a high-profile change in policy because the administration does not want to appear to be rewarding the Cuban government. Second, the administration feels that the embargo can continue to serve as leverage for political reform, and maintaining it will avoid strengthening the Cuban government symbolically and economically. The United States will, however, end its policy of "regime change" toward the island. With these constraints in mind, the secretary of state hopes that the United States would be able to forge a partnership and join strengths with its partners and allies. She has convened the meeting to get an understanding from those around the table what a partnership might entail and areas where the United States might hope to combine strengths.

A Post-Raúl Transition

As a first step in framing a coordinated policy, the secretary of state probed whether those at the table could agree on what a post-Raúl transition might look like. If the international community would not be able to agree on the nature, dynamics, and possible indicators of a transition and its prospective leaders, how could they move in sync in their tactics and tools to engage Cuba? If the United States and its partners and allies could agree on the strengths and weaknesses of a post-Raúl government, would this enable them to come together to influence an in-house succession so that over time Cuba might move toward democratic reform? Could the United States learn from its allies' insight into public attitudes and the level of cohesion among civil society actors in ways that would allow it to better respond to a succession or transition and have influence within the next government?

All of the participants were uncertain in their assessment of what a post-Raúl transition might look like, throwing into relief the lack of information other partner countries might possess about the inner workings of the Cuban hierarchy. Cuba would undoubtedly be affected by the global economic downturn; the stability achieved through Raúl's cabinet reshuffle in March 2009 may mean that the armed forces and their cadre of political military officers will remain in charge of the state economy, which would imply a weakened Communist Party. In the long term, some ministers thought that this dynamic would erode state capacity as corrupt practices within the armed forces become more widespread and gain visibility. Within this context, would Cuban state institutions be flexible enough to manage conflict within the political elite as they confront economic and political challenges? And would such an environment, in the absence of enhanced grassroots economic opportunity, create a tipping point for demands for deeper democratic change among the wider population? Disagreements among participants quickly became apparent regarding the nature of a post-Castro Cuba. Some participants emphasized that the Central and Eastern European institutional models of democratic transitions are not relevant to Cuba, and that the Chinese and Vietnamese transitions may be more relevant.

The participants who were playing the role of foreign ministers agreed that with or without the Castros, Cuba will go through a protracted period of liberalization, starting with selected economic openings that play into the interests of key power brokers, especially in the military. This type of transition opened possibilities for the governments represented around the table to press for greater economic openings. Since it was unlikely that the Cuban government would collapse and democracy would suddenly take root in Cuba, the most productive measures the international community might take would be to design and agree upon incentives for more internal openings that might be attractive to a post-Castro government. If Cuba's new leaders were confident that an external embrace would not directly interfere in the transition, they might be willing to risk greater openness that would lead to a democratic process over time.

Such an approach by the international community would entail international assistance, especially through international financial institutions and integration into hemispheric political bodies. A post-Castro government anticipating major political and economic instability would undoubtedly tighten its political and economic grip. Political change was thus seen as being inextricably linked to stability. The international community should look for a balance that promotes political change without prompting the new leadership to close down political space for fear of instability. The Cuban government would be unlikely to give Cubans enough political and economic space to advance their freedoms if it did not have some confidence that doing so would not result in a loss of its own power. One participant predicted that at some point the tensions between change and stability will clash. For those who advocate fundamental change, the challenge will be to use engagement as a tool that fosters greater political openness, rather than affirms the status quo.

A New Objective and Yardstick for Policy

Participants urged the United States to move away from "regime change" as an explicit policy objective and adopt a policy designed to lead to the normalization of relations through a policy of critical and constructive engagement. Given that the justification for such a policy would be to assist the Cuban people to become voices for change, what measures should be adopted to assess progress? Further, what parts of current U.S. policy should be recalibrated to move from regime change to supporting change from within? Would it be necessary to end hostile rhetoric and dismantle sanctions that prevent the United States from improving the well-being of the Cuban people? Would such an approach also require revising the U.S. strategy on dissidents, and Radio and TV Martí? (Radio y Televisión Martí is a U.S.-government-financed radio and television broadcaster based in Miami that transmits Spanish-language news and current affairs programming to Cuba. Modeled on Radio Free Europe, Radio Martí was started under President Reagan in 1985 and TV Martí in 1990.) Should the United States reconsider how it relates to Cuba economically? How can the international community engage the Cuban government to encourage it to allow Cuban citizens to play a consistent and greater role in Cuban politics and to press for economic freedoms?

U.S. policy toward Cuba faces a fundamental tension: the United States seeks to strengthen Cuban civil society so that the Cuban people can play a role in defining Cuba's future, yet the United States will want to avoid any measures that may strengthen Cuba's authoritarian government. If the United States is to help empower the Cuban people and decrease their dependence on their government, it will need mechanisms to support and engage the Cuban people. This is the underlying rationale to remove restrictions on remittances, communications, and travel. Although these actions may also provide some economic benefit to the Cuban government, U.S. inaction would serve the interests of the Cuban government as it aims to maintain the status quo and resist all external action that might threaten its hold on power. The yardstick for the United States in determining whether certain actions that aim to strengthen civil society should be taken should be whether the Cuban people benefit more than the Cuban government.

The international community must also come to terms with a core tension in its own policies toward the island. Unless the Cuban government tolerates the emergence of civil society and an entrepreneurial class, a strategy of "change from within" will likely amount to mere rhetoric. With U.S. leverage on Cuba sharply diminished, the international community will have a critical role in taking up this dialogue with Cuba's leaders. Such a dialogue should not be construed as policy conditionality—it is a matter of political realism. If Cuba wants to take its place among the Western Hemisphere's democracies and establish confidence in its role as a supplier or producer in global markets, it will have to match the performance of other countries that adhere to international norms. The more countries other than the United States take up and coordinate such a dialogue with Cuba, the greater the prospects that the message will have an impact.

Obstacles to Coordinating Policies

While international participants urged well-publicized changes as a sign of a new U.S. willingness to engage the wider hemisphere, participants acting in U.S. government roles were undecided as to whether a move toward engagement should occur as a high-profile policy change in order to maximize impact, or whether policy changes should be undertaken quietly so as not to appear to reward the Cuban government.

Participants also debated whom the United States should work with in the region. Some in the roles of foreign ministers from countries friendly to the United States argued that selective multilateralism, such as seen in the current simulation, would not be a solution. Venezuela, Bolivia, Ecuador, China, and Russia are the countries that must be brought on board with the new synthesis. Still, even if that effort succeeded, the United States was unlikely to work closely with governments that it did not consider committed to a democratic Cuba. Coordinating with those with fundamentally different perspectives would also carry the risk of undermining policy coherence.

Even among countries that consider themselves friends of the United States, differing historical perspectives led to tensions in suggested policies and tactics. This raised questions concerning U.S. options if coordinated engagement does not lead to the intended effects, and the Cuban government is unwilling to respond to good-faith negotiations. Should the United States continue to align its policies with a common multilateral policy? Fifty years of acting alone provides empirical evidence that reverting to a unilateral policy of isolating Cuba will not achieve U.S. objectives. For the United States, the dialogue underscored the need to moderate its policies, even if this process proves difficult and is accompanied by new tensions. But the international community should also accept that unleveraged engagement is a weak strategy. To this end, U.S. partners should grant the United States some leeway to manage the sensitive politics of shifting strategies after fifty years, while at the same time reinforcing the importance of pressing Cuba to improve its human rights and rule-of-law profile.

Creating an Enabling Environment: A Two-Pronged Multilateral Approach

Participants agreed on a two-pronged policy framework of engagement in which multilateral cooperation would aim to further two common goals:

engaging the Cuban government and supporting the development of broad-based civil society.

ENGAGING THE CUBAN GOVERNMENT.

Participants highlighted that a policy of engaging the Cuban government and civil society could not coexist with a policy of imposed "regime change," aimed at forcing the Cuban hierarchy from power. Only after putting aside this objective might the United States gain access to both the Cuban government and civil society entities and possibly identify interlocutors within both settings with whom it could work.

The United States will be more likely to increase space for debate and dissent within the government if it coordinates its engagement of the Cuban leadership with its partners and within the inter-American system. This in turn might result in a larger voice for the wider Cuban population in how it is governed, allow fissures to gain visibility, and encourage leaders to take risks. The challenge with the Cuban government will be to demonstrate that engagement brings benefits, and thus to create incentives for individual leaders and the government at large to make structural changes and adhere to the rule of law.

STRENGTHENING CIVIL SOCIETY

The United States has politicized the acceptance of U.S. assistance by limiting U.S. civil society assistance to a small portion of Cuba's population, the dissident community, at times even making recipients targets of government oppression. This has made some civil society groups in Cuba afraid to accept U.S. help. As a result, U.S. assistance has not been an effective vehicle to engage or strengthen broader civil society. The European Union representative urged that the United States channel civil society assistance funds through multilateral initiatives in the short and medium terms.[3] Latin American participants urged that a motion be introduced at the next OAS General Assembly to establish a regional civil society fund. Participants recommended that the United States, after it has lifted restrictions on travel within the twelve categories permitted under executive authority (see appendix A for a detailed overview of the legal

3. The European Union launched a new project in 2007 that solicits proposals from and provides support to a broad range of EU-based NGOs who assist Cuban civil society groups.

parameters of the U.S. embargo on Cuba), disseminate assistance funds more broadly and encourage U.S. NGOs to engage their counterparts.

Cuba and the OAS

As of 2009, every OAS member state except for the United States maintains diplomatic relations with Cuba, and among these states a consensus has emerged to allow Cuba to take up its seat in the OAS. The question that remains is whether OAS membership could be offered in a way that creates incentives for reform in Cuba. Given Cuba's historic disdain for the OAS, however, it is not at all certain that Cuba desires to be reinstated if it is required to meet standards for membership.

Participants were concerned that the OAS's commitment to democracy as embodied in the Inter-American Democratic Charter might be eroded if Cuba were reinstated without preconditions. One suggestion was that a group of countries might review Cuba's progress toward the objectives of the charter and make recommendations that, if met, would lead to Cuba's full reinstatement. But many doubted Cuba would have any interest at all in such an invasive process. The participant in the role of the OAS secretary general believed that most members would seek a measured and orchestrated process for Cuba's reinstatement, in which all members would be invited to have their say. In his view, such an effort would strengthen the OAS's representative decisionmaking mechanism and reinforce the message that Cuba has a stake in its reintegration to the Inter-American system. There was some support for providing an incentive to Cuba by linking economic and political reforms in Cuba to a process that would eliminate commercial and financial sanctions.

Although Cuba cannot participate in the inter-American system (including the Inter-American Development Bank) until it is a full member of the OAS, there is no legal provision prohibiting representatives of the OAS from talking with the Cuban government.[4] To this end, the United States should encourage discussions between the Cuban government and a small working group of member states; the latter would also

4. Specifically, the Cuban government and its representatives and employees cannot participate in activities of OAS bodies, with the exception of the Pan American Health Organization, which is a part of the UN system. Cuba can participate in UN activities of which the OAS is a co-sponsor, but they would have to be considered primarily activities of the UN, not activities of the Inter-American system.

issue an invitation to Cuba to participate in technical, issue-specific working groups on education, public health, labor rights, rule of law, disaster relief, counternarcotics measures, and public security, framed within a parallel timetable to reinstate active membership.

The exclusion of the Cuban government from the OAS does not apply to its citizens or civil society organizations independent of the Cuban government.[5] Establishing a multilateral civil society fund that fosters the rule of law, human rights, and micro-enterprise, through which the United States could channel assistance funds, should be a priority in the multilateral agenda.

Several months after this simulation exercise, on June 3, 2009, the OAS General Assembly passed a resolution lifting the 1962 resolution that suspended the Cuban government's membership and allowing Cuba to retake is seat once it demonstrates that it upholds the purposes and principles of the organization, including democracy and human rights. Even with this major change in policy, the key findings from this discussion remain relevant. First, to be engaged by the inter-American system, Cuba must act pursuant to this new OAS resolution. Second, a consensus within the organization is still lacking on how to assess whether Cuba meets the purposes and principles of the OAS. Thus, central elements of a U.S. diplomatic strategy should be both practical engagement with Cuba and the creation of a shared international perspective on upholding the purposes and principles of the OAS.

International Financial Institutions

Participants were unanimous in considering Cuba's integration into the international financial system as more pressing than reinstatement in the OAS. Membership in international financial institutions such as the World Bank, the International Monetary Fund, and the Inter-American Development Bank (the latter requiring active OAS membership) might become more attractive to Cuba as external financial support to the Cuban government possibly diminishes in the wake of the global economic recession, making Cuba's leaders less resistant to financial reforms.

5. Cuban citizens must provide assurances that they are participating as private citizens, not as government employees or representatives, and civil society organizations must be able to demonstrate that they represent independent civil society, not government-controlled groups.

Participants proposed that international financial institutions involve Cuba in assessment and planning operations and eventually offer membership if Cuba would be willing to meet their requirements. The group believed, further, that Cuban engagement with international financial institutions would give Cuba's leaders access to the kind of advice and support that would be required to reduce painful dislocations if the government undertook structural reforms in a planned manner. Involving these institutions now can also set the stage for investments to develop market-based infrastructure. Bilateral trade credits would be available to reinforce multilateral engagement as Cuba is integrated into an international rule-based financial system. The engagement of international financial institutions would require broad-based diplomatic support; participants believed that Mexico, Brazil, and Canada, with U.S. encouragement, could sponsor a motion to build such support among the international community.

Simulation Exercise No. 5, Part II:
A Meeting of the National Security Council and Foreign Ministers Concerning Multilateral Engagement and Crisis Management, November 13, 2010

Participants were confronted with an emergency scenario in which the secretary of state reconvened the foreign ministers at the National Security Council one month after their previous meeting in the hope that the group might coordinate a response to a leadership crisis unfolding in Cuba, precipitated by Raúl Castro's death. Already it had become evident that there was a breakdown in law and order and mass migration to the United States was a distinct possibility.

The ministers sought to determine an appropriate response that would allow them to assess the situation and work with Cuba's leaders to stabilize the situation. They were determined to avoid unilateral action by the United States for fear that it would only exacerbate matters. They hoped that by making early contact with Cuba's leaders they could avoid the deployment of an OAS-UN peacekeeping mission, which might otherwise be needed in the case of widespread violence or developments requiring a humanitarian response.

In spite of a lack of contacts in Cuba, participants agreed that the United States would be able to manage a mass migration crisis through the combination of diplomatic contacts and the interception of refugees on the high seas. However, they were concerned that violence and lawlessness might require a swift humanitarian response and intervention. The ministers warned the secretary of state that unilateral action by the United States would be unwarranted and unwanted and would have disastrous diplomatic consequences, and in any case a unilateral response would be unlikely to increase stability.

The ministers argued that violence and lawlessness would be unlikely to materialize since the Cuban armed forces would continue to be the strongest institution on the island in a post-Raúl succession. In the event of a breakdown of law and order, in their view, the armed forces were capable of reestablishing public order and acting as a government that international actors, including the United States and its allies, could work with to initiate humanitarian relief. Ministers considered it unlikely that instability would lead to a split between the armed forces and the rest of the governing hierarchy or between reformers and hard-liners, as both believe that the Revolution can best be sustained through continued centralization of power and authority. The greater unknown was the subject explored in chapter 6: the strength and coherence of independent civil society and its capacity to press for meaningful change from within. Whether the international community and the United States could deal with this type of volatile situation would be determined by their access to good information to events unfolding in Cuba. None of those acting as foreign ministers had sufficient understanding and access to the armed forces to make reliable judgments.

This lacuna of access and information again reinforced the importance of expanding and broadening contacts with the Revolutionary Armed Forces and Cuban civil society. Although some ministers and U.S. representatives worried that Venezuela would try to assert influence by providing military support for the hard-liners, most considered this unlikely. Their main concern was that U.S. intervention should be avoided for fear of resultant global perceptions of U.S. interference and the inability to judge accurately whom to support. United action should be sought through the OAS to build a common hemispheric understanding and response to the unfolding situation in Cuba.

Regarding migration, the ministers suggested that the United States reopen discussions with the Cuban government before a migration crisis unfolded. This would allow for common actions that would improve access to legal migration as well as facilitate the return of illegal migrants to Cuba. The resumption of migration talks would also open channels of communication to those in the Cuban government who could, in the event of a crisis, help ensure accurate communications with U.S. authorities and thus help the United States avoid miscalculations.

Considerations for U.S. Policy

The philosophical and policy distance between the United States and its partners and allies on Cuba has been vast, and building sustainable international cooperation will not be a simple task. Other countries believe that U.S. policy to isolate Cuba is driven by domestic politics, in particular the agenda of the Cuban American community. This certainly was true in the past, but now, with changing demographics and politics within the Cuban American community, a majority of Cuban Americans favor an engagement policy toward Cuba (see appendix B of this volume, "2008 Florida International University Poll of Cuban American Opinion"). Public diplomacy regarding the changing views of the Cuban American community would lessen some of these concerns and help improve the perceptions of the Cuban American community in the outside world, as well as inside Cuba. But reversing the dynamic of international engagement on Cuba will be a more challenging task.

Most of the international community has focused its primary policy efforts on trying to convince the United States to change its policy of isolating Cuba; encouraging Cuba to respect democratic governance and the rule of law has been secondary. The international community needs to shift its focus to methods to encourage the Cuban government to open up political and economic space for its citizens. The Obama administration's early steps to ease restrictions on travel and remittances have started to shift the debate, as has U.S. support for the OAS resolution passed in June 2009 that has made political reforms the central issue on whether Cuba takes its seat at the OAS.

If sufficient goodwill were developed to foster a strategically coherent common policy around the premise that change in Cuba must come from within and be based on the desires of the Cuban people for a voice in the running of their country, what measures will convince the Cuban government to grant the Cuban people space for change? How, too, can the international community build the capacity and knowledge base of

Cuban civil society actors to ensure that they play a constructive role in Cuba's future? The United States and the international community need to sustain a dialogue around these themes and turn principle into actionable strategies.

A key to an effective international strategy will be managing the combined and seemingly contradictory principles of stability and change. Before Cuban leaders will consider giving the Cuban people greater political space, they will need to believe that doing so will also produce stability. Allowing Cuba to participate in regional and international forums such as the OAS, the World Bank, the International Monetary Fund, and the Inter-American Development Bank could open up the prospect of political and economic inclusion that would improve the well-being of the Cuban people and provide a more stable environment for evolving political space. Yet stability has to be balanced with building capacity and allocating resources in a manner that promotes an open, competitive, and democratic Cuba. This is a delicate balance. Tipping too far toward stability could protect the Cuban government. There is also the potential for clashes among international actors that weigh stability and change differently. For U.S. policymakers, managing the delicate balance between stability and change will be the most important and difficult goal of its international diplomacy.

In this context, early engagement of international financial institutions in Cuba would provide a foundation for changing the status quo. Cuba will need massive investments in infrastructure, but also in the software of its economy and commercial framework. This will entail new approaches to everything from education and health policies to taxation to business regulation to judicial systems that enforce the rule of law. As Cuba expands its commercial relationships, especially with Brazil, Canada, and Spain, it will feel pressure to comply with international practices. The earlier key international institutions can help set the directions for change, the more likely it is that Cuba will evolve further along principles rooted in international market practices that complement personal freedoms and political change.

The OAS has been an undervalued and underutilized player that could help promote change in Cuba. The June 2009 resolution on Cuba's membership that was passed eight months after this simulation exercise reinforced the conclusion of Brookings advisers that the OAS could support a constructive outcome, one that the hemisphere could agree on and that could provide incentives for Cuba to become an active member in the OAS. That said, there is as yet no consensus within the organization on how Cuba will be judged to have fulfilled the purposes, practices, and principles of the OAS charter. Growing international engagement with Cuba will expand the dialogue on democracy and human rights. The more other hemispheric players participate in furthering this agenda, placing the onus on Cuba to act, the greater the potential will be to sway the Cuban government to act.

The simulation suggested observing caution about how the United States and the international community deal with a crisis in Cuba. Lacking solid information on an unfolding situation and contacts with Cuba's armed forces, the international community could overreact and easily reach bad decisions that would only fuel a crisis. Few participants in the roles of representatives of national governments wanted to engage in calming internal political instability in Cuba, but they agreed that the initial actions to do so should be united and led by the OAS. Intervention was to be avoided and, if absolutely necessary, should only be undertaken after a request from the Cuban government, and in agreement with the UN and the OAS.

Some participants dismissed the chances that such instability would occur. Yet Hurricane Katrina threw New Orleans into a state of instability and looting until the U.S. military eventually exerted control. Instability in Cuba may also be more likely than commonly imagined, and this may make countries unprepared to cooperate. That could in turn result in a disproportionate burden falling on the United States. The lesson for U.S. policy is to engage international partners now on the prospects for instability, debunk the myths that instability could not occur in Cuba, and plan for it with others in such a way that the burden is shared internationally. In addition, international engagement of the Cuban armed forces and civil society will help to reduce the unknowns in the event of a crisis. Unchecked migration or other crises should never be allowed to entrap the United States into taking an interventionist position that would not be good for the United States, Cuba, or hemispheric relations.

Finally, it is striking that debates on policy within the United States and at times with other governments have been more acrimonious than exchanges among professionals, including the military, when they have had the opportunity to engage directly. The United States, Cuba, and others in the hemisphere have a common interest in working together on issues that impact the hemisphere such as humanitarian emergencies, improving the environment, preventing disease, and dealing with organized crime. The link between organized crime and drugs has become pernicious in the hemisphere, affecting every country on the supply or demand side of the chain or on transit routes; weaknesses at any point in the chain can provide a safe haven for criminals. Depoliticizing cooperation on such issues is a practical necessity for all countries; practical and professional cooperation in these areas can then set the foundations for tougher discussions on politics.

For the United States, reorienting its approach to Cuba by working with other hemispheric actors and the Cuban government will be essential to creating wider and more meaningful capacity to leverage change in Cuba. A strategy that develops a common perspective with our partners will be most likely to encourage Cuba's leaders to undertake measures that will allow Cuba to begin an evolution toward democracy, respect for human rights, and transparent and equitable development. In pursuing such a shift in strategy, the United States also wins diplomatically, both by eliminating a policy of isolation that has been perhaps the most acrimonious issue is U.S. relations with the rest of the hemisphere and by depriving Cuba of the argument that its failures are due to U.S. policies rather than to its own shortcomings.

SIMULATION SCENARIO NO. 5, PART I
CONTEXTUAL BACKGROUND OF EXERCISE

The following scenario was given to participants:

October 14, 2010. Raúl Castro has suffered his first stroke in June, following the Pope's visit to Cuba in the same month, but was able to speak at the July 26 celebrations. The event was moved to Havana from Camagüey to ensure that he would be close to medical assistance if needed. The Canadian trade minister, who has recently met with Raúl, has informed the U.S. secretary of state that Raúl Castro is dying.

The new Democratic president has improved bilateral relations, and over 250,000 Cuban Americans have visited the island in 2009 and remittances were estimated at US$2 billion that year alone. United States and Cuban interest section diplomats are again allowed to travel throughout Cuba and the United States. Bilateral talks have been held on the environment, counternarcotics efforts, and migration. Sales of U.S. agricultural products to Cuba remain at approximately US$600 million annually, and U.S. multinational oil companies are pressing Congress for legislation, or a change in sanctions regulations, that would allow them to develop Cuba's offshore oil.

Religious freedom was substantially enhanced by the tremendously popular visit of Pope Benedict XVI in early June 2010. Raúl agreed to the construction of new churches, and Catholics and Protestants have expanded their provision of social services. In some areas of healthcare they have replaced the state.

Spain negotiated the release of ten political prisoners and continues to seek the release of those remaining, numbering about twenty. A disagreement arose over Oscar Elías Biscet, who refuses to be freed if he must leave the island. According to Elizardo Sánchez's human rights monitoring group, the major problem is no longer the detention of political prisoners but the suppression of dissident groups such as those associated with Oswaldo Payá and Martha Beatriz Roque.

A new phenomenon in Cuba, the rise of independent groups that carry out social and cultural activities, is worrying authorities. Strengthened by the Cuban government's decision to permit greater access to the electronic media, Los Jóvenes por Dios used Internet and cell phones to establish a youth network that extends throughout Cuba. The group is nondenominational but enjoys support from another, larger, group known as the Coalición Nueva (New Coalition), which has united religious and cultural groups, youth groups, Afro-Cubans, and dissidents under one umbrella. Although Los Jóvenes por Dios and the Coalición Nueva programs are apolitical, Cuban security forces are concerned about their popularity and reach. They have held unannounced but well-attended musical events in many of Cuba's major cities.

Disparities and tensions have grown between Cubans with and those without access to dollars and goods from the United States. Cuban Americans are often silent partners who provide financing to thriving illicit businesses that provide services to tourists and all types of goods to Cubans. The new dollar-based black market, where dollars can be converted to pesos at a better exchange rate than that offered by the state, has contributed to corruption and rising inequality.

Destructive hurricanes during the summer of 2009 led Raúl Castro to accept the U.S. administration's offer to sell and donate materials for the repair of homes and lands. In order to permit all Cubans to purchase these supplies, the Cuban Central Bank announced that it was issuing a new currency, the Castro. Its dollar and euro values are significantly lower than the convertible peso's. Holders of nonconvertible and convertible pesos were given two weeks to turn in their pesos for the new Castro.

Role-Play No. 5:
"A Meeting of Foreign Ministers at the National Security Council"

Characters in the Role-Play–
U.S. Secretary of State (host)
U.S. Secretaries of the Treasury, Homeland Security, and Defense
Director of National Intelligence
Assistant Secretary for Western Hemisphere Affairs
Commandant, U.S. Coast Guard
Senior Director for Western Hemisphere Affairs of the National Security
    Council
Foreign Ministers of Brazil, Canada, Chile, Mexico, Spain, and the
    United Kingdom
High Representative for the Common Foreign and Security Policy
    of the European Union

Secretary General of the Organization of American States
Secretary General of the United Nations

Instructions, Part I: Background and Meeting Agenda

The foreign ministers invited to the meeting anticipate that the United States is ready to reestablish diplomatic relations with Cuba, ease sanctions, and open talks on the status of the territory occupied by the U.S. Naval Base at Guantánamo Bay. Although they understand that this might not happen during Raúl's presidency, they envisage a discussion with the new U.S. administration about a process that would align U.S. policy with that of its allies and partners.

The U.S. president has discussed with the Secretary of State his desire to see an evolution toward democracy on the island and a formal U.S.-Cuba bilateral relationship once the Castro brothers are no longer in power. He believes that it will be helpful to explore the value of coordinating U.S. policy toward Cuba, understand what a partnership might entail, and explore areas where the U.S. might hope to combine strengths with its partners.

The Secretary of State will have to probe the extent to which its allies would press the United States to modify its approach to Cuba while ensuring that U.S. policy continues to place a high priority on the new Cuban president's commitment to a process of political and economic reforms. Although the Secretary of State remains determined not to make unilateral concessions to Cuba, she is prepared to agree to Cuba's reinstatement in the OAS and to ask the Secretary of the Treasury to use his licensing power to further increase Cuba's access to information without a quid pro quo.

I. Cuba after Raúl Castro

—As Cuba moves toward a succession or transition, will Raúl Castro have the institutional backing and authority to choose his successor and ensure the continuation of the Revolution?

—What are the vulnerabilities and challenges facing the Cuban hierarchy? Will corruption erode authority or create new sources of power?

—Can Cuba survive the global recession or the loss of Venezuelan subsidies?

—If the U.S. threat recedes, will the international community put more pressure on Cuba to reform and conform to international standards?

II. A Common Approach toward Cuba

The Secretary of State hopes to probe whether those present can agree on common tactics and tools to engage Cuba, and what they expect from Cuba in return. The U.S. administration's objective is to empower the Cuban people to press for further political change that will lead to progress on democracy, human rights, and economic development.

III. A New International Strategy for Cuba

The foreign ministers of Brazil, Canada, Chile, Mexico, Spain, and the United Kingdom laid out the principles that they felt were critical to effectively deal with Cuba's leaders and engage the Cuban government and people to permit a faster evolution toward democracy, transparency, and human rights in Cuba. They believe this approach will only be truly effective if the United States joins in a united effort.

Instructions, Part II

In part II the simulation exercise sought to test the cohesion of the international community in case of a crisis situation in Cuba.

November 13, 2010. The Secretary of State has urgently reconvened the same foreign ministers and U.S. officials. Raúl Castro's death on November 1, 2010, has precipitated a crisis in Cuba that threatens to result in a humanitarian disaster and mass migration. The Secretary of State has told the foreign ministers that the international community must be prepared to step in to prevent a breakdown of public order in Cuba. She added that the president had asked the Secretary of Defense to review options for the deployment of an international humanitarian peacekeeping mission under the auspices of the OAS and the UN.

NATIONAL SECURITY ADVISER'S BRIEF
Following Raúl's death on November 2, over 100 youths breached the residences of the United States' chief of mission and the Swiss ambassador, demanding visas for entry to the United States from Havana. Acting President José Ramón Machado Ventura warned the diplomatic establishments to remove protestors from their premises within forty-eight hours, for fear that others

would join them. Otherwise a repetition of the 1980 Mariel mass migration could not be ruled out.

In Florida, 100,000 Cuban Americans marched down Miami's Calle Ocho demanding that the protestors be allowed to enter the United States. Florida ports were closed. Vessels sailing toward Cuba were turned around, but two large vessels sailing from Belize tied up at Havana's Marina Hemingway. Rumors spread that thousands of Cuban Americans had made arrangements with Mexican and Cuban smugglers to evacuate their relatives from Cuba to Mexico or the United States.

Several thousand Cubans congregated at the port of Mariel and several hundred were waiting outside the Northeast Gate at the U.S. Naval Base at Guantánamo Bay after walking there from Guantánamo City. Two protestors were shot dead during demonstrations in Camagüey and Cienfuegos.

Alexander Castro, Fidel Castro's son, announced that he had been chosen to succeed his uncle, Raúl Castro. NBC and ABC reporters in Havana broadcast that younger military officers were backing Castro, but that Minister of the Interior General Abelardo Colomé Ibarra remained loyal to Machado Ventura, the first vice president.

Abridged Minutes

Abridged minutes of the simulation are provided to enable study of the kinds of exchanges that took place among the participants.

Role-Play No. 5, Part I

The Secretary of State thanked her guests for agreeing to participate in this discussion. Raúl Castro's poor health brought into stark relief the fact that after almost half a century, Cuba may no longer be governed by a Castro or by one of the revolutionaries who fought with him in the Sierra Maestra. She emphasized that the United States should begin now to coordinate its policies in ways that would advance the cause of the Cuban people and the principles and values of democracy across the hemisphere.

The Secretary of State stated that in her view there was ample room to find common ground to positively influence Cuba's future. The administration had already made a step toward improved relations with Cuba by allowing greater travel and remittances and opening talks on issues of mutual concern, including migration, countering of the illicit narcotics trade, and the environment. However, although Raúl Castro's government had created some openings—launching a new currency and granting space for increased religious freedoms—there was much yet to be done in the realm of democracy and human rights. She stressed that the United States had quietly given up its isolationist policy, but Raúl had done little to ease his government's authoritarian policies and human rights abuses. The United States, she said, is willing to do much to reduce tensions and reduce sanctions, but does not want to take actions that could strengthen the Cuban government practically or symbolically as long as it holds political prisoners. The embargo would continue to be used as leverage for political reform.

She suggested that they begin their discussion by exchanging information on perceptions of the coming transition. If the international community cannot reach an agreement on the nature, dynamics, and possible indicators of a transition and its prospective leaders, in what ways can they move together in their tactics and tools to engage Cuba?

I. Cuba after Raúl Castro

The Foreign Minister of Mexico responded sharply that the United States should not link its actions to Cuba's. Cuba would not meet U.S. expectations because it feared losing power, and the United States would not end the embargo because it wanted a change in Cuban leadership resulting either from isolation or from the impact of reforms that would undermine the government. The United States should accept the reality of the Raúl Castro government and its successor and begin working with, and not against, the region. This in turn would give hemispheric actors more influence with the current and future Cuban government.

The British Foreign Minister made the point that Raúl already had consolidated power and by doing so would have control over the choice of his successor. Those closest to Raúl were his colleagues from the armed forces and security forces; it is highly plausible that a military man might follow Raúl, whether Machado Ventura as an interim leader, who at seventy-nine would not hold the presidency for long, or a younger member.

The Secretary of State predicted that Cuba would be vulnerable to the global financial downturn and cautioned the international community to take into account the potential political impact of further economic shortfalls. Although increased remittances might offset the impact of a recession and support citizens' economic independence from the government, they will likely create deep divisions between the Cubans who have access to dollars and those who do not, leading to potential unrest.

The Secretary General of the OAS responded that serious social unrest was unlikely. The Cuban hierarchy had survived the loss of a third of its GDP when the Soviet Union halted its four-billion-dollar annual subsidy; Cuba had found a new source of support from President Hugo Chávez. Nevertheless, as the Secretary General pointed out, the importance of remittances to sustaining the populations' well-being and independence from the government should not be underestimated.

The Spanish Foreign Minister pointed out that corruption in the military could undermine the transition. Fidel had recognized the threat to political control posed by narco-trafficking, and Raúl had ruthlessly stamped out involvement in the drug trade within the Revolutionary Armed Forces and the Ministry of the Interior. If Russia became involved in the economy, its commercial mafias could corrupt high officials. Cuban society in great part lives by petty corruption that has eroded the social fabric of the Revolution; remittances from the United States created a thriving illegal trade in dollars; only time would tell whether the pervasiveness of corruption would undermine the Revolution.

The European Union Foreign Affairs Chief believed that the strength of Cuba's governing institutions—the armed forces, the Interior Ministry, and the Cuban Communist Party—would ensure the Revolution's survival. He urged that Cuba's institutions be compared to those of China and Vietnam, not the weaker Central and Eastern European models. As long as Raúl was in power these institutions would remain loyal to him. The United States should seek to fortify, not undermine, these institutions to avoid a corrupt and unstable island in its offshore waters.

The Assistant Secretary for Western Hemisphere Affairs remarked that for years the United States believed Raúl to be a hard-liner and an ideologue, yet he had emerged as a pragmatic president. Since the United States still lacks the insight it needs into the key decisionmakers and decisionmaking mechanisms of the Cuban government, a coordinated approach to sharing information with allies would form the basis for combined strategies. Talking with a diverse cross-section of the military, security forces, and the Communist Party on issues of concern to the United States and its allies would enhance their ability to decipher the shrouded internal workings of the Cuban government. By combining forces to reach out to civil society, the international community could also help increase civic participation and thus could put pressure on the Cuban government to permit assistance programs on the rule of law, human rights, professional training, and micro-enterprise, among others.

II. A Common Approach toward Cuba

The Secretary of State reaffirmed her commitment to coordinating U.S. policy with key allies and other states in the region and urged that they reach an agreement on common goals for Cuba that could serve as a yardstick for measuring progress. If U.S. policy moves away from "regime change" as its objective and moves toward creating an "enabling environment" that will bring about change spearheaded by Cuban actors, what will be the metrics to measure progress? Although the Secretary of State acknowledged that it might not be prudent to link policy to Cuba's actions, she believed it to be useful to define common objectives.

The Mexican Foreign Minister advised against such thinking, fearing it would lead to the use of a carrot-and-stick approach that has repeatedly failed for the United States as well as the EU. The Brazilian Foreign Minister asked participants to explore practical actions that might form part of a program dedicated to engaging the Cuban government in ways that would help the Cuban people have a greater voice in their government and become the agents of change. Such an environment can come about only if the United States and its allies are willing to work with the Cuban government. The United States cannot effectively provide assistance to the Cuban people unless the Cuban government allows it to do so. The United States and its allies must beware of placing conditions that Cuba might not meet because it will be difficult to continue them when Cuba's leaders fail to reform. Yet the Cuban people, not the government, are the ones that would suffer. Finally, he urged the United States to reconsider how it relates to Cuba economically. Current U.S. policy is predicated on the concept that Cuba can have a weak, resource-deprived government while building a prosperous civil society.

He urged Washington to recognize that its sanctions hurt Cuba's citizens and civil society more than their government. If Washington is serious about empowering the Cuban people through grassroots economic stimuli, the government too will benefit; even so, a resource-deprived Cuba is not in U.S. national interest.

The Canadian Foreign Minster believed that the region would be ready to work with the United States on a common approach to Cuba, but substantial progress would not be made until the United States changed its entire apparatus set up to promote regime change (including Radio and TV Martí) and lifted or substantially modified the embargo.

III. A New International Strategy for Cuba

After a lengthy discussion, the foreign ministers asked the Secretary of State to thank the president for consulting them on Cuba policy and on the formulation of a common strategy. They recognized that their suggestions would be difficult to implement, but it was their firm belief that if their ideas were adopted, they would permit a new international strategy that would move Cuba toward democracy:

1. *Engaging Cuba.* The United States should coordinate engaging the Cuban leadership with its partners and within the inter-American system. Doing so would give the administration greater access to the Cuban government and people, strengthening its ability to press Cuba to undertake reforms that would create greater space for debate and dissent within the government and civil society more broadly. If the United States no longer sought retribution, Cuba's leaders would be more open to compromise and reconciliation. In addition, a multilateral approach within the Inter-American system toward the Cuban government would lead to pressures for change from within by demonstrating to the Cuban government the benefits of engagement and dialogue, in which individual leaders and the government have a stake within the system.

2. *Strengthening Civil Society.* The foreign ministers agreed that by giving assistance only to Cuba's dissidents, the United States has politicized its program and made it more difficult to engage with Cuba's broader civil society actors. The EU Representative advised that in the short and medium terms, the United States should channel civil society assistance funds in support of multilateral initiatives. Participants from the region urged that a motion be introduced at the next OAS General

Assembly to establish a regional civil society fund. In the medium to long term, when restrictions on the twelve categories of travel beyond family travel have been lifted, the United States should disseminate assistance funds more broadly and encourage U.S. NGOs to engage their counterparts.

3. *Reinstating Cuba into the OAS.* The United States should encourage the OAS Secretary General to review the criteria for Cuba's reinstatement. Cuba should be allowed to participate in the technical and issue-specific regional groups that cooperate on education, disaster relief, health, justice, public security, and labor. Cuba's reinstatement as a full member of the OAS would revitalize the inter-American system, but discussions would have to be held with the membership and with Cuba to make sure that the Inter-American Democratic Charter is not undermined. Full reinstatement was thus likely to be a measured, orchestrated process.

4. *Participating in International Financial Institutions.* Cuba's integration into the international financial architecture would require broad-based international diplomatic support, including acquiescence by the United States. The process would likely be lengthy, considering Cuba's resistance to economic reforms, but one way to begin would be to permit Cuban officials to participate in training programs. Some foreign ministers also proposed that international financial institutions could involve Cuba in their operating programs through quiet ad hoc backroom lending, with low conditionalities, outside the framework of a specific structural assistance package. Such lending would eventually support structural reforms in a more principled way than bilateral trade credits, would sustain consistent multilateral engagement in an international rule-based architecture, and would have a significant impact on Cuba's technical work environment.

Role-Play No. 5, Part II: Multilateral Engagement and Crisis Management

November 13, 2010. One month on from the group's last meeting, the Secretary of State again convened participants in the hope that together they would take action to deal with the crisis unfolding in Cuba. The president had asked the Secretary of Defense to prepare a plan for the deployment of an international humanitarian peacekeeping mission under the auspices of the OAS and the UN.

The National Security Adviser informed the group that Raúl Castro's death had precipitated a leadership crisis. The following was the assessment of the intelligence community:

—Ramón Machado Ventura and General Colomé Ibarra will attempt to reestablish order by clearing the ports and swiftly and ruthlessly repressing demonstrations around the county. The Cuban leadership is divided, and it is unclear whether the situation can be resolved peacefully.

—A mass migration is already in the making. The United States will take no action to remove protesters in the diplomatic residences, and it will not make use of Guantánamo Naval Base to hold would-be migrants because doing so would encourage more Cubans to seek entry into the base.

The Secretary of Defense's major concern was the potential breakdown of order in Cuba. Should this occur, the international community would need to mount a rapid humanitarian response and intervention to provide food and basic necessities and to protect the civil population.

The Mexican Foreign Minister warned that unilateral action of almost any type would not be accepted by the Cuban government or people, and one or the other contender for power could use the presence of a U.S. force to rally the population to its side. Even a U.S.-led international coalition would likely be seen or misinterpreted as a U.S. invasion. Should an international force be deployed, the United States would have to maintain a very low, behind-the-scenes profile. The Chilean Foreign Minister agreed that the only way that humanitarian relief and a peacekeeping force could be deployed to Cuba would be with the agreement of the Cuban authorities. The UN and the OAS would not approve of a mission that was not endorsed by the Cuban government and people.

The British Foreign Minister said that although it certainly was not too early to plan, there was time to find other solutions that would not require the deployment of an international force, which would take time to authorize and organize. The Secretary of State responded by saying that the president would welcome a solution brokered by those around the table, which would preempt the need for deploying peacekeeping or humanitarian assistance forces.

There was disagreement among participants as to the role of Venezuela in crafting a common hemispheric response to unrest in Cuba following Raúl Castro's death. The Assistant Secretary for Western

Hemisphere Affairs stated that the Revolutionary Armed Forces could be relied on to reestablish order, but he feared that in case of divisions within the army, with younger officers supporting Alexander Castro to succeed Raúl instead of the first vice president, Venezuela would provide military support to the old-guard hard-liners loyal to Machada Ventura, led by Colomé Ibarra. The Secretary of Defense assumed that the OAS and the UN would take steps to avoid any outside unilateral intervention. The Mexican Foreign Minister felt that Venezuela needed to be included in any policy discussions and decisions to take action, not only to head off their unilateral intervention in Cuba but also to make use of Venezuela's contacts within the Cuban government and grasp of the internal situation. The Secretary of State thought that including Venezuela in such multilateral discussions, however, would be divisive.

The Secretary of State asked whether any of the governments present had been in touch with Machado Ventura or Alexander Castro, or had contacts within the Cuban military who could provide information needed to determine how to proceed. The Canadian Foreign Minister responded that he had already spoken with everyone in the room but no one had been able to reach Machado Ventura or Castro, and their contacts with the military were limited. The Secretary of State concluded that this incident highlighted the need for significantly enhanced communications and understanding of the inner workings of the Cuban power structure, especially the security apparatus and the armed forces.

All participants agreed that they must gain a better understanding of events in Cuba. This would involve establishing contacts with both the Castro and Machado Ventura factions, as well as with the Communist Party, and civil society. The OAS should be involved immediately by sending a delegation to visit Cuba, and should reach out to Venezuela in the process. Participants also said that they hoped the United States was fully prepared to deal with a mass migration, but would urge that the United States resume talks on migration policy in the future in order to forestall the migration response in a crisis.

The British Foreign Minister summed up the discussion by confirming that his government would immediately join with others to open up channels of communication in order to seek solutions and avoid miscalculations or misunderstandings. The OAS Secretary General responded that he would convene a regional working group that would be open to Venezuela. He would also work with the Secretary of State and other governments to ensure that humanitarian relief would be made available promptly if it was needed. The UN Secretary General said that he would ask the UN Department of Peacekeeping Operations to look at what countries might participate in a peacekeeping mission should it be requested by Cuba and the UN membership.

Following the meeting, the Secretary of State called Ricardo Alarcón, president of the Cuban National Assembly. They agreed on bilateral talks that would aim to achieve the following goals:

—The U.S. attorney general would rescind the wet foot, dry foot policy that had allowed Cuban migrants who reached U.S. soil to remain there legally.

—Cuban authorities would announce a new lottery in which winners would be eligible to apply for permanent residence in the United States.

—The United States would agree to process and provide permanent residency visas for 30,000 Cubans annually, an increase of 10,000.

CHAPTER EIGHT

Creating Consensus in the Cuban American Community

The sixth simulation exercise, held shortly after the U.S. presidential election, on December 2, 2008, focused on the dynamics and motivations of the Cuban American community and divisive issues that relate to U.S. policy toward Cuba. Changing demographics inside the community have produced new perspectives on contacts with the island. More Cuban Americans want to see and support their families. Cuban American youths who are growing up in the United States increasingly want to understand their heritage. Some in the older generation want to see change in Cuba in their lifetimes and have grown frustrated with the embargo. Recognizing this growing trend toward consensus on questions of both travel and remittances, this last simulation was planned to focus on whether the Cuban American community could reach consensus on the next steps in U.S. policies beyond the opening stages of engagement that would be critical to drive change in Cuba.

The following pivotal issues emerged from this simulation:

—Will there be a tipping point when the fervor to isolate Cuba becomes a liability, not a strength, in the eyes of Cuban Americans?

—Will Cuban Americans be a force for change in the United States and Cuba, or will their internal divisions render them a community to be managed in order to minimize the roadblocks to creative new ideas?

—Should the Obama administration defer to the Cuban American community and risk being caught in fractious debate? Or, alternatively, should it seek to lead and build constituencies around innovative approaches?

—Can the Cuban American community build a consensus? Will a strong Cuban American leader emerge who can forge consensus? How much time is there to build consensus? At what point does inaction and stalemate risk further divisions in the community?

—What will the Cuban government do to exploit tensions among Cuban Americans? How can Cuban Americans respond?

—Can Cuban Americans establish common ground on economic and diplomatic initiatives, and those that foster contact between U.S. and Cuban citizens, allowing Cuban Americans to become ambassadors for change, or will internal turmoil undermine their potential?

The Exercise

The day was divided into two parts. First, Brookings Institution advisers and special guests assessed the diversity of experiences, motivations, and visions for change within the Cuban American community. For the first time in fifty years, a significant number of Cuban Americans urged the administration to engage with Cuba in order to help the Cuban people create the conditions for democratic change from within. Yet significant numbers of older, more conservative members of the community adamantly oppose change. Those who desire a more open policy have not reached a consensus on the next steps of a new U.S. policy toward Cuba. The discussion assessed the perspectives of a diverse group of Cuban Americans concerning U.S. policy: a politician, a young professional, an academic, and a business leader. Their ages cut across the spectrum of Cuban Americans who have come to or were born in the United States since 1959. Although they all advocated a shift away from isolating Cuba, there was no agreement on whether President Obama or the Cuban American community should lead the effort to build political consensus around a new policy. Some lamented the lack of a strong Cuban American leader who would represent the new majority and urged the administration to design a policy that would be both forward-looking and help forge consensus in the community.

In the second part of the day, participants assumed fictional roles of community leaders who meet in December 2010 at the Biltmore Hotel in Miami. The simulation exercise assumed that by this point the Obama administration has implemented policies to reduce restrictions on travel and remittances. Contacts have increased between Cuban Americans and their families in Cuba. Although some conditions on the island have improved, change has been minimal. Raúl Castro and the Communist Party remain firmly in control. Youths have limited prospects for jobs or economic opportunity. Now, young Cuban American professionals have convened a cross-section of the Cuban American community to reach consensus on a new U.S. policy toward Cuba. The goal is to move beyond this stalemate and use the aspirations of Cuban Americans to reach out to the Cuban people as a foundation for a new coherent policy toward the island.

A Demographic Profile of the Cuban American Community Today

Since 1959 four waves of Cubans have migrated to the United States, each group with its own socioeconomic experiences, political outlooks, and motivations for leaving Cuba.[1] According to the 2007 American Community Survey, just over 1.6 million people of Cuban descent lived in the United States: approximately 980,000 (61 percent) were born in Cuba and 630,000 (39 percent), in the United States. Of those born in Cuba 415,000 (26 percent) were not U.S citizens.[2] The profile of this population—when and under what circumstances its subgroups left Cuba and their socioeconomic backgrounds—is central to understanding the divisions within the Cuban American community and predicting where the future balance of political power in the community will be.

1959 to 1962: The Cuban Elite

The shifts in Cuba during and in the wake of the Revolution drove the first wave of Cubans to U.S. shores, constituted primarily of Cuba's elite. They numbered just 144,732 persons and currently make up 15 percent of all Cubans who left Cuba for the United States after 1959.[3] They had close ties to U.S. businesses and capital and most were in favor of militant action against the Revolution's leaders, in order to reclaim Cuba.[4] These

1. Silvia Pedraza, *Political Disaffection in Cuba's Revolution and Exodus* (Cambridge University Press, 2007).
2. 2007 American Community Survey estimates, available at http://factfinder. census.gov/servlet/SAFFFactsCharIteration (select population group "Cuban").
3. Calculations based on 2007 American Community Survey figures (see note 2). Does not include those born in the United States.
4. Nelson Amaro and Alejandro Portes, "Notas para una sociología del exilio: Situación y perspectivas de los grupos cubanos en EEUU" [Notes on a sociology of exile: situations and perspectives of Cuban groups in the USA], *Aportes* 23: 7–24.

first, upper-class, émigrés were followed by a middle-class wave (merchants, professionals, and skilled workers) in the aftermath of the silencing of the Catholic Church and the closing of private schools and universities in Cuba, which occurred in 1961. In contrast to later waves, this second wave was not pulled by opportunities offered in the United States but was motivated to emigrate because of concern about Cuba's internal politics. With the cessation of flights between the two countries in the aftermath of the Cuban Missile Crisis in October 1962, large-scale legal migration came to a temporary halt. Post-1962 emigrants—most of whom were skilled and unskilled blue-collar workers who were spurred to leave by the introduction of rationing and conscription—arrived on U.S. soil illegally or via third countries.

1965 to 1979: Frustrated Workers

The next wave of migration, consisting of 277,234 persons, or 28 percent of all Cuban emigrants, was spurred by Lyndon B. Johnson's open policy for refugees from Communism, made possible with the Freedom Flights (*los vuelos de la libertad*), the air bridge between Havana and Florida that started in 1965. It transformed what had been an exodus in disorganized spurts into a coordinated movement of people. For these migrants, the economic pull of opportunities in the United States was matched by a political and economic push from Cuba. Cuba prevented professionals, technical and skilled workers, and young men of military age from leaving, and so 57 percent of arrivals were blue-collar, service, or agricultural workers, and only 12 percent were professionals or managers.

This more heterogeneous group of migrants displayed variations in social class and values that were reenacted in exile.[5] As Cuban American leaders opened dialogue with the Cuban government in 1978 to promote family travel and reunification, the Cuban American community split into two political camps with opposing views as to whether or not to support or oppose dialogue, and whether or not to visit Cuba. This schism continues to this day, with the pro-engagement side of the debate fortified by the views of the third and fourth waves of immigrants, the so-called "children of the Revolution."

5. Silvia Pedraza, "Cuba's Refugees: Manifold Migrations," in *Cuban Communism, 1959–1998*, edited by I. Horowitz and Jaime Suchlicki (New Brunswick and London: Transaction, 1998), pp. 496–518.

1980 to 1981: The Marielitos

Orderly migration came to a halt in the 1980s with the exodus of the 125,313-strong *Marielitos*—disproportionately young, male, Afro-Cuban, and politically disaffected. Seventy-one percent of the *Marielitos* were blue-collar workers. They constitute 13 percent of all Cuban emigrants today. Fleeing to the United States from the Cuban port of Mariel as part of the Mariel boatlift in 1980, they left as new generational strains developed inside Cuba, caused by limited economic and political opportunities. They encountered a changed situation on the ground in Miami: whereas the first two waves of Cuban Americans arrived in a city bursting with opportunity in the 1960s and 70s and brought resources—education and professional expertise—that aided their integration, the *Marielitos* and later immigrants found themselves in a very changed society and had fewer transferable resources to bring.

Today 28 percent of *Marielitos* live below the poverty line; the figure for the overall Cuban American population is just 16.5 percent. Race, too, has been a challenging factor in the *Marielitos'* integration: Earlier immigrants were predominantly white Cubans. For Cubans of mixed race who began to participate in out-migration in the 1980s, their predicament in the United States became one of uncertainty. They were not accepted into the white Cuban American establishment, and African Americans viewed them as Cubans. Increasingly they formed their own separate community.

1982 to Today: The Balseros

The mass migration of 1980 and 1981 led to a bilateral migration agreement in 1985, under which the United States would issue up to 20,000 visas to qualified applicants. In reality, only 7,500 visas were granted over the next five years, because fewer Cubans were naturalized in the United States than anticipated, reducing the number of Cubans who could petition for their family back in Cuba to be granted visas under the program. Despite the limited opportunities for legal migration, the number of illegal departures between 1982 and 1990 was extremely low.

The collapse of Soviet subsidies and the beginning of the Special Period ushered in the phase of undocumented migration aboard *balsas*, or rafts. The number of *balseros* who arrived illegally each year rose steadily, from a few dozen a year in the 1980s to 467 in 1990, 2,203 in 1991, 2,557 in 1992, and 3,656 in 1993.[6] By 1994, a year marked by massive riots in Havana, the unmet demand for migration resulted in a mass migration of 37,000 Cubans taking to rafts to reach U.S. shores. In order to avoid another mass migration, migrants who were interdicted at sea were directed to the Guantánamo Naval Base. Most were resettled in third countries; however, it is assumed that many found their way either legally or illegally to the United States.

The *balsero* crisis, as it came to be known, led to the 1994 U.S.-Cuba Migration Accords, which guaranteed entry to 20,000 Cubans who would be granted permanent resident status. The migrants were made up of Cubans who were granted refugee status, those who met the requirements for legal entrance, and winners of both a Cuba-specific lottery and the international visa lottery. The United States expanded the U.S. Interests Section's personnel in Havana in order to carry out in-country processing of lottery winners and those seeking refugee status.

This agreement did not, however, stop illegal migration: under the so called wet foot, dry foot policy, Cubans who took to the seas were granted entry into the United States if they reached U.S. soil. Those picked up at sea were interviewed and, if found not to qualify for refugee status, were returned to Cuba. Since 1995 between 1,000 and 3,000 Cubans have entered the United States without documentation annually, and since 2000 yet more Cubans have reached the United States via Mexico. Undocumented migration peaked in 2007, when 4,825 made it safely to the United States across the Florida Straits (2,868 were interdicted at sea by the U.S. Coast Guard) and 8,194 entered across the U.S.-Mexico border (4,295 were apprehended by border patrol in Mexico).[7] In this way, since 1981 over 500,000 Cubans—comprising legal immigrants admitted through the preference system, those gaining visas via immediate relatives, and those entering as refugees and parolees—have been granted legal permanent residency status. Over half have arrived since 1994.[8]

6. William M. LeoGrande, "From Havana to Miami: U.S. Cuba Policy as a Two-Level Game," *Journal of Interamerican Studies and World Affairs* 40, no. 1 (Spring 1998): 76.

7. Congressional Research Service, *Cuban Migration to the United States: Policy and Trends* (Washington: 2009).

8. U.S. Department of Homeland Security, "U.S. Legal Permanent Residents: 2006," *Annual Flow Report* (Washington: 2007).

In Miami, the integration of the *balseros* went largely unassisted by the older members of the Cuban American community. Having grown up under the Revolution, most *balseros* came from a lower socioeconomic class than earlier emigrants, and in Miami they were often seen as having supported the revolutionary government because they had lived in Cuba under the Castros. Of all the members of the Cuban American community, their ties to the island are the strongest and most extensive. Seventy-six percent of those who send remittances to Cuba left the island since 1990, even though 70 percent of the people in this group earn less than $30,000 annually (39 percent of the *balseros* live below the poverty line). Furthermore, 77 percent of the post-1990 arrivals are not U.S. citizens, so they wield little political power and their views of and preferences for U.S. policy toward the island are less visible than those of earlier immigrant groups.

New Attitudes: "No Change without Exchange"

Shifting demographics have moved the center of Cuban American politics away from isolating Cuba to a greater acceptance of engagement. In presentations from a cross-section of Cuban Americans in the first part of the exercise, the common theme was the need to engage Cuba, but the rationales for this varied. There was no agreement as to what type of engagement should be sought nor how far the administration ought to go to engage with Cuba.

A Cuban American politician stressed that the changing political landscape in Miami no longer compelled many Cuban Americans to vote Republican. In line with national trends, several long-time members of the community showed concern for broad, domestic social issues, whereas more recent arrivals who registered to vote in one party or the other did so on the basis of socioeconomic interests and their desire to maintain family connections with Cuba. Engaging Cuba and progressive socioeconomic policies both respond to an emerging new constituency of Cuban Americans as they register to vote.

In the 2008 election, the Democratic Party began to take advantage of this shift in attitudes by fielding candidates for the U.S. House of Representatives, registering voters, and raising funds from within the Cuban American community, where 69 percent had in the past been registered Republicans. Now new voter registrations indicate a shift away from the

Republican Party toward independents and Democrats. Increasingly, Cuban Americans who arrived since 1980 are represented among new voter registrants: an exit poll of 2,500 Cuban Americans in Miami-Dade County found that 27.6 percent identify themselves as "strong Democrat," 27.1 percent as "Democrat," 19.6 percent as "Independent," 15 percent as "Republican," and 6.8 percent as "strong Republican."[9]

For the first time, the "Cuba issue" cost votes in Florida. A few months prior to Barack Obama's visit to south Florida, the Democratic Party of Miami-Dade County voted and agreed on a policy to ease restrictions on Cuban Americans' travel and remittances to Cuba, and to support grass-roots economic activity in Cuba. A Florida International University poll, detailed in appendix B and conducted in the immediate aftermath of the U.S. presidential elections, revealed a rise in the political influence of those supporting a policy shift. The results cut across party lines: far exceeding the 38 percent of Cuban Americans who voted for Barack Obama, 72 percent think the embargo has not worked well or at all, 56 percent of support reestablishing diplomatic relations with Cuba, and 72 percent would like to see direct talks between the U.S. and Cuban governments on issues of bilateral concern.[10]

The Miami-Dade exit poll had similar results: of the 35 percent of Cuban American voters who voted for Barack Obama, almost 75 percent thought that the embargo had failed. One Cuban American businessman observed that President Obama does not owe anything to the hard-liners in Miami, but those who did vote for him want and expect significant changes in Cuba policy.

More recent arrivals seeking to facilitate contact with family in Cuba are converging with the younger generation of Cuban Americans, who fear the loss of opportunity to discover and establish links to their own Cuba. A young Cuban American participant emphasized that growing up in the shadow of the Elián González, the *balsero*, and Brothers to the Rescue crises had made exile politics part of the inheritance of U.S.-born

9. Benjamin G. Bishin, Feryal M. Cherif, Andy S. Gomez, and Casey Klofstad, "Miami Dade's Cuban-American Voters in the 2008 Election," *Cuban Affairs* 4 (2009): 1.

10. The poll distinguishes between registered and unregistered voters (many of whom are more recent arrivals from Cuba and therefore non-U.S. citizens) in order to discern political influence.

Cuban American youths. However, despite their solidarity with their family's commitment to human rights and democracy in Cuba, they aspire to explore their roots and find ways of connecting with their families back home. Consequently, young Cuban Americans increasingly speak out about the need for linkages with Cuban society so that they can be relevant to a future Cuba. One young participant expressed this with the slogan *"No hay cambio sin intercambio"*—there can be "no change without exchange."

This evolving environment has made it possible for Cuban Americans to take hitherto untenable positions on opening up relations with Cuba and on steps toward phasing out the embargo. The proliferation of Cuban American organizations promoting increased contact with Cuba, including several youth groups, indicates that the pro-embargo establishment has been losing its monopoly on Cuban American opinion.

Has a tipping point been reached in the community such that fervor to isolate Cuba has become a liability, not a strength, in the eyes of Cuban Americans? Parts of the older generation have emerged at the forefront of this debate, many breaking with "first-wave conservatism" to recognize that a peaceful, prosperous, and democratic Cuba can only be achieved through change from inside the island and cannot be forced by outside actors. Their conversion to this view has given weight and depth to the argument that a policy of engagement might give the United States the chance both to press the Cuban government to allow greater space for the emergence of civic institutions and to direct support to Cuban civil society, which over time would create broader and deeper demands for change from within.

In their view, engaging Cuba and Cubans more systematically would also give the United States a better opportunity to understand Cuba's internal dynamics and identify potential change agents. With increased linkages, the United States could more effectively press for adherence to human, civil, and labor rights in a principled way. These leaders also advocate a proactive policy, independent of Cuban actions, in an effort to end the inertia caused by Cuba's effective veto over U.S. policy: the United States sets conditions for Cuba, Cuba resists. In effect Cuba has manipulated the Cuban American community into stalemate. To shift the momentum and break this stalemate, the United States should set a policy agenda to strengthen the capacity of Cubans to drive change from within Cuba, and not get trapped by Cuba's self-interest in preserving the status quo.

Simulation Exercise No. 6:
A Meeting of Representatives of the Cuban American Community, December 13, 2010

Two years into the Obama administration, young Cuban American professionals, members of the Iniciativa Cuba en el Siglo 21 (Cuba Initiative for the Twenty-First Century), convene a broad cross-section of Cuban Americans to shape a common vision for U.S policy toward Cuba beyond the initial openings undertaken by the Obama administration. Key Cuban American groups, academics, and civic and religious leaders attend the meeting. The new administration has authorized more widespread "people-to-people" travel under the twelve authorized categories that are within executive authority (see appendix A), including travel for educational, cultural, humanitarian, religious, and professional purposes. It has also relaxed restrictions on remittances and launched bilateral dialogues on migration and counternarcotics policy. So far, however, the Raúl Castro government—still firmly at the helm—has not announced further economic and political liberalization since formally assuming power in 2008.

Many Cuban Americans have welcomed the chance to see and support their families, but already patience with the administration's Cuba policies is fraying, pulled at by differing interest groups within the Cuban American community. Members of the older generation who supported change want more, whereas those who favored isolation have become even more agitated in their opposition. As the Raúl Castro government becomes further entrenched and Cuba takes first steps toward developing its energy resources, these dynamics have led to a fear among the pro-engagement groups that the window of opportunity for change is closing. Younger Cuban Americans wonder whether there will be another opportunity to connect with their families and Cuba. Even though the embargo has not worked to force change in Cuba, some parts of the community cannot come to terms with lifting the embargo or changing legislation that symbolically might be seen as rewarding the Castros.

Thus, the challenge for the meeting is one not just of advancing policy but of determining whether there would be enough consensus within the

Cuban American community to make it a positive and constructive force on U.S. policy. There is no doubt that parts of the community can block new ideas, but can those in the community who aspire to a U.S. policy of critical and constructive engagement rise above these obstacles and assume a new mantle of leadership? Can Cuban Americans forge common strategies that engage the Cuban government to expand the space for civil society without appearing to reward the Cuban hierarchy? How should the community deal with the Cuban government's intent to maintain control over politics and the economy?

The group went into the meeting with a sense that the diversity among its ranks would allow the movement to transcend the framework of established opinion and allow it to appeal to a broad cross-section of the population. It ended with a sober acknowledgment of the difficulty of keeping the community together, and of the fragility of the consensus arrived at regarding support for liberalizing Cuban American travel and remittances.

An Elusive Consensus?

The importance of building consensus on U.S. policy was intuitive to the Cuban Americans playing the scenario. A new approach to U.S. policy is needed: attempts to isolate Cuba have not produced change on the island and have marginalized the United States in the international arena. The initial measures on travel and remittances and engagement on migration policies taken by the administration are positive but will not by themselves produce the democratic Cuba the participants desire. If the Cuban American community can unite around a common engagement platform, it will have a more powerful impact on policy.

President Barack Obama is seen in Cuba as an agent of change. A large portion of the Cuban population, 62 percent of which is Afro-Cuban, identifies with him, and his election has raised awareness of institutional racism in Cuba. To deal with this phenomenon, the Cuban government has taken some steps toward integrating Afro-Cubans into the hitherto white-dominated workforce of the tourism sector. The positive image of the United States would be reinforced if the Obama administration were to fully lift the travel ban on U.S. citizens, which would build contacts with the island that go beyond those within the Cuban American community and Americans traveling under people-to-people licenses.

Some participants emphasized that Cuba today is not the Cuba of fifty years ago. Telecommunications have progressed and many business ties between the island and foreign firms have been created. For many Cuban Americans who left Cuba after 1980, family is more important than politics. These facts, one participant who played a Cuban American academic said, bode well for the future of reconciliation between Cubans on the island and abroad.

Yet from this common ground, consensus eroded. A Cuban American businessman said that the administration had done too little, too late. Frustration among Cuban Americans was growing because Cuba's leaders, by continuing to reject real reform, were impeding any form of meaningful political and economic change. The Cuban American community itself may be an inadvertent obstacle to change in Cuba. Cuba's leaders have used the community's traditional isolationist views to justify stronger central control, to deflect blame for bad policies at home in Cuba, and to avoid making anything more than cosmetic changes in policy. The United States for its part has conditioned its actions on Cuba's behavior, and in so doing ceded political leadership to Cuba.

Consensus quickly became an elusive ideal. Some participants advocated that the Obama administration use its bully pulpit to help Cuban Americans in Miami understand alternatives to the status quo. Still others pointed to the political risks, arguing that the Democratic Party loses among all Cuban American voters when it takes positions on Cuba, and not only within the core group of Cuban Americans who would likely vote for a Democrat. U.S. policy toward Cuba is a Republican issue. Since a Democratic candidate is seen as unlikely to gain votes by trying to erode Cuban American support for the status quo in Cuba policy, a better Democratic Party strategy within the community is to address wider social issues not directly related to U.S. relations with Cuba.

If the administration were to take its lead from the Cuban American community it would find it impossible to formulate a coherent Cuba policy. Although there is consensus on issues around engaging and supporting family connections, it quickly erodes when policy veers toward paradigm-shifting initiatives that are needed to underpin a strategy focused on helping Cubans achieve change from within Cuba. To achieve such a radical policy shift, the administration may have to accept that it must sacrifice consensus within the Cuban American community.

Who Provides Leadership?

The discussion highlighted the risk of a serious void in leadership on U.S. policy toward Cuba. The Cuban American community wants to lead and feels that it should, but as the previous discussion has demonstrated, participants could not overcome the vastly divergent outlooks within the community. Given the sharp divides on Cuba policy, those role-playing administration officials were reluctant to lead: they preferred that the Cuban American community drive the process to arrive at a consensus on the components of a new U.S. policy of critical engagement.

Participants were concerned that this stalemate could actually reinforce the preference of the Cuban hierarchy for the status quo by serving as a convenient scapegoat for the government's own shortcomings. In summary, it was easy to reach consensus within the community on basic principles of supporting family ties and people-to-people travel, but moving beyond such measures ran aground as a result of limited drivers and initiative from inside the U.S. administration to propel a principled policy forward.

One Cuban American academic highlighted that any issue on the agenda of U.S.-Cuba relations was burdened with fifty years of history and legislation that make it very difficult to move forward. Many in the community recognized that progress on policy toward Cuba will require bold measures and will entail taking risks, yet that would appear to be exactly what the Cuban American community was not prepared to do. Linking this to U.S. policy, the academic lamented that the United States, by following the lead of the Cuban American community since the 1970s, had forfeited any semblance of an independent foreign policy toward Cuba; this would continue to be the case until the administration cuts the Cuban American community's apron strings.

For the administration, showing leadership may be the only effective option, but it would not be a comfortable one, as Cuban Americans have not agreed on a course beyond the very basics of engagement. Some parts of the community will criticize administration policies that are seen to go too far; others, for not going far enough. The latter argue that the United States must embark on a path of more radical change because an incremental approach will not produce the desired outcome. One community leader said that only the White House could essentially rise to the occasion and begin to lead Cuban Americans in Miami toward a new policy

approach, because no significant political leader has ever argued for anything different than the status quo. Cuban American attitudes are more
realistic than they were, but not as advanced as Washington might wish.
Consensus will remain elusive.

For the administration and any part of the Cuban American community that aligns with it, credibility will have to be sustained by results. If
relations with Cuba start to demonstrate the potential for change, and if
Cuban Americans see that their families have some sense of hope for
improved well-being, then progress will generate a new dynamic. But
that will be tricky. Cuba will want to release pressure within its society,
but the Cuban government will want to avoid any threats to its future.
Internal change may come slowly, and if it is not clearly visible to the
outside world, Cuban American public opinion may coalesce around yet
another kind of shift in policy—perhaps to some variant of isolating
Cuba internationally while at the same time encouraging family contacts—potentially leading to a policy of contradictions. Effective leadership in Washington will require clarity of purpose and the crafting of
tools to support Cubans who are open to change, a clear strategy to
engage the Cuban government that does not further entrench its hold on
power, and the political capacity to maintain consensus within the
Cuban American community around core issues such as travel and
remittances.

Formulating a Policy Agenda

Despite participants' differing views on policy, useful perspectives
emerged as the group grappled with defining a policy course that would
create the conditions to normalize relations with Cuba and end the
embargo. The administration had already taken the easy steps by authorizing people-to-people and cultural exchanges, but these were deemed
insufficient by a majority. The group struggled to come up with a set of
unilateral actions, not conditioned on any response from Cuba, that the
United States could take. The Cuban government could, however, hold
them hostage, either through inaction or obstinacy. What measures could
the administration implement to signal significant change to the Cuban
government and its people, as well as to the international community? If
the objective of policy is to create an enabling environment that would,
over time, assist the Cuban people to take a part in forging Cuba's political future, how can top-down and bottom-up U.S. engagement be made

operational without provoking the Cuban government to shut down civic and political spaces?

1. Diplomatic Relations. To understand internal dynamics in Cuba, both at the grassroots and among the political leadership, the United States will need a stronger diplomatic presence on the island. Politically, a swift move to widen diplomatic relations, bringing U.S. diplomacy toward Cuba in line with U.S. diplomacy with the vast majority of countries in the world, would carry huge symbolic weight. Cuba could no longer credibly blame its woes on its northern neighbor. How can such a change in the diplomatic relationship be structured?

If the administration wishes to send an ambassador to Cuba, it could begin by establishing, or reestablishing, lines of communication. Beginning in the fall of 2002, the Bush administration used its diplomatic presence in Cuba to articulate an ideological point of view, rather than to manage a relationship. To create a new strategy, the United States will need to give substance to the bilateral relationship, reestablishing and taking further bilateral initiatives on migration, counternarcotics policy, and the environment that in the past established trust and formed the basis for moving diplomatic relations and dialogue forward.

An ambassador can only be effective if he or she has sufficient tools to manage an effective embassy, one that provides the information and insights necessary for the president and the secretary of state to make informed decisions for a judicious and thoughtful Cuba policy. The United States could establish the underpinnings of a long-term relationship by negotiating reciprocal diplomatic representation, including reciprocal access to government officials, unrestricted in-country travel for diplomats, and the option for U.S. government representatives to establish relations with independent civil society entities. With these underpinnings in place the United States can then send an ambassador to carry out the full range of diplomatic duties necessary to represent the United States.

The group could not agree on the timing of such measures; it was unclear whether an ambassadorial appointment would be seen as a reward to the Cuban hierarchy or understood as a necessary diplomatic tool. To counter a negative perception in Cuba, the group agreed that the decision to send an ambassador should be coupled with a rationale, such as a new agreement on migration, or cooperation on drug policy or counterterrorism measures. Diplomacy is a tool to make the complete policy agenda for change work more effectively. Participants agreed that if the United States is to be fully present on the field, it will need to establish full diplomatic relations.

2. *Economic Relations.* The administration can maintain consensus among Democrats and independents as it moves forward on the relatively easy issues of opening up people-to-people travel and cultural and educational exchanges. The consensus fractures when it takes bolder measures. Participants proposed starting with small economic openings in line with U.S. interests, to include the export to Cuba of nonagricultural products such as textiles, computers, hardware, and other items. But promoting real structural change in Cuba will be difficult as long as investment of U.S. capital in Cuba is off the table.

Cuba still owes more than $500 million to one of its preferred trading partners, Sherritt, a Canadian mining company, and it depends on Venezuela for approximately $3 billion dollars' worth of annual subsidies. Thus, in 2009 Cuba's economic standing resembles its pre-1991 dependence on the Soviet Union. Aware of this vulnerability, Cuba will have to diversify its partners and adopt market-based transparency if it is to survive and reduce its dependency on a single-source provider of subsidized oil, until its own oil comes online. If the United States opens the economic gate, a large number of U.S. corporations will seek commercial and trade relationships on the island. In the first years this will not include risky capital investments, but many U.S. companies will set up commercial relationships, and their presence will have the potential to encourage change within Cuba, particularly on labor rights and financial transparency.

Cuban Americans have become an important element in the calculations of the Cuban government because remittances are a large and growing source of income. Such support could become more widespread if the United States were to allow the community to be more directly involved in financing small businesses and in systematically providing greater economic resources to grassroots economic activities. Such engagement would give some relief to the Cuban people and allow the government to capture tax revenues from remittances—but would the Cuban government allow this? Participants concluded that the damage would be greater if the experiment in increased Cuban American financial involvement in Cuba were not attempted at all.

Stronger economic ties could also enhance political leverage on issues such as the release of political prisoners, if a broadly representative group of Cuban Americans could come together around an initiative to open a dialogue with the Cuban government directly. In 1977 talks between the Cuban American community and the Cuban government resulted in the release of political prisoners in Cuba. But one Cuban American participant rejected a positive prognosis from such dialogue at this point in history, asserting that the danger of a direct dialogue between Cuban Americans and the Cuban government is that neither the United States nor the Cuban American community would be able to control its outcome.

3. *People-to-People Contacts.* There was wide agreement that the focus of U.S. policy should shift away from dislodging the Cuban government to supporting the Cuban people. Recognizing that the Cuban government may seek to obstruct a policy that aims to increase the independence of the Cuban people from it, the administration should promote enhanced contact, access to information, and economic resources that help the Cuban people. People-to-people travel to permit contacts between U.S. and Cuban citizens should be undertaken unilaterally and on a broad scale, and in coordination with multilateral engagement of the Cuban government. The purpose of such strategies is to support those on the island who are open to change, as well as to allow the United States to better understand the dynamics of Cuban society. People-to-people contacts, the group felt, should not be contingent on anything. They are a fundamental tool serving a new strategic perspective: change in Cuba must come from within.

At the same time, participants emphasized the need for a robust cultural diplomacy strategy, one that is not contingent on regime change. Cultural initiatives cannot be effective if they are linked to regime change, as was the case with many USAID-funded activities, especially those tied to Cuban American groups that advocate a specific ideology or political agenda. New mechanisms are required to expand and fund educational exchanges, promote the arts, and allow NGOs to interact freely with civil society. Fostering the interaction of civil society on both sides of the Florida Straits was deemed most likely to promote diverse voices and reform in Cuba.

The discussion detoured to Radio Martí on a regular basis; the Miami-based broadcaster is an example of the United States' advocating independent media while funding a radio station that is seen as neither independent nor professional. Participants agreed that its programming should be reviewed and realigned to reflect those of Radio Free Europe and Radio Liberty; it should use local journalists to broadcast locally, as they gain the political space to do so. The vested interests in jobs and commitment to an isolationist approach on the part of some Radio and TV Martí personnel would undoubtedly complicate efforts to professionalize these broadcasts. The administration should be prepared for a negative reception and even backlash by Martí personnel if it eases restrictions on Cuba and opens up policy.

The administration should also establish funds for micro-enterprises and civil society entities, which would foster entrepreneurship, support a wide range of civic actors, and assist vulnerable groups, such as Afro-Cubans and youths. U.S. government funding should be made available for such programs, and U.S. NGOs should also be licensed to reach out to their Cuban counterparts across a diverse set of activities and interests. If such activities were internationalized with donors from multiple countries, the Cuban government would encounter greater difficulty in shutting down funds and would effectively eliminate the scapegoat of U.S. meddling. In addition, travel should be permitted in the twelve categories authorized under the Trade Sanctions Reform and Export Enhancement Act of 2000. Furthermore, participants strongly recommended that the Commission for Assistance to a Free Cuba be dissolved, as its policy recommendations had become associated with the Bush-era focus on regime change.

Considerations for U.S. Policy

A poll conducted by Florida International University in November 2008 demonstrates the shift in attitudes within the Cuban American community toward greater engagement and a recognition that the embargo has not worked (see appendix B). The sixth simulation exercise served as a de facto focus group to get a deeper understanding of attitude shifts captured by the poll. The diversity in the waves of migration from Cuba helps explain the differences in perspective among Cuban Americans. The overall shift in perspective toward engagement creates an opportunity to consider new policy solutions, but the simulation underscored the limits and fragility of any consensus among Cuban Americans. Although consensus is strong around issues of family ties, travel, financial support, and cultural engagement, it fractures at the formulation of the next round of policy initiatives needed to sustain the momentum for change in U.S. policy toward the island and in Cuba itself.

Recognition of this fragility should prepare the Obama administration to confront a political reality: if it wants an effective policy on Cuba that can break with the status quo, it will have to lead the process. Even though many Cuban Americans see the need for a real break in strategy, the community itself cannot generate this kind of change-focused agenda. Even while taking the initiative to move forward with new policies, the administration will have to find ways to engage Cuban Americans and win their support, yet avoid being entrapped by the divisions within the community.

Without such leadership from the administration, one can expect a stalemate in U.S. policy, which in effect hands the Cuban government the lead in shaping U.S.-Cuba relations. As underscored throughout this book, the Cuban government's interests are to preserve power. Incremental and cosmetic changes will help buy the Cuban government time until energy revenues come online and relieve the financial pressures on the Cuban state. The risk here is not with a strategy of engagement. Rather, it is with a failure to innovate and create a policy that sustains the pressure for change, mobilizes international consensus toward this end, and keeps the focus on supporting Cubans who are committed to shaping their own political and economic future.

The discussions in the simulation highlighted that there is a window of opportunity—or perhaps a window of necessity—for the United States and the international community to support policies that can help diversify access to resources and power in Cuba. The global recession has affected the generosity of Cuba's traditional friends, exacerbating economic hardship on the island. The Cuban state may see itself obliged to permit small-enterprise development and to grant people titles to their homes and land, so that they can use their property as a source of capital. These measures, if introduced soon, may provide a counterbalance to the resource infusions into state coffers when energy revenues come online. Politically, this kind of concrete agenda is important in the United States to sustain the interest and commitment of Cuban Americans, especially those in the older generation who want to see progress in their lifetimes.

Misconceptions and lack of information concerning existing legislation can end up constraining the creation of more effective policies. They should not. For example, during the simulation some participants seemed resigned that the Helms-Burton Act would preclude significant policy change and that building coalitions in Congress to change the law would be an insurmountable task. For some, the idea of amending legislation touched a raw nerve, since many saw changing a law such as Helms-Burton as offering permanent change to Cuba in return for little or nothing from the island's leaders. These misperceptions led to a subsequent special session on the legal underpinnings of the embargo (see appendix A), in the course of which it became clear to the group that authority to change most aspects of the embargo lies with the president and does not require legislative action. This realization boosted the group's morale and strengthened its interest in pursuing the policy road map laid out in chapter 2.

This session also taught participants important lessons about perspectives on "making concessions to the Castros" and how to present the concept of a unilateral U.S. approach to policy. After fifty years of stalemate, the perception is entrenched in the Cuban American community that any change in policy is a "concession." Within this group, a driving point became that the goal of U.S. policy had to change to a focus on change from within and that, by consequence, changes in policy that entail engaging Cubans are not concessions, but tools in implementing a strategy to reach this goal.

Still, some tensions emerged when participants delved into more fundamental questions of trade, investment, and political engagement. The question arose as to whether U.S. policy should reflect reciprocity from the Cuban government. Should the United States unconditionally move to deepen engagement and provide more support, such as engagement through the international financial institutions that could benefit the Cuban government? The group agreed that formal conditionality would be counterproductive. If conditions are codified on paper, it is guaranteed that the Cuban government will never meet them. Rather, the United States can make clear what policy direction it wishes to take and then decide when it wishes to take those steps. In that sense, U.S. policy would be unilateral, not tied to specific Cuban benchmarks. But it would not be blind to Cuban actions.

In a very general sense, the Brookings Institution's Cuba project may be instructive for the administration and its leadership on Cuba policy regarding its approach to the Cuban American community. From this simulation it became clear that members of the Cuban American community working on the project wanted consensus if they could get it. When presented with a road map that eventually became the policy recommendations in chapter 2, the Cuban American representatives and others in the group engaged fervently to merge substance and politics to create a viable agenda. Consensus on a strong agenda may well be within reach if the administration is willing to put forward creative ideas and consult with the community.

SIMULATION SCENARIO NO. 6
CONTEXTUAL BACKGROUND TO EXERCISE

The following scenario was given to the participants.

December 2, 2010. Young Cuban American professionals, members of the group Iniciativa Cuba en el Siglo 21 (the Cuba Initiative for the Twenty-First Century) have convened a broad cross-section of the Cuban American community at Miami's Biltmore Hotel. The initiative's membership consists of all ages and political trends, but has considerably more moderates and liberals than conservatives. There are no hard-liners in their ranks, but many are protesting outside.

The chairman of the event is a former ambassador who believes that it is time to shape a common vision toward Cuba that the majority of the community can endorse.

This bold initiative reflects the fact that much has changed since the election of President Barack Obama in 2008.

Over 150,000 Americans have traveled to Cuba over the past year, following the administration's decision to license people-to-people group travel for educational, cultural, humanitarian, religious, and professional purposes. The annual flow of remittances is estimated at two billion dollars.

The House of Representatives voted overwhelmingly to lift the travel ban entirely, but it is unclear whether the bill will pass the Senate. A bill permitting U.S. oil companies to develop Cuba's offshore oil passed the Senate in November 2009 but has not passed the House. The U.S. Treasury may license U.S. oil companies to work with Cuba to develop its offshore oil reserves, in order to counter the concern that if U.S. companies are prevented from doing so, Russian or Venezuelan companies may acquire concessions located less than sixty miles off the Florida coast.

The Organization of American States is debating conditions for Cuba's reinstatement as a member, and Cuban officials are attending OAS meetings on regional issues.

The Cuban government has doubled the number of family businesses permitted to operate in the tourist sector. More Cubans are seen in tourist hotels, usually visiting with Americans or Cuban American family members and friends. There are an estimated million cell phones on the island; Internet access has improved, but government restrictions on connectivity continue.

Cuban civil society is growing, and there are about fifty political prisoners. Generous donations from abroad have enabled Catholic and Protestant churches to take on unprecedented responsibility for the provision of community services, providing employment and learning opportunities for Cuban youths. The New Coalition and the Jóvenes youth groups put on popular musical and cultural events throughout the island.

Ironically, political change may be greater in south Florida than in Cuba. The Obama administration's decision to allow the unimpeded flow of Cuban Americans to Cuba has changed the terms of the debate within the community.

In Miami's Cuban American community, visiting Cuba is a popular and acceptable way of linking to family and friends and exploring roots. Cuban Americans have financed businesses and repaired homes of family members in Cuba. They also provide capital for informal loans, small businesses, food, medicines, and much more. Increasingly, they talk about playing a role in Cuba's future. Many Cuban Americans plan to trade and invest and to build second homes on the island.

Conservatives still vehemently demand that the Cuban government hold elections before the U.S. government makes any "concessions." They are determined that the travel ban for all Americans not be lifted. Their position is well defended by Cuban American legislators in the Senate and House.

The Obama administration prefers to move forward cautiously, fearing that Cuban authorities are unlikely to undertake democratic or economic reforms and that it will be criticized by conservatives if it moves too fast. Its bottom line is to position the United States so that it will be able to seize the initiative once both Raúl and Fidel Castro are out of power.

But most in the Cuban American community want a proactive policy and are ready to accept an end to the embargo. Some fear that the administration is moving too slowly and that they will be left out. Some anxiously await a leader who will unite the community behind a new strategy.

Most of those attending this summit hope that they can devise an agenda of common actions and objectives. With such an agenda in hand, they hope to push the administration to adopt a much more for-ward-looking approach to Cuba.

Role-Play No. 6: "A Meeting of the Cuban American Community"

There were no assigned roles for this simulation exercise. Brookings advisers and special guests were invited to present what they believed would be the position of Cuban American leaders and organizations of these leaders' choice.

The following instructions were given to participants in this simula-tion. Knowing these instructions increases understanding and helps readers interpret the course of the dialogue.

All the major Cuban American groups, academics, and civic and reli-gious leaders are attending the summit organized by young profession-als and chaired by a prominent Cuban American diplomat, Ambassador Carlos Martinez. Public commentary in the run-up to the meeting has been broadly favorable, but the Cuban Liberty Council has been out-spoken in its opposition and is boycotting the event.

Ambassador Martinez opens the discussion by stressing that the time has come for the community to reach a consensus on U.S. policy toward Cuba because the old policy of regime change has failed. There is a win-dow of opportunity now. The Obama administration is open to a more moderate policy, and the aging Castro brothers cannot withstand the march of time much longer. Most important, both Cuban Americans and Cubans want to reconcile their differences and prepare for a demo-cratic, prosperous, and peaceful future for Cuba.

I. The Role of Cuban Americans in U.S. Policy toward Cuba

Ambassador Martinez and the young professionals believe that if the Cuban American community develops a consensus strategy, it will play a powerful, proactive, and positive role in shaping U.S. relations with Cuba. To this end, the meeting will address the following issues in the hope that doing so will help them chart a way forward:

—Is a consensus on Cuban policy possible in the community?

—Is there a Cuban American champion—an individual or an organi-zation—that has the vision and courage to bring the community together behind an agenda for engagement?

—Should Cuban Americans continue to attempt to control U.S. policy toward Cuba? Would it be better to lower the level of Cuban American influence in order to allow the administration to fashion a Cuba policy that reflects U.S. national interests rather than Cuban American opinion?

II. A Positive Cuban American Agenda for Change

Assuming that the Cuban American community wants to shape U.S. policy, it must devise a strategy that will articulate its members' common views and an agenda of priority actions that they would like the administration to take.

—What should be the principal issues on the U.S. government's diplomatic agenda with the Cuban government? Should there be bilateral talks? Should the president or other high-level officials meet with Raúl Castro? Should a U.S. ambassador to Cuba be appointed?

—What should the United States expect of Cuba in the areas of human rights, democracy, economic reform, and the resolution of longstanding issues such as Guantánamo and expropriated property?

—What should the strategy be for integrating Cuba into the hemispheric architecture (OAS) and international financial institutions?

Abridged Minutes

Abridged minutes from the simulation are provided to enable study of the kinds of exchanges that took place among the participants. The first half of the minutes consists of presentations made by various representatives of the Cuban American community. These presentations helped frame the evolving views in the community, and set the context for the simulation that followed. The second part of the minutes records the exchange during the simulation exercise.

Presentations by Representatives of the Cuban American Community

A transition in the balance of power within the Cuban American community is under way. The hard line is losing ground as its adherents age, while the desire for greater engagement is taking ever more dynamic forms and gaining adherents as younger second-generation Cuban Americans and more recent emigrés seek to take the reins. They perceive that the greater the engagement between the exile community and

Cuban society in Cuba, the greater the chances for them to move positive changes along in Cuba. Brookings advisers and special guests presented their views on this transition.

1. THE VIEWS OF A CUBAN AMERICAN POLITICIAN

There has been a generational change in Miami. The Democratic
Party has recently begun to take advantage of this by fielding candidates
for the U.S. House of Representatives in the Florida district, by registering voters, and raising funds. For the first time, Cuba-related issues,
rather than gaining votes for the Republican incumbent, have cost votes
because more and more Cuban Americans are opposed to the hard line.
They and many others who have arrived from Cuba more recently will
shift the vote from the hard line—which is to maintain the isolation of
Cuba—to one that favors closer ties with Cuba. Today there are more
Cuban Americans who arrived after 1980 than those who came before,
and they're having an impact on the debate in Miami. Whereas the
older generation was de-linked from Cuba, more recent immigrants
wish to be linked to Cuba, as do younger U.S-born Cuban Americans
who wish to discover their roots. The opening up of travel to Cuba by
Cuban Americans is going to lead to a policy that is more responsible
and responsive toward the Cuban people.

2. A SECOND-GENERATION CUBAN AMERICAN

A series of crises between the United States and Cuba was instrumental in influencing the views of the younger generation, including the
balsero crisis (mass migration of 1994), the shoot-down of the Brothers
to the Rescue civilian aircraft by the government of Cuba, and Cuban
American outrage over the return of Elián González, the child found at
sea in 1999, to his father in Cuba. Regardless of the stance taken, the
events shaped the framework of the younger generation's view of Cuba.
It contributed to a narrative of good and evil, one where good was said
to triumph eventually, reinforcing the belief that the Cuban system
would fall apart once Fidel Castro died. But when Fidel Castro fell ill
and the transition was at last at hand, events did not unfold as anticipated. The narrative that this generation believed was based on the
older generation's vision and it did not materialize. These facts created
considerable frustration for young second-generation Cuban Americans
and drove a shift in attitudes: young Cuban Americans grasp that in

order to understand their heritage, they must be linked to Cuba. The Cuban American exile community must realize that the Cuban American cause will evaporate if young second-generation Cuban Americans do not have direct contact with the island; they will become nonplayers. Change toward democracy is unlikely to come about without exchange. There can be *no hay cambio sin intercambio*—no change without exchange.

3. A FIRST-WAVE CUBAN AMERICAN

Like more and more members of his generation, this man who arrived in Florida without his parents as a Peter Pan child shortly after the 1959 Revolution recently came to believe that a democratic Cuba with a prosperous economy is in the long-term interest of the United States. Many first-wave Cuban immigrants, recognizing the shortcomings of a policy of isolation that is more stringent today than during George W. Bush's first term, now see that the United States cannot impose democracy from outside and so must help to create an enabling environment that will allow the Cuban people to make their voices heard in Cuba. The United States, by engaging both the government and civil society, will have a greater opportunity to get to know the players, identify potential change agents, and help break the monolithic Cuban government. If the U.S. government engages with the Cuban government, it will be able to advocate for political prisoners and more effectively help improve human, civil, and labor rights in a principled way that is respectful of Cuban sovereignty. The role of U.S. civil society organizations, too, will be paramount in helping Cuban civil society free itself of government control.

This participant emphasized that the United States ought to act in its interest and that of the Cuban people, and move away from a dependence on what the Cuban hierarchy does or does not do—which has in effect given Cuba veto power over U.S. actions. The United States should not expect too much in terms of immediate results from the process nor should it be surprised if the Cuban government turns a cold shoulder: the status quo has been convenient and valuable to the Cuban government, and it has a history of resorting to confrontation, occasionally creating crises whenever U.S. presidents tried to relax relations in the past. It is time to take Cuba out of the context of a bilateral conflict and place it into a multilateral setting. The president and secretary of state should engage the OAS and a group of key nations to lead the way in terms of engaging Cuba and returning it to a hemispheric context.

4. A FIRST-WAVE CUBAN AMERICAN BUSINESSMAN

Agreeing with the earlier participants on the rationale to open policy toward Cuba, this participant emphasized that the Obama administration should lift the travel ban but not expect receptivity from Cuba. The United States ought to do what the Cuban hierarchy doesn't want it to do, namely, open up to Cuba and allow the vast powers of U.S. civil society to permeate Cuba and begin to prompt change.

5. A FIRST-WAVE CUBAN AMERICAN ACADEMIC

Cuban Americans themselves are becoming the catalysts for change in U.S. policy toward Cuba. The administration needs to consider how it can encourage Cuban Americans to develop a serious relationship with Cuba. Conservative Cuban Americans, who desire an isolationist policy, have been traditionally and hope to remain the gatekeepers of U.S. Cuba policy. But today, moderate Cuban Americans who want to engage Cuba are in the majority and therefore ought to have more influence, especially because they represent a large and growing bloc of Democratic voters. They want a more open U.S. policy so that they can both engage and maintain the Cuban American community's relevance to new policy. The difficulty, of course, is that there are trade-offs. Permitting Cuban Americans to travel allows them to remain to some degree in the center of U.S. policy, whereas allowing all Americans to travel would reduce Cuban American influence and, potentially, opportunity in Cuba.

Simulation Scenario No. 6:
"A Meeting of the Cuban American Community"

On December 2, 2010, Ambassador Martinez opened the meeting at the Biltmore by pointing out that the administration's decision to permit Cuban Americans to travel and send remittances to Cuba had led to an even greater realization that there was a need for a common strategic approach to Cuba. He stated that there was agreement within the community that sustainable change would materialize in Cuba only from within, and the community did not know how to move that agenda forward. The United States government had done the easy things: restrictions on Cuban American travel and remittances had been eased; exchange programs are already under way; the sale of medicines and agricultural commodities to Cuba had increased, and there was greater openness on the issue of humanitarian relief. Where should policy go next?

Martinez suggested that the group begin by identifying the cornerstone policy issues, so that the participants would be aware of what was needed to change these policies, then systematically discuss these policy areas. The group could begin by discussing how the United States might phase in the normalization of relations and discuss the impact of lifting economic sanctions. Would the group be prepared to advocate for this? Finally, the group would end with a discussion about reconciliation.

I. The Role of Cuban Americans in U.S. Policy toward Cuba

A former Cuban activist said that no previous U.S. election had had so much impact on Cubans as that of Barack Obama. Everyone in Cuba was pleased with Barack Obama's election, and this in turn made it more difficult for the Cuban hierarchy to portray the United States as a threat. The fact that Cubans identify with the U.S. president had led the Cuban government to take some steps toward allowing Afro-Cubans to be integrated into the formerly all-white tourist-sector workforce. This positive image of the United States would be reinforced if the Obama administration lifted the travel ban and authorized private remittances to Cuban citizens and civil society entities. Visits by North Americans, not just Cuban Americans, are important. They are called the "Yuma" and represent prosperity and liberty. Money transfers provide capital for informal "banks" that with a phone call from a person in the United States will lend to the Cuban borrower who might be an individual setting up a small business or a civil society organization carrying out good works.

But even the Obama administration is subject to Miami's influence, and this slows or stops measures that could help Cubans and could grow civil society. Therefore he advocated that U.S. policy should not pass through Miami. U.S. policy must be freed of Miami's passions if it is to bring about change in Cuba.

A Cuban American academic responded that Miami is not entirely the problem because it has been changing for the better, not only in the recent past but over the twenty years since the end of the cold war. Initially, the political leadership of Cuban Miami thought of itself as deciding the future of Cuba. Slowly and sometimes painfully, over the course of the 1990s, this began to change because of the connections between Cuban Americans in Miami and dissidents on the island. Miami came to understand that change in Cuba was going to come from within Cuba, and not be imposed from the outside by Cuban Americans. They also began to acquire an understanding of what the real Cuba was like. It was not the Cuba of fifty years ago. Too much had changed. And for many Cuban Americans who had arrived since the 1980s, family was more important than politics. These circumstances bode quite well for the future reconciliation of Cubans and, along with President Obama's lifting restrictions on Cuban American travel and remittances, have once again allowed Cuban Americans to be ambassadors to the Cuban people.

A prominent Cuban businessman said that what the administration had done was too little, too late. There is growing frustration among Cuban Americans because Cuba's leaders, by continuing to reject real reform, are blocking the process. Yet the Cuban American community itself has been an obstacle to change because Cuba's leaders have manipulated the views of Cuban Americans in order to maintain internal control. The Cuban government is jeopardized by a more open relationship with the Cuban American community and the United States. Cuba's leaders have found and continue to find it easier to make only marginal changes. The United States then conditions its actions on Cuba's behavior, and in so doing continues to cede influence over how events in Cuba play out.

Still, an opinion leader pointed out, as the amount of information flowing to Cuba increases and as the internal opposition expands in breadth and bravery, the Cuban hierarchy will be pressed to change. It is very difficult for proud and determined Cuban leaders to come to terms with this. An influential part of the Cuban American community in Miami is equally stubborn and proud. Both sides are intent on a zero-sum game. Both have a need to win. That makes it very difficult to begin a process of national reconciliation.

An academic said that reaching consensus would be an elusive ideal; it had never worked in fifty years. For the Obama administration to expect a consensus to emerge out of Miami would therefore be illusory.

Rather, the administration should not underestimate the power of its bully pulpit to help the Cubans in Miami understand alternatives to the policy status quo. In her view only the White House could rise to the occasion and begin to lead Cuban Americans in Miami toward acceptance of a new policy approach. This is true simply because there has never been a significant political leader who has argued for anything other than the status quo.

If the administration fails to lead those in Miami who hold moderate views, they may become weary and worried and withdraw from the debate, a Cuban American opinion leader stated. The window of opportunity is closing. If the United States and Cuba are to reconcile, the Obama administration will have to take decisive action on game-changing policies. The administration's failure to lead on Cuba policy will again cede the whole issue to the Republicans.

An academic asked if this might be the moment for the Cuban American community to take the initiative by engaging not just the United States government but the Cuban government as well.

Cuban Americans have become an important element in the calculations of the Cuban government because remittances are a large and growing source of income. If the United States allowed the community to be more directly involved in the financing of small businesses and in providing greater economic resources in a more systematic and global way rather than just one family member to another, the Cuban American community could bring to bear substantial pressure on the Cuban government. If the administration provided the opening, Cuban Americans could become directly involved in financing small businesses. If Cuban Americans were permitted to increase their economic relationship with Cubans it would enhance their political influence because without this assistance, the livelihoods and well-being of the Cubans would be reduced, and the Cuban government would not want to lose this source of foreign exchange. Therefore a broad group of Cuban Americans would have leverage if it could come together around an issue to open a dialogue with the Cuban government directly. The release of political prisoners might be one such issue.

Another participant disagreed with this vision: the danger of a direct dialogue between Cuban Americans and the Cuban government is that neither the United States nor other Cuban Americans can control its outcome.

Another Cuban American worried that little could be accomplished if such a position were adopted. In his view, an odd, unstable dynamic has emerged on the island. Meanwhile, Cuban American attitudes have become more realistic than they were, but are not as advanced as might be hoped. This will potentially cause a fork in the road for the community. Some will argue that the community will need to do something much more radical because incremental changes don't produce the desired outcome. Others will argue the opposite. The ensuing divisions might make consensus elusive.

Ambassador Martinez then asked how the community might proceed if it cannot reach consensus. Should it tell the White House to advance its own policy, even though the community cannot guarantee that it will back the policy?

A Cuban American opinion leader thought that the administration could avoid being denounced by hard-liners within the community if the White House, like the Republicans, used surrogates to forge policy, relying on select Cuban American organizations for this purpose. President Obama wouldn't have to be the architect of a controversial Cuba policy, because there are enough points of consensus within the Cuban American progressive community to allow the president to design and lead a more open and engaged approach to Cuba using surrogates. According to a Cuban American academic, a very robust cultural diplomacy strategy would be the top priority for policy. Fostering the interaction of civil society on both sides of the Florida Straits is most likely to promote diverse voices and reform in Cuba. Miami is already culturally engaged, but more is needed.

Mechanisms to expand and fund educational exchanges, promote the arts, and allow NGOs to interact freely with civil society in Cuba would need to be found. But no new policies can be effective if they are linked to a strategy of regime change or state building, as has been the case with many of USAID-funded activities, especially those tied to Cuban American groups that hold a specific ideology. The Obama administration should therefore align itself with the progressive sector of the Cuban American community. This is the sector that voted for him and expects that he will spearhead a real change in policy, even if there is no consensus within the community.

II. A Positive Cuban American Agenda for Change

Next, Ambassador Martinez asked what the Cuban American community expected from its relationship with Cuba and with the Cuban people. How should policy promote democracy and human rights? Can policy give a voice to people who are imprisoned for expressing their views?

Ambassador Martinez reminded the players that they are in 2010; the international situation, though similar to today's, is starting to change. Venezuela's President Chávez has amended the constitution and been reelected. He and the Russians are creating commotion in eastern Europe and in the Middle East to keep oil prices high, and Chinese growth has resumed at a double-digit pace. Cuba retains the support of Venezuela, Russia, China, and other countries, insulating the government from the necessity of relinquishing state control of key sectors of the economy. So, reluctantly, the group agreed that it would take a complete change in the structure of the Cuban economy before the country can hope for further Western and U.S. influence to have a positive impact on the Cuban government.

A Cuban American businessman picked up on this theme, pointing out that this view is not necessarily correct, because after the 2008 hurricanes, even with Chávez's support, Cuba continued to owe more than $500 million to one of its preferred trading partners, Sherritt International. Thus, Cuba in 2010 is in the same situation as prior to 1991, when it was dependent on the Soviet Union. Cuba will have to diversify its partners and adopt market-based transparency if it is to survive and reduce its dependency on Venezuela. Cuba's leaders recognize that this dependency makes Cuba extremely vulnerable, just as in 1991. If the United States opens the economic gate, a large number of U.S. corporations will seek commercial and trade relationships on the island. In the first years, this will likely not include capital investment, because making large investments in Cuba is too risky, but many U.S. companies will set up commercial relationships and their presence will lead to positive relations and potentially to a dialogue for change within Cuba.

Ambassador Martinez pointed out his concern that as the administration moved toward a more open policy it would begin to lose consensus. How could it maintain consensus as policy advanced beyond easing Cuban American travel and initiating strategies to empower the Cuban people?

A Cuban American politician reminded participants that every time Democrats take hard-line positions on Cuba, they lose not only within the core group of Cubans who would likely vote for a Democrat, but among all Cuban American voters. Since U.S. policy toward Cuba is a Republican issue, a Democratic candidate cannot gain votes by trying to erode Cuban American support for status-quo Cuba policies. Rather, he or she gains votes by addressing wider social issues not directly related to Cuba. This in turns allows Democratic candidates more freedom to take game-changing positions on Cuba. Nevertheless, Democrats should not leave the Cuban American community behind because of a lack of consensus. Rather, they should take positions that have relatively wide support within the progressive community and build consensus around them.

Still, a Cuban American academic pointed out, the concern about splitting the community remained valid. As the administration moves forward on the relatively easier issues of opening up people-to-people travel and cultural and educational exchanges, it will retain the support of Democrats and independents. But it will lose support across party lines when it takes the paradigm-shifting initiatives. Yet it can only promote the big changes in Cuba if it risks losing support, because only a radical shift in policy, including allowing trade and investment with Cuba, will succeed in fostering a democratic Cuba.

In response to Ambassador Martinez's question about establishing normalized diplomatic relations with Cuba, a former U.S. diplomat pointed out that if the United States wishes to send an ambassador to Cuba, it will have to begin by establishing, or reestablishing, lines of communication. The United States will need a bilateral relationship on a number of issues. In the past this dialogue was on migration, the narcotics trade, and the environment. The United States must also reestablish the underpinnings of a long-term relationship that includes diplomatic representation providing Americans access to Cuban officials, permission and ability to travel freely, and ease of social interaction with Cuban civil society. With these underpinnings the United States can then send an ambassador because he or she will be able to carry out the full range of diplomatic duties necessary to represent the United States. A United States ambassador must have sufficient tools to manage an effective embassy that provides the information and insights that the president and the secretary of state need to make informed decisions for a judicious and thoughtful Cuba policy. In the recent past, U.S. emissaries in Cuba have been used by the administration to articulate an ideological point of view rather than to manage a relationship with the Cuban government.

Within this framework, Ambassador Martinez asked whether there is a symbolic importance of opening a full embassy in Cuba, and if so, what should the timing of such an act be? Should an emerging relationship with Cuba be top-down or bottom-up? In other words, should there be a greater emphasis on opening up cultural exchanges, economic exchanges, and travel, or on trying to have high-level dialogue between the American and Cuban governments?

A Cuba expert responded that the one advantage to naming an ambassador to Cuba is that it has symbolic weight. The United States accredits ambassadors to friendly as well as relatively hostile governments. A Cuban American academic noted that bilateral relations would be strengthened by rebuilding the diplomatic functions of the United States and Cuban Interest Sections that currently exist in Washington and Havana so that they could begin to function more like embassies. During the Carter administration, opening the interest sections in the two capitals was a major first step toward normalization of relations. To be on the field fully, the United States will need diplomatic relations.

However, a Cuba expert warned that the political logic of upgrading diplomatic relations would be difficult to justify absent foreseeable practical gains. It would be unprecedented for the United States to have diplomatic relations and also retain the embargo. Normalization of relations and the accreditation of an ambassador would need to be coupled with a rationale—a new agreement on immigration, narcotics trafficking, or counterterrorism cooperation might make the exchange of ambassadors valuable.

A Cuban American warned that the United States should not assume that the Cuban government shared its motives. For the time being, the Cuban government doesn't want a prosperous society that might unravel its system of control.

A U.S. diplomat challenged this idea, asserting that the Cuban hierarchy will have to change. He cited the fact that the Chinese leadership had acknowledged that it couldn't resist political and democratic change within China, and its focus turned to managing the change from the provincial level instead of the village and municipality level. Chinese leaders seem to believe that if they don't make these political changes, their hold on power will fade: economic prosperity, communication, and external travel make future political change a certainty.

A Cuba expert responded that although he believed that in time the same dynamic would take hold in Cuba, it would not happen in the near term. The Cuban people are still in an early stage of developing contacts and communications with the rest of the world, and the economic dynamism necessary to create social pressures for change are not in full force.

Ambassador Martinez returned to the question of what the United States should do next—how it could build on cultural, educational, and other openings toward the Cuban people and civil society.

An American journalist responded that removing Cuba from the State Department's list of state sponsors of terrorism would improve the political environment between the two countries. A Cuban American added that the embargo should have been lifted when the Soviet Union fell apart. Another participant disagreed with both of them: two issues that he would not change until normalization occurred were lifting the U.S. embargo and taking Cuba off the terrorist list.

An academic suggested that the best thing to do would be to dissolve U.S. government–funded assistance programs devoted exclusively to dissidents as well as the position of special coordinator for Cuba affairs, created by the Bush administration and now vacant. Doing so would promote a process of dialogue.

The history of conditionality shows that continuing that policy will be unlikely to put the two countries on a path toward normalization, whereas economic engagement is a force that cannot be controlled and opens up doors. Small-business formation could stimulate change, as could foreign investment, but Cuba's labor laws and monetary policy do not provide for a competitive environment. Property claims and demands for access to U.S.-held frozen Cuban assets will have to be resolved before real progress can be made on the economic side.

One participant concluded that touching any subject on the agenda of U.S.-Cuba relations would be burdened with fifty years of history and legislation that make it very difficult to move forward. The new U.S. administration probably would not have the time and patience to

deal with each of these difficulties one by one. The United States has
not had a foreign policy toward Cuba since the 1970s, and this will
continue to be the case unless the administration shows some independence from the Cuban American community.

A diplomat pointed out that Congress, not only the president and secretary of state, has a role to play in a new policy toward Cuba. He
advised that legislators repeal the restrictive Helms-Burton Act in order to
free up the president to design a policy of his own choosing toward Cuba.
Repealing restrictive legislation would allow the president to pick and
choose the elements of his foreign policy toward the island. He wouldn't
have to lift the embargo or establish normal diplomatic relations.

A Cuban American asked what the U.S. position might be with
regard to Radio Martí. Shouldn't the Obama administration at least
change the top management, which has followed an aggressive hard line
on Cuba? It would be important for new management to make a commitment to good journalistic practices on the air, including standardized
language. When Radio Martí moved from Washington to Miami, it
became politicized and thus forfeited any claim to meeting international
journalistic standards. Radio Martí should be run like Radio Free
Europe and the Voice of America. The amount of pain and heartache
that any administration would have to go through to make the station
more professional would be considerable, but new and credible management would go a long way toward meeting this goal.

Ambassador Martinez asked what a meeting between President
Obama or Secretary Clinton and Raúl Castro would signify. It would
certainly be a bold moment symbolically and could potentially have a
major impact on setting a substantive direction for policy, but would it
be wise and could the potential of such a meeting be realized?

A U.S. diplomat responded that the lead-up to such a meeting could
establish a process for the resolution of tough bilateral issues such as
property claims, cooperation on the narcotics trade, and crime, and set
an agenda for a dialogue on migration, the environment, and dealing
with natural disasters. It could also lead to discussions in areas of concern such as human rights, democracy, and political transparency. It
might also establish a list of easy deliverables agreed to in advance that
would be announced regardless of progress on other issues. Other topics to be discussed at such a meeting might be educational and cultural
exchanges with Cuba that lead to people-to-people contacts. In the

event that nothing more happens via government channels, there could still be very visible and positive developments on a people-to-people level. Also under discussion would be potential actions that could be sponsored by the Cuban American community—actions that demonstrate outreach from the Cuban American community to Cubans on the island.

A Cuba expert's summary was that if and when the administration formulates a policy toward Cuba, it should be done like a big guy, not timidly. For too long the United States has relied on the timid and small-minded to dictate policy toward Cuba. If the United States wants to see a democratic Cuba, it must formulate a policy toward Raúl's government that includes a dialogue on sensitive issues such as human rights and race. How would President Obama deal with the dual narrative of racial politics in Cuba? The land of equality versus the land of inequality?

To close the meeting, Ambassador Martinez turned to the question of whether the United States should consider approving or not objecting to the engagement of the OAS and other multilateral institutions with Cuba.

An opinion leader pointed out that regional and multilateral engagement would tend to promote change and would be an opportunity to press Cuba to live up to the standards required for membership in international institutions. This could be achieved by the United States simply by not objecting to Cuba's participation. Participants considered that the Helms-Burton Act's requirement of a presidential veto of Cuba's membership in the OAS and other international organizations might tie the president's hands, despite the executive branch's official power to set foreign policy. Assuming, however, that there are no legislative obstacles to formal or informal engagement of Cuba by the Inter-American Development Bank, the International Monetary Fund, and the World Bank, these institutions could develop important frameworks for future assistance programs. The reintegration of Cuba into the international community was well under way: the desire of the international community to engage Cuba through multilateral initiatives has been reinforced by Cuba's choice to be an active and important player in the UN system. Indeed, Cuba's cooperation with the UN Human Rights Commission presents opportunities for multilateral engagement on the most fundamental issue for the United States and its partners, the human rights situation in Cuba.

Participants concluded that a multilateral engagement with Cuba by the OAS, the UN, and international financial institutions could form part of a holistic approach toward Cuba in which the United States could either take unilateral action or coordinate with its allies and international partners, as part of a high-level dialogue or at the technical-working-group level.

APPENDIX A

Understanding the Legal Parameters of the U.S. Embargo on Cuba

This appendix addresses the nature of the U.S. embargo on Cuba. It lays out what is permitted under the embargo, elements that can be modified through regulation, and aspects where legislative changes are necessary to allow for travel and commercial activities.

Included are two articles, one by Vicki Huddleston and Carlos Pascual, first published in the *Miami Herald* on February 24, 2009 (reproduced by permission), and a policy brief drafted by Robert Muse, a Washington, D.C., attorney, and Dóra Beszterczey, a research assistant at the Brookings Institution.

Both writings make clear that the president of the United States, acting through the Treasury Department's Office of Foreign Asset Control (OFAC), has considerable authority to adjust the embargo through regulations and licenses to allow greater flexibility in travel, remittances, and trade. However, congressional action would be needed to change the law so as to permit U.S. citizens to travel to Cuba as tourists.

In addition to explaining the legal underpinnings of the embargo, the piece by Muse and Beszterczey further clarifies the nature of the role of Congress. The Helms-Burton Act of 1996 codified not only the restrictions imposed by the embargo but also the authority of the president to modify it through regulations and licenses. This has important operational significance. In the past, the perception that the act was a barrier to engaging Cuba has deterred innovative approaches to policy, but such perceptions are based on a misinterpretation of the actual parameters of the legislation. There is indeed significant scope to creatively engage Cuba and to use travel, remittances, and trade as tools to get resources to a nascent civil society in that country.

Use "Smart Power" to Help Cubans[1]
VICKI HUDDLESTON AND CARLOS PASCUAL

Contrary to popular myth and public misunderstanding, if President Barack Obama wishes to change the U.S. policy toward Cuba, he has ample authority to do so. If he takes charge of Cuba policy, he can turn the embargo into an effective instrument of "smart power" to achieve the United States' policy objectives in Cuba.

Obama's leadership is needed to change the dynamic between the United States and Cuba. The status quo is no longer an option. Not only has it failed to achieve its goals; it has tarnished our image in the hemisphere and throughout the world. Waiting for Congress to act will only further delay change. Fortunately, even in the case of Cuba, Congress has not materially impaired this country's venerable constitutional arrangement under which the president has the ultimate authority to conduct our foreign affairs.

Executive Authority

Again and again we hear that the embargo can't be changed because the Helms-Burton law codified it. Nothing could be further from the truth. Whether you agree or disagree with the current commercial embargo, the president can effectively dismantle it by using his executive authority. Helms-Burton codified the embargo regulation, but those regulations provide that "all transactions are prohibited except as specifically authorized by the Secretary of the Treasury by means of regulations, rulings, instructions, and licenses."

This means that the president's power remains unfettered. He can instruct the secretary to extend, revise or modify embargo regulations. The proof of this statement is that President Bill Clinton issued new regulations for expanded travel and remittances in order to help individuals and grow civil society.

1. This piece first appeared in the *Miami Herald* on February 24, 2009. Reproduced by permission of the *Miami Herald*.

Obama will have to modify Office of Foreign Assets Control regulations to fulfill his campaign promise to increase Cuban-American travel and remittances. If he wants to reproduce the more open conditions in Cuba that led to the "Cuban Spring" of 2002 and Oswaldo Payá's Varela Project, he could reinstate people-to-people and educational travel. By a simple rule change, he could also speed the entry [into the United States] of life-saving medicines from Cuba, rather than subjecting them to delays from cumbersome OFAC licensing procedures.

Since 1992, U.S. law—the Cuban Democracy Act—has sought to expand access to ideas, knowledge and information by licensing telecommunications goods and services. Yet, in practice, regulations are so strictly interpreted that the United States in effect is imposing a communications embargo on Cuba. To lift it, the president can authorize a general license for the donation and sale of radios, televisions and computers. In addition, rather than helping Cuban state security keep Yoani Sánchez [a prominent award-winning blogger in Cuba whose "Generation Y" blog gets more than one million hits each month] and others off the Internet, the Obama administration could make Internet technology readily available so that any barriers to communications would be clearly the fault of the Cuban government, and not ours.

Environmental concerns rate high with the Obama administration. So it might open bilateral discussions, exchange information and license the provision of scientific equipment to improve the health of the ocean and success of commercial fisheries.

The United States Geological Survey estimates that the North Cuba Basin holds 5.5 billion barrels of oil and 9.8 trillion cubic feet of natural gas reserves. If the president wishes, he can instruct the secretary of the treasury to license U.S. companies to explore, exploit and transport these resources that we and the region so badly need.

Failed Policy

After a half-century of failed policy, there is enormous support in the Cuban-American community for initiatives that will improve the well being and independence of the Cuban people. What they didn't know—but know now—is that there is no reason they can't reach out to the Cuban people and still retain the embargo as symbol of their concern about the Cuban government's failure to live up to international norms of human rights, democracy and transparency.

The U.S. Embargo on Cuba:
What Is Required to End It and How Might That Happen?
ROBERT MUSE AND DÓRA BESZTERCZEY

The statute that authorizes the U.S. embargo on Cuba is the Trading with the Enemy Act (title 50, United States Code), which provides the president, in the broadest terms, with the authority to institute and maintain economic sanctions on countries deemed hostile to the United States.

The Treasury Department's Office of Foreign Assets Control (OFAC) has been delegated the authority to administer the U.S. embargo on Cuba and does so under the Cuban Asset Control Regulations (CACR). Therefore, as a practical matter, the embargo is a set of provisions that have been promulgated one by one, individually, through OFAC rulemaking.

Executive Branch Authority and the Helms-Burton Act

The executive branch's power to extend, revise, and modify the CACR's embargo provisions is virtually unfettered. Because the Helms-Burton Act of 1996 codified the Cuban regulations verbatim, it also codified C.F.R. §515.201, which provides that "all . . . transactions are prohibited except as specifically authorized by the Secretary of the Treasury . . . by means of regulations, rulings, instructions, licenses or otherwise."

The Helms-Burton Act thus left untouched the executive branch's authority to modify the embargo on Cuba. Indeed, OFAC's authority to modify and suspend elements of the CACR-based embargo on Cuba is reiterated periodically in the regulations. Given OFAC's express power to modify the embargo through the creation of new regulations (either by rulemaking or by the creation of new generally licensed exceptions to the embargo), specific elements of the embargo may thus be rescinded in one of two ways: deletion of the specific regulation from the CACR through an OFAC rulemaking, or the promulgation of a general license authorizing a new activity.

This finding counters two common misapprehensions about the embargo: first, that the embargo on Cuba was "codified" and therefore it will take an act of Congress to rescind its various provisions; and, second, that the Helms-Burton Act conditions lifting the embargo on Cuba on that country's meeting multiple requirements (such as that a democratically elected government must be in power that does not include Fidel or Raúl Castro), with the result that either Helms-Burton must be repealed or its conditions met before important provisions of the embargo can be lifted. Although Helms-Burton must be repealed in order for fully normalized relations to resume between the United States and Cuba, it is not a ban to incremental relaxations and even rescissions of key aspects of the current embargo.

Easing Elements of the Embargo

The executive branch can modify substantial elements of the embargo in three ways:

1. By promulgating new regulations
2. By issuing specific licenses permitting new activities involving Cuba
3. By generally licensing hitherto prohibited dealings with that country

Should the president wish to pursue a calibrated rapprochement with Cuba to create the foundations for a negotiated normalization of relations, the broad resumption of travel to Cuba under §515.565(b)(2) by U.S. citizens would be an obvious place to start. President Clinton acted under this authority in January 1999 when he created new categories of approved travel to Cuba via a general license, allowing U.S. citizens to compete in athletic competitions in Cuba, and created a new license specifically for so-called "people-to-people" educational travel to Cuba, which authorized travel-related and other transactions directly incident to nonacademic educational exchanges organized by private foundations and research and educational institutes for noncommercial purposes "to promote people-to-people contact."

Modifications affecting permitted commercial activities, usually seen as the last vestiges of the policy, can also be made. A bilateral trade gesture may thus be the next logical step, for which regulations prohibiting trade may be rescinded by the Treasury Department through a rulemaking, or that agency may generally license a class of products for importation into the United States. For example, a rule change to 31 C.F.R. §515.204 would generally license the importation of Cuban-origin agricultural products. Such a step would reciprocate U.S. producers' current access to the Cuban market, which renders making the case for the change reasonably simple. It would also support Cuba's small farmers, who are increasingly cultivating formerly state-controlled agricultural land and are selling the produce to the Cuban government. In a similar way, U.S. products may be generally licensed for export to Cuba.

The Peculiar Problem of Travel Restrictions

In 2000, the Trade Sanctions Reform and Export Enhancement Act (TSRA) became law. Section 910 of TSRA provides that the Treasury Department may not authorize travel-related transactions in Cuba for what the statute terms "touristic activities." The statute defines "touristic activities" as any activity not "expressly authorized in any of paragraphs (1) through (12) of Section §515.560 of the CACR," since that regulation was already in effect on June 1, 2000.[1] As a result of section 910 of TSRA, the general ban on U.S. citizens' travel to Cuba cannot be rescinded through the issuance of an OFAC rule, nor may it be permitted through the creation of a general license. A formal and comprehensive rescission of the ban on tourist travel to Cuba by U.S. citizens will require an act of Congress.

Nevertheless, a large increase in U.S. citizens' travel to Cuba can be achieved by reinstating §515.565(b)(2) "people-to-people" visits to Cuba, a category created in 1999, as well as the other eleven categories of travel authorized in the TSRA. A resumption of such travel can be authorized by executive branch fiat because that category of authorized travel existed on June 1, 2000, when the travel regulations were codified, and is therefore exempt from the prohibitions of that codification. Programs offered by holders of §515.565(b)(2) licenses included Afro-Cuban religion and culture; architectural preservation; Cuban music, art, and dance; natural history; agricultural organization and production, and rural development. Group travel for such broad educational and cultural purposes may be reinstated by the president.

1. The Cuban Asset Control Regulations authorize travel-related transactions to, from, and within Cuba for twelve categories of purposes under the following sections (http://law.justia.com/us/cfr/title31/31-3.1.1.1.4.5.1.54.html): 1. Visits to immediate family (§515.561); 2. Official business of U.S. and foreign governments and intergovernmental organizations (§515.562); 3. Journalistic activity (§515.563); 4. Professional research (§515.564); 5. Educational activities (§515.565); 6. Religious activities (§515.566); 7. Public performances, athletic and other competitions, and exhibitions (§515.567); 8. Support for the Cuban people (§515.574); 9. Humanitarian projects (§515.575); 10. Private foundations or research or educational institutes (§515.576); 11. The exportation, importation, or transmission of information or informational materials (§515.545); 12. Certain export transactions that may be considered for authorization under existing Department of Commerce regulations and guidelines with respect to Cuba or engaged in by U.S.–owned or controlled foreign firms (§515.533 and 515.559).

Helms-Burton versus Lifting the Embargo

Must the conditions mandated by the Helms-Burton Act for the lifting of the embargo be satisfied before the embargo can be lifted? The "termination" of the economic embargo is permitted under section 204(c) of the Helms-Burton Act when the president submits a determination to Congress that "a democratically elected government" is in power in Cuba. Section 206 of the act defines such a government as one that, in addition to meeting the requirements of a transition government, is also a result of free and fair elections; shows respect for the basic civil liberties and human rights of the citizens of Cuba; is substantially moving toward a market-oriented economic system; is committed to making constitutional changes to ensure regular free and fair elections and the full enjoyment of basic civil liberties and human rights; and has made demonstrable progress in returning to U.S. citizens property confiscated by the Cuban government or in providing equitable compensation.

This provision means that the U.S. embargo on Cuba must remain in place until the Helms-Burton Act is repealed or its conditions are met. However, it does not define the embargo itself. Thus, even though only a comprehensive act of Congress can remove all vestiges of the embargo and make possible a full normalization of relations between the United States and Cuba, a multiyear process can be envisioned whereby the secretary of the treasury substantially and progressively removes embargo provisions through licensing. In addition to dismantling provisions that prevent the United States and its citizens from helping the Cuban people and licensing the aforementioned items, the executive branch can permit the sale and donation of communications equipment and the transfer of funds to civil society entities and the Cuban people for activities such as starting and operating micro-enterprises.

The investment of significant U.S. capital in Cuba will likely be constrained until the embargo is formally terminated, because U.S. companies will have to consider the risk that executive branch regulatory provisions could be reinstated as easily as they were rescinded. Investors will also consider the wisdom of investing before the United States and Cuba have completed a bilateral investment treaty, which will have to take into account U.S. citizens' and companies' expropriation claims against Cuba that were certified by the U.S. Foreign Claims Settlement Commission in the 1960s.

APPENDIX B

2008 Florida International University Poll of Cuban American Opinion

In December 2008, the Brookings Institution, in collaboration with Florida International University (FIU) and the Cuba Study Group, released the results of a poll of public opinion among Cuban Americans in south Miami-Dade County, Florida, regarding U.S. policies toward Cuba. The questions focused particularly on travel, remittances, bilateral dialogue, and the embargo. The poll also explored voting patterns in the 2008 presidential and congressional elections. Conducted by the Institute for Public Opinion Research at FIU, the poll was concluded on December 1, 2008, and the results were released the next day. This chapter presents a summary of those results (full results and demographic data are available at www.brookings.edu/~/media/Files/events/2008/1202_cuba_poll/1202_cuba_poll.pdf).

Poll Results in a Historical Context

FIU began polling the Cuban American community in 1991. In 2008, for the first time, the poll found that a majority of participants, 55 percent, favor ending the U.S. embargo against Cuba. This figure has been steadily rising over the past decade: in 1997 only 22 percent of Cuban Americans favored ending the embargo, but by 2004 the percentage had risen to 34 percent; since then the naysayers have slowly given way to this year's majority. With this shift in attitudes, the deeply rooted symbolic construct of the embargo is slowly breaking down and making space for a more realistic and pragmatic approach to crafting an effective policy toward Cuba.

FIGURE B-1. Shifting Attitudes on the U.S. Embargo on Cuba, 1997–2008

Percent

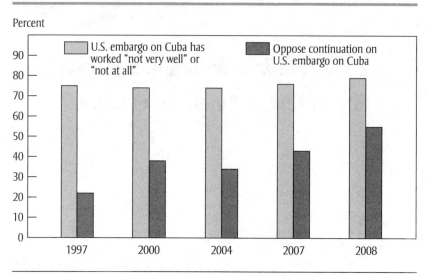

Note: "Don't knows" have been excluded from above data.

With this change, a discrepancy between pragmatism and ideology is growing, evident in a comparison of responses on whether the embargo has "worked" (ideology) versus whether it should be continued (pragmatism). Between 1997 and 2004 the percentage of respondents who were staunch believers in the embargo's effectiveness (ideology) held steady, between 25 and 26 percent, dropping a mere 4 percentage points, to 21 percent, in 2008. Nevertheless, support for the embargo's continuation (pragmatism) fell consistently after 1997, from 72 percent in 1997 to 66 percent in 2004 and to 45 percent in 2008.

The table and chart below provide a detailed comparison of views on the U.S. embargo on Cuba between 1997 and 2008.[1]

The strength of the support among Cuban American voters and the wider community for ending current restrictions on travel and remittances and engaging in direct talks with the Cuban government on issues of mutual concern such as migration shows that pragmatism is coming out on top of ideology—engagement is winning out over isolation. A large portion of the shift is accounted for by those who emigrated after

1. For a historical overview of shifting attitudes to a variety of questions asked in FIU polls over the years, see www.fiu.edu/orgs/ipor/IPORpastProjects.htm#Cuba.

1980 and from younger age groups, but by no means all; this poll also discerns support for engagement from those who left Cuba before 1980, traditional supporters of an isolationist policy toward Cuba.

Democratic and Republican Support: A Bipartisan Movement

It is significant that the high percentage of respondents who expressed support for greater engagement with the Cuban government and contact with the Cuban people crossed party lines. Even though Cuban American votes in the presidential election were split 62 to 38 percent with the majority of Cuban American votes going to the Republican presidential candidate, John McCain, the poll showed that support for a change in U.S.-Cuba relations has a bipartisan base.

It is also important to discern whether U.S. policy toward Cuba was an important motivation among Cuban American voters to vote along party lines. This does not in fact seem to have been the case. Although both Republican presidential and congressional candidates won majorities of the Cuban American vote, the poll revealed the community's support for a departure from Bush administration policy toward one more in line with Barack Obama's policy as outlined in his speech to the Cuban American National Foundation on May 23, 2008—an indication that support for the Republican Party was in large part separate from opinions on Cuba-related issues.

Implications of the Poll Results for U.S. Policy

President-elect Barack Obama came into the White House having campaigned for a return to the more liberal travel and remittance policies of 2003, and this poll demonstrates strong support within the Cuban American community for implementing those changes, as well as for launching direct discussions with Cuba. This poll also shows inroads of Democratic Party influence within the Cuban American community and a continuing shift to more liberal attitudes concerning Cuba policy. Though the results highlight a growing generational gap, the community as a whole is showing increased receptivity to greater engagement with Cuba. As Cuban Americans who arrived in recent years register to vote, the president could find even greater political support for a new policy toward Cuba in the future.

Methodology

The poll surveyed 800 Cuban American respondents randomly selected from a sample representing all Cuban adults living in Miami-Dade County. The sample was based on 2007 American Community Survey (ACS) estimates, and results were weighted to reflect ACS demographic data. Since a large proportion of young adults use only cell phones, the FIU pollsters interviewed 300 cell phone users and 500 landline users. Interviewees included 354 respondents who had arrived from Cuba since 1989. In order to discern effects according to age and voter registration status, the survey disaggregated results along the categories of the respondents' age groups, the year they left Cuba, and their status as registered versus not registered to vote (the latter including non-U.S. citizens as well as citizens).

The question on continuing the embargo had the same context and wording as the question on this topic that has been asked in eight FIU Cuba Polls conducted since 1991. Accurately gauging opinion over time on the often competing symbolic and practical aspects of the embargo is a challenge. To provide a more thoughtful and consistent response, in the 2008 poll as in previous polls, the question was asked after a series of questions about specific policies of the embargo and a question about the overall efficacy of the embargo.

TABLE B-1. 2008 Poll Results

Percentage of Cuban Americans polled who . . .	2008	Registered to vote	Not registered to vote
Favor ending currents restrictions on sending money to Cuba by Cuban Americans	65	54	69
Favor ending current restrictions on travel for Cuban Americans	66	56	63
Favor ending current restrictions on travel for all Americans	67	58	63
Think the embargo has worked not very well or not well at all	79	72	78
Oppose continuing the embargo	55	44	53
Favor reestablishing diplomatic relations	65	56	65
Favor direct talks between the U.S. and Cuban governments about migration and other critical issues	79	72	85
Voted for John McCain	62	62	
Voted for Barack Obama	38	38	

TABLE B-2. Poll Results for Selected Questions

Summary of responses to selected questions in the FIU 2008 Cuba Poll. All figures are percentages.

Would you favor or oppose ending current restrictions on sending money to Cuba by Cuban Americans?

	Favor	Oppose
All respondents	65	35
By age group		
18–44	70	30
45–64	64	36
65 and older	55	45
By period left Cuba		
Before 1980	50	50
1980–98	68	32
After 1998	78	22
Born outside of Cuba	58	42
By whether registered to vote		
Not registered	69	31
Registered	54	46

Would you favor or oppose ending current restrictions on travel for Cuban Americans?

	Favor	Oppose
All respondents	66	34
By age group		
18–44	71	29
45–64	64	36
65 and older	53	47
By period left Cuba		
Before 1980	48	52
1980–98	68	32
After 1998	78	22
Born outside of Cuba	62	38
By whether registered to vote		
Not registered	63	37
Registered	56	44

Would you favor or oppose ending current restrictions on travel to Cuba for all Americans?

	Favor	Oppose
All respondents	67	33
By age group		
18–44	75	25
45–64	64	36
65 and older	51	49

(continued)

TABLE B-2. **Poll Results for Selected Questions (*continued*)**

By period left Cuba		
Before 1980	49	51
1980–98	67	33
After 1998	80	20
Born outside of Cuba	67	33
By whether registered to vote		
Not registered	63	37
Registered	58	42

Overall, do you think the U.S. embargo on Cuba has worked very well, well, not very well, or not at all?

	Very well	Well	Not very well	Not at all
All respondents	9	12	23	56
By age group				
18–44	6	10	23	61
45–64	10	13	23	54
65 and older	16	16	22	46
By period left Cuba				
Before 1980	15	17	24	44
1980–98	11	12	18	59
After 1998	4	4	23	68
Born outside of Cuba	6	20	29	45
By whether registered to vote				
Not registered	7	15	23	55
Registered	13	15	23	49

Do you favor or oppose continuing the U.S. embargo on Cuba?

	Favor	Oppose
All respondents	45	55
By age group		
18–44	35	65
45–64	47	53
65 and older	68	32
By period left Cuba		
Before 1980	65	35
1980–98	43	57
After 1998	29	71
Born outside of Cuba	48	52
By whether registered to vote		
Not registered	47	53
Registered	56	44

Do you favor or oppose the United States' reestablishing diplomatic relations with Cuba?

	Favor	Oppose
All respondents	65	35

(continued)

TABLE B-2.   **Poll Results for Selected Questions (*continued*)**

By age group
18–44	77	23
45–64	60	40
65 and older	42	58

By period left Cuba
Before 1980	45	55
1980–98	63	37
After 1998	80	20
Born outside of Cuba	68	32

By whether registered to vote
Not registered	65	35
Registered	56	44

Should the U.S. and the Cuban governments engage in direct talks about migration and other critical issues?

	Yes	No
All respondents	79	21

By age group
18–44	88	12
45–64	74	26
65 and older	62	38

By period left Cuba
Before 1980	62	38
1980–98	80	20
After 1998	90	10
Born outside of Cuba	80	20

By whether registered to vote
Not registered	85	15
Registered	72	28

In the presidential election did you vote for John McCain or Barack Obama (registered voters only)?

	McCain	Obama
All respondents	62	38

By age group
18–44	49	51
45–64	56	44
65 and older	80	20

By period left Cuba
Before 1980	74	26
1980–98	56	44
After 1998	58	42
Born outside of Cuba	49	51

FIGURE B-2. **Overview of Aggregate Responses**

Percent

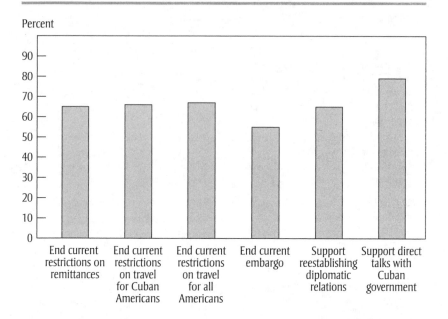

FIGURE B-3. **Overview of Poll Results by Year of Immigration**

Percent

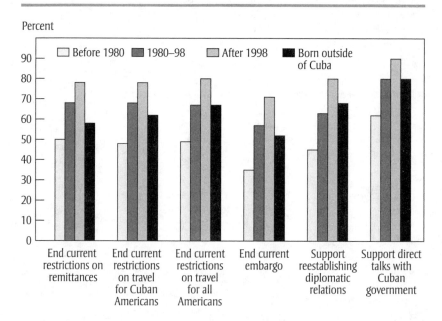

FIGURE B-4. Overview of Poll Results by Voter Registration Status

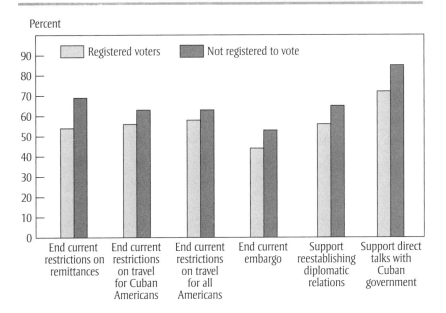

FIGURE B-5. Demographic and Political Profile of Respondents—
Citizenship and Political Preferences by Year of Immigration

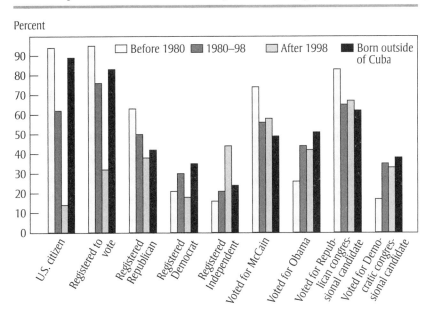

Index

94b–95b, 98, 101–02, 116–17; speech
of July 26, 2008, regarding aqueducts,
124; as successor to Castro, Fidel, vii, 1,
35, 60–61, 101; visitors to, 149–50. *See
also* Simulations—No. 3: Meeting of
Raúl Castro and His Advisers
Catholic Church, 118–20, 121, 184
CDA. *See* Cuban Democracy Act
Centro de Formación Cívica y Religiosa
(Center for Civil and Religious
Formation), 119
Chávez, Hugo, 40, 151, 174. *See also*
Venezuela
Children of the Revolution, 184
Chile, 17
China, 2, 19, 60, 152, 153, 158
Christian Democrats, 125, 137
Christian Liberation Movement, 125
Civil society (Cuba): activists and
dissidents, 117, 125–26; affirmative
social policies and, 124; Afro-Cubans,
119, 122–25, 130–31; in Cuba, 134,
157; human rights groups, 119;
initiatives to promote, 26–28, 29; key
sectors of, 115, 118; religious groups,
118–21, 129–30; organized opposition
of Democrats, dissidents, and activists,
125–26; role in Cuban change, 39,
115–16; support to activists, 41; U.S.
policy considerations and, 133–35;
women, 119; youths, 119, 121–22, 123,
130. *See also* Catholic Church;
Simulations—No. 4: Meeting of Cuban
Grassroots Activists
Clinton, William J. ("Bill"), 22, 73, 77
Clinton (William J.) administration, 23, 38
Coast Guard (U.S.), 37
Commerce, Department of (U.S.), 26
Commission for Assistance to a Free Cuba
(CAFC), 47
Common Market of the South (Mercosur),
151
Congress (U.S.), 22, 31, 32, 37, 61
Convivencia (online forum), 119
Council of State (Cuba), 100
Crime and drugs, 42, 63, 123, 167, 174
Cuba: agriculture and food issues in, 92,
93, 94b, 97, 151; assistance and aid to,
27–28, 66, 132; Cuban hierarchy, 134;

currency in, 93, 94–96, 102; democracy
and democratization in, 2, 8–11, 14, 28,
41, 125, 147, 153, 165; economic issues
of, 17, 59–60, 65–66, 87b, 91–96, 102,
123, 125, 134–35, 165, 196, 199–200;
energy issues of, 17, 29, 59–60, 63–64,
80–81, 151, 199; EU and, 17, 40,
151–52; human rights issues in, 17, 66,
152; integration in, 122–23; political
prisoners in, 23, 40–41, 48, 66, 197;
military in, 90; nationalism in, 132;
recommended new U.S. policies for,
14–33, 150, 153, 156–59, 163–64, 167;
relations with hemispheric nations,
150–51, 165–67; stability of, 36, 39, 47,
48, 53–55, 86b, 107, 156, 165; as a
terrorist state, 28; U.S. policies for, viii,
1–4, 11–12, 14–16, 19–21, 35–36, 66,
147–49; Venezuela and, 9, 17, 29, 59,
60, 64, 66, 151. *See also* Castro, Fidel;
Castro, Raúl; Civil society; Embargo
(U.S.); Engagement road map; Miami
(Fla.); Simulations
*Cuba: A New Policy of Critical and
Constructive Engagement* (report;
2009), ix, 14–33
Cuban Adjustment Act (rev. *1995, 1996*),
34–35, 37, 38
Cuban American community: *balseros*,
185–87, 189, 206; demographic and
ideological shifts of, 2–3, 12, 184, 210;
demographic profile of, 183–87;
frustration with embargo, viii, 2;
Marielitos, 185; new attitudes of,
187–90, 198, 206–07; poll of Cuban
American opinion (*2008*), 229–37;
views of U.S. policies toward Cuba,
16–17, 18. *See also* Simulations—No. 6:
Meeting of Representatives of the
Cuban American Community
Cuban Communist Party (PCC), 3, 42,
86b–87b, 89–90, 98–100, 121. *See also*
Cuban Revolution
Cuban Constitution (*1976*), 125–26
Cuban Democracy Act (CDA; *1992*), 22,
25, 32, 61, 73, 77
Cuban Liberty and Democratic Solidarity
Act. *See* Helms-Burton Act of *1996*
Cuban Missile Crisis (*1962*), 184

Cuban Revolution (*1959*): Afro-Cubans and, 123; anniversary of, vii, 15; benefits of, 123, 131; change and, 82; Cuban migration and, 183; preservation of, 76, 90–91, 111–12. *See also* Cuban Communist Party
Cuban Spring (*2002*), 23–24, 75
Cuban Study Group, 12, 18
Cultural issues, 129–31

Democracy and democratization, 14, 38–39, 40. *See also* Cuba
Democratic Party (U.S.), 187–88, 192, 214. *See also* Simulations—No. 6: Meeting of Representatives of the Cuban American Community
Deng Xiao Ping, 60–61
Diplomacy, 21, 24, 31, 32, 37, 39–40, 195–96. *See also* Simulations—No. 5, I: Meeting of Foreign Ministers in Washington, D.C. (*2010*); and No. 5, II: NSC Meeting on Multilateral Engagement and Crisis Management (*2010*)
Drugs. *See* Crime and drugs

Ecuador, 158
Educational issues, 121–22
Elections of *2008* (U.S.), 187
Embargo (U.S.): Bush speech of October 24, *2007*, 35–36; communications and information embargo, 67, 78–79, 92; effects of, 8, 10, 15, 33, 40, 41, 150; failure of, 1; frustration with, viii, 2; legal issues and regulations for, 10–11, 12, 22, 74, 200, 221–27; Obama, Barack, and lifting restrictions, 16, 18, 19, 22, 164; permission for travel to Cuba, 22–23, 24, 31, 73, 77–78; road map for lifting, 10–11, 201; United Nations and international community views of, 17, 164; views of Cuban Americans toward, 16–17, 18, 188–90, 198. *See also* Helms-Burton Act; Simulations—No. 2: NSC Meeting on New U.S. Strategies toward Cuba (*2009*); Simulations—No. 6: Meeting of Representatives of the Cuban American Community (*2010*); Travel
Emigration. *See* Migration

Energy issues: Cuban energy, 17, 21, 59–60, 63–64, 66, 80–81, 96, 151; U.S. and, 29, 66; Venezuela and, 59, 60, 66, 80, 151. *See also* Simulations—No. 2: NSC Meeting on New U.S. Strategies toward Cuba (*2009*)
Engagement road map, 10–11, 23–33, 201
EU. *See* European Union
European Commission for Democracy through Law (Venice Commission), 132
European Union (EU), 17, 40, 151–52, 153. *See also individual countries*
Europe, Central, 2
Executive branch (U.S.): authority and prerogatives of, 20, 21–23, 30–31, 32, 61, 73, 77, 78, 200; wet foot, dry foot policies and, 37, 151. *See also individual presidents and administrations by name*

FAR. *See* Revolutionary Armed Forces
FDA. *See* Food and Drug Administration
Financial issues, 27, 30. *See also* Cuba; Energy issues; International financial institutions
Florida International University poll (*2008*), 2–3, 12, 16–17, 18, 188, 198, 229–37
Food and Drug Administration (FDA), 25
Foreign Assistance Act of *1961*, 32
France, 65, 152
Freedom Flights (*los vuelos de la libertad*), 184
Free Trade in Ideas Act (Berman Act; *1988*), 25

González, Elián, 52, 189, 206
Gorbachev, Mikhail, 4, 60–61
Grupo do Rio. *See* Rio Group
Guantánamo Bay, 22, 31, 33, 41, 64, 186

Havana riots (Cuba, *1994*), 186
Havana Talibans, 87b
HB. *See* Helms-Burton Act of *1996*
Health and medical issues, 25, 151
Helms-Burton Act of *1996* (HB; Cuban Liberty and Democratic Solidarity Act), 11, 22, 30, 32, 46, 61, 73, 77, 78, 200. *See also* Embargo